Verda Ashuna

JUST TO
ILLUSTRATE

LeGrand Richards

JUST TO ILLUSTRATE

BY

LEGRAND RICHARDS

BOOKCRAFT, INC.

SALT LAKE CITY, UTAH

Litho in U.S.A.
by

PUBLISHERS PRESS
PP
SALT LAKE CITY, UTAH

FOREWORD

One cannot help loving Elder LeGrand Richards. Love seems to be his distinguishing characteristic — his love of the gospel and his love of people. To hear him preach a sermon is a delight, for he not only enlightens but he cheers his listeners. When he is through speaking one is filled with the joy of the gospel and the desire to go forth and accomplish good and bring glory to the name of our Heavenly Father.

Elder Richards is so filled with enthusiasm for the gospel that his thoughts roll forth in a steady stream — almost faster than he can put them into words. One interesting illustration after another emphasizes the point he wishes to make. His love of humanity, and his keen power of observation give us insight into the lives and problems of people — and what is more interesting than people!

Everyone loves a storyteller. Elder Richards' retentive memory and skill in relating true stories has made him one of the great speakers of the Church. When asked to record his wealth of stories from years of experience as a missionary and leader in the Church, Elder Richards reluctantly complied though he has been asked to do so by many of the saints over the years.

So here we have before us a book filled with fascinating true stories as they relate to the wonderful gospel of salvation. Prepare yourselves for a treat, for Elder Richards is a keen salesman, a resourceful leader, an enthusiastic missionary, a loving father and friend, and most of all — a simple, practical man with a simple, straightforward speech.

Part of his success in life is due to the fact that he stresses the positive approach. A born psychologist, he recognizes that each person is individual, and he seems to have an uncanny sense of how to appeal to each individual he meets.

This book is unconditionally guaranteed to increase your enjoyment of the gospel and your desire to share it with others. Its pages are packed with wisdom, wit, and scholarship.

Enthusiastically,
The Editor

CONTENTS

A Father's Example

Personal Integrity

I want to say a few words about my father and his example and teachings. We were raised on the farm and I never heard Father use an unclean word in my life or swear. His worst swear word was 'oh, fiddle sticks'. I saw him dismiss a man once from his employ because he told us boys an unclean story. We were so young that we didn't know any better than to go and repeat it to our Father. So Father told him he thought he ought to find work elsewhere.

Father was so honest that if he were to run through a red light unintentionally he would go around the block and come through again just to show that he wanted to observe the law.

While we were living in the country we used to take our wheat to the grist mill and then draw on it until our credit was gone. A new miller came into the town to run the mill, and I went to the mill to get a grist, and we had no credit, so he wouldn't give it to me. I asked him to check with the owner of the mill. I went back within a few days with a load of wheat and got our grist and when I said, "Did you check with the owner of the mill?" His reply was, "Yes." I said, "What did he say?" He said, "The next time one of those sons of George F. Richards comes to this mill, if he wants the mill, get out and give it to him." It is wonderful to have a father so honored that you can look up to him and be proud to say, "He is my father."

A Unique Occasion

We boys used to enjoy working with Father. One year my cousin, President Stephen L Richards, as a young man from the city, spent a summer on our farm.

When we were cutting hay, since there were no trees or buildings nearby for shade, we would drop the tines of our hay rake and cover them with new mown hay; then we would spread more new mown hay underneath, and crawl underneath to eat our lunch. It was rather unique that under that hay rake on that dry farm one summer were three future apostles of the Church, though not one of us knew at the time. There was my father, George F. Richards, President Stephen L Richards and myself. During one of our lunch periods, Father asked Stephen which he would rather have—his father's knowledge of medicine or the dry farm. Stephen replied, "If my father's knowledge were law instead of medicine, I would rather have that." As it turned out, Stephen did study law and became one of the finest speakers and thinkers in the Church, and was honored in being a counselor to President McKay.

Sabbath Day Observance

The last year that I spent on the farm, I ran Father's header cutting grain around the valley. We expected to finish a certain grain patch on a Saturday afternoon, but we had a little trouble with the header and didn't get quite through. I sent word in to Father that we would finish on Sunday morning. As soon as he got that word he saddled up our old buckskin riding horse and came out to that farm almost before you could say "Jack Robinson" to let us know that no son of his would run his header on the Sabbath day. That was a lesson I never forgot.

When we were boys the greatest sport the young people could have on Sunday was to go buggy riding in the afternoon. Father would never let us boys do that. So my younger brother and I went to him one day and decided that we would have it out. Well, Father explained that his children had to set an example to other children, but that he did not like to deprive us of the enjoyment we should have. So he offered to let us leave one of the teams at home any day during the week, quit our work at noon and come home, have a fresh team so we could buggy ride. Of course, we thought it would be ridiculous for us to be the only boys out buggy riding during the week when the other boys did it on Sunday but it taught us a lesson. Father was willing to sacrifice a day's work of the team, and half a day's work of his boys in order that we might have the enjoyment we desired, but he taught us that it was not appropriate on the Sabbath.

Good Measure

At the end of each year, Father would gather us three boys around the table with him and we would figure our tithing for the year. Father never overlooked anything. We figured the pigs, the chickens, the eggs, the garden and what it had produced, the fruit, the milk, the increase or growth of the calves during the year, and after we had figured everything together, Father would always throw in a little for good measure. It was that example, I am sure, that so impressed us as boys. I am sure that if the record were examined it would be found that no year ever closed without his sons having paid a full tithing.

I never saw my father neglect a Church duty. Many times when he served as a Counselor in the Stake Presidency, we hitched the horses on the buggy for him to fill an appointment in the stake when he would have to travel 10 or 15 miles in a heavy snow storm, but he always went.

Father's Love

I never heard my father criticize a brother.

We all had a deep affection for our Father. While he expected us to follow his counsel and advice, his leadership in the family was one of deep love and affection. He lived within a few months of being 90 years of age. Shortly before his death, I went to his apartment one day. As he saw me enter, he arose and took me in his arms and calling me by my kid name, he said, "Grandy, my boy, I love you." You can't get very far away from love like that.

When I returned from my first mission my father met me in Chicago, having been called into the Quorum of the Twelve while I was in the mission field. As we slept together in the pullman on the way home, he prayed for me that I would get a companion that would entitle me to be the father of some of the choice spirits of heaven. He explained that it was his feeling that the choice spirits of heaven might have the right to choose the lineage through which they were born.

My mother bore Father fifteen children. When that fifteenth child would wrap his big arms around his mother and say, "Mother, you don't know how grateful I am that you didn't stop at fourteen," it paid the bill.

When we would meet in our family gatherings, and there were many of us present, Mother would remark, "Father, look what we started." In a family gathering shortly before his death, Father made this statement, "I don't think you children are going to have to provide many more entertainments for me. I am going to be promoted." I am sure there isn't one of his children but what feels that when the Lord called him home, he truly had been promoted.

On February 23, 1961 we celebrated the one hundredth anniversary of his birth. At that time he had 277 living descendents without counting the in-laws. What a kingdom!

A Serious Consideration

United Parents

Mixed marriages are a major cause of unhappy homes and broken marriages. Marrying within one's church is essential to happy and successful family life. Parents should be united in their spiritual and church convictions. Here are a few experiences to illustrate this fact:

While I was serving as President of the Hollywood Stake in Los Angeles, I was sitting at my desk one day and a lady came in selling neckties. She said, "I guess you don't remember me, do you, President Richards?" My reply was that I was afraid I didn't. She reminded me that she had taught Sunday School when I was the Superintendent in Salt Lake. Then, of course, I placed her. I said, "What is the rest of the story?"

"Well," she said, "I fell in love with a Catholic boy. I loved him so much I didn't think it would make any difference to the Lord how I served Him as long as I served Him. We were married by his Priest, and I agreed to raise the children in the Catholic Church, so I have been going to church with him and taking part in the prayers, attending mass, and so on. Recently I told him that I was the biggest hypocrite in the world — that I didn't believe a thing that was going on in his church — that I knew that Joseph Smith was a Prophet of God and that the Book of Mormon was true, and that the Lord had established His kingdom upon the earth for the last time. I said I didn't know what was going to happen to him or myself or the children, but that I was going back to my church."

I always tell the young people that they cannot run away from the Lord — no matter where they go they will find that He is there.

Difficult Choice

In Holland, we brought a wonderful family into the church. One of the young men of the family was keeping company with a young lady who finally told him that if he joined the Mormon Church she would have nothing more to do with him. He chose to join the Church and their courtship ended.

He later immigrated to America and was here in this land without any of his relatives during a time when employment was difficult to obtain. He couldn't speak the English language, so he had quite a struggle to get along. Being somewhat despondent, his health broke, so in the depths of his discouragement, he wrote to his former sweetheart in Holland. She offered to take him back provided he would give up his Church. So, he returned to Holland and married this young lady, and went to Church with her. He stood it as long as he could. After they had two children, he returned to his own Church and then to America, but his wife would not accompany him. He left with the promise that the money would be available for her and the children if she ever decided to join him.

When Sister Richards and I returned from the mission, we brought this woman with her two children to Utah with us. She later joined the Church and died a faithful Temple worker.

Deathbed Regrets

You can't run away from the Lord when once He has given you a real testimony of the truth.

A Stake President in New York told this story. He said he and the Bishop were invited to visit a woman who was very sick in the hospital. She was raised as a good Mormon girl, but she fell in love with a Catholic man and married him. He took her East to live but would not let her have anything to do with her Church. He had passed away, leaving her with a son and daughter nearing twenty. He had named his spinster sister the executrix of his estate, with provision that if his wife made any attempt to raise the children in the Mormon Church she should be cut off from all benefits from his estate.

Here she was apparently on her deathbed, realizing that her children had been taught nothing concerning her own Church but had been raised in the Catholic Church. Now she was suffering the regrets of her actions, and said, "If I had my life to live over again, I would have gone back to my Church and people even if I had to crawl on my hands and knees to do so, and had I had to go out working every day to raise my children in the Church."

A Western Girl

It would be wonderful if we could help all our young people to avoid such mistakes and the almost certain regrets and sorrow.

While attending a Conference in Chicago, I saw a young woman holding a baby in her arms sitting on about the third row back. At the close of the meeting she came up and said, "Bishop Richards, could I shake your hand?" I replied that I couldn't think of anything I would rather do. As we shook hands the tears came into her eyes and I said, "You are one of our Western girls, aren't you?" Her emotions were such that she could not speak, but she nodded 'yes'. Then I said, "And you married out of the Church." I got another affirmative nod. Then I added, "Your husband doesn't want you to come to Church." I got another nod. Then I said, "You are homesick for your church and your people." With that she dropped down on the front bench and covered her face in her baby's shawl and wept as if her little heart would break.

She found that she could not find happiness by running away from her church and her people.

Poor Partners

A young woman from Southern Utah came into my office one day and told me her experience.

She said she heard me speak at their Stake Conference, when I advised our Mormon girls to marry members of the Church. She said that at the time she was keeping company with a young man who was not a member of the Church, but feigned to be interested, so she married him feeling that I had been talking to the other girls and not to her. She said, "We had been married but a few months when he left me, and I have never heard from him since."

A good sister called at my office one day and told me about her son who had gone to California in the armed forces. He met a girl whom he finally married. He said, "Mother, I married her because she was so much like you." She claimed an interest in the Church, but after they were married, she did all she could to try to lead him away from the Church. At Christmas time, she bought him a pipe and a carton of cigarettes although she knew that he never smoked.

This reminds one of the words of the Lord through Moses when the children of Israel were told that they should not marry out of their own group. In Deuteronomy 7: 3-4 we read, "Neither shalt thou make marriages with them. Thy daughter thou shalt not give unto his son, nor his daughter shalt thou take unto thy son, for they will turn thy son from following me, that they may serve other Gods; so will the anger of the Lord be kindled against you."

Before Marriage

It is better to get your companion in line in spiritual matters before marriage than to take chances on achieving that result after marriage. Just to illustrate:

A young man called me at my home one evening by phone. When I answered, he said, "Is this Bishop Richards?" When I replied in the affirmative, he said, "Well, I am in trouble." I asked him what his trouble was. He answered: "I have been keeping company with a young lady for three years. Since she heard you preach a few days ago, she won't go out with me any more." I inquired, "Why not?" He said, "Because I am not active in the Church." My comment was, "Good for her — I am happy to know that there is at least one young woman in the Church who will take the advice of an old man like me." Then I added, "Now what are you going to do about it?" He said, "What can I do?" I answered, "Get active in the Church; then go back to her." He replied, "How can I?" I told him to get in touch with his Bishop and he would help him. Then I said, "If he doesn't help you, you come back to me." He has never returned.

How I admire that girl for the stand she took!

A Father's Advice

At the close of the second world war, a young man called me at my office for an appointment. When he came in he explained that he was from the East; that he had been studying for the ministry and that his father was a minister of the gospel.

He had met, courted and married a young Mormon girl who was in his locality serving as a Wave or a Wac. She would not give up her church, so this young man went to his father, the minister, and said, "Now, Father, what am I going to do about my church?" His father thought for a few minutes and then replied, "My son, I think you had better join your wife's church; she would have to give up more to join your church than you will have to give up to join hers." So he joined her church and he said, "The more I learn about it the more wonderful it becomes."

The purpose of his call was to see if there was any branch of the church service he could devote himself to in earning a living, explaining that he had always wanted to teach religion. I explained our Seminary and Institute program and our Church Schools and informed him that we paid our teachers for such service. "But," I said, "of course you couldn't teach in one of these if there were any question in your mind as to the divine mission of the Prophet Joseph Smith, because you couldn't plant a testimony in the hearts of the youth of the Church unless you had a testimony yourself." He said he was surely getting one fast.

A Warning

A mother called me one day and asked me to come out to her home and talk with her daughter and the young Catholic boy she wanted to marry.

I told this young man that if he thought he could get this girl to give up her church to marry him, with a promise that she would raise their children in the Catholic church, that he was mistaken — that even if she promised to do so, she would ultimately return to her own church, for she knew it was true. I told him he could know it was true if he would take time to find out. I promised him he could know if he wanted to, and that they each owed it to their unborn children to raise them in a home where they were both united in spiritual matters. I pointed out how selfish they were if they thought only of themselves and not of their children.

I told him that if he wanted to know that Mormonism was the truth that we would help him to find out, but that if he was not interested, I would advise them to discontinue their courtship, and he should find some good Catholic girl and marry her.

A couple of years later this young woman came into my office and said, "I thought you would be interested to know the result of your visit to my home and the counsel and advice you gave. Well, we discontinued our court-ship. I have since married a returned missionary in the Temple. We are very happy, and I want to thank you for your advice."

A Rejected Suitor

Sister Richards and I were attending a Relief Society Bazaar in Los Angeles when we were told this story:

A young Mormon girl from Los Angeles, a daughter of one of the families we knew well when I presided over the Hollywood Stake, went to attend the Brigham Young University at Provo. She started keeping company with a young man whose parents were members of the church, but he was not active in the Church. When he became serious with her and proposed marriage, she told him she wouldn't marry a man who was not active in the church, honoring his Priesthood, and living so she could tell her children to follow the example of their father. Well, this brought an end to their courtship.

Soon thereafter she commenced keeping company with another young man. When their engagement was announced, the rejected boy received a copy of the paper containing the announcement. He called the girl clear from Chicago to Los Angeles and told her he could not live without her — that if she would reconsider and call off her engagement he would come back on her terms and would promise to do anything she asked him to do in the church. The night we met them both at the Bazaar, he was a member of the Ward Bishopric.

We need more such girls in the church who will stand up for their ideals, to assure happy homes and worthy fathers.

Under the Oak Tree

During the war we had a son working during the summer at Zion's National Park, along with other Uni-

versity students. He played in the Orchestra and was
master of ceremonies in entertaining the tourists. I received an assignment to attend the Zion's Park Stake
Conference. I invited my wife to accompany me with the
suggestion that we go a day early and spend a night at
the Lodge and visit our son.

Upon our arrival at the Lodge, my son told me that
there was a Mormon boy there who said he would never
marry out of the Temple. Now he had met a young
college student from the East — so cultured and refined
that he had rather let his heart go out to her. When he
heard we were coming, he asked my son if I would
be willing to talk with her for him, and, of course, my son
accepted the invitation for me. So while the dance went
on that evening, I sat out under an oak tree with this
young man and this young lady from the East. I told
her the story of Mormonism as best I could in an hour
and a half — how we got the church and what our philosophy of life was, including our teachings regarding
eternal marriage and the eternal duration of the family
unit. Then I asked her if she knew that what I had told
her was true would she be interested, and she replied,
"Very much." Then I bore her my testimony and told her
how she could know that what I had told her was true.

I didn't hear from this young couple for possibly
two years. I was sitting at lunch in the Lion House when
a young lady came up and tapped me on the shoulder.
As I looked up she said, "Do you remember me?" I replied, "Yes, all but your name — who are you?" She said,
"Do you remember sitting," and before she could say
'under the oak tree at Zions Park Lodge,' I replied, "Yes,
what is the rest of the story." "Well," she replied, "I
married that young man, but we were not married until
we could be married in the Temple (we make them wait
a year after joining the church before permitting them

to go through the Temple.) He is now over in Korea, and I am working over in the Genealogical Department. I have since been back east teaching the gospel to my people, and they are interested." "Then," I said, "is it all I told you it was?" Her face brightened, and she replied, "And more too."

I didn't hear anything more from this couple for a number of years. A few days before leaving to attend a Stake conference, I received a letter from the wife of the Stake President. She expressed her pleasure with my assignment to their conference, adding that she was the young lady to whom I taught Mormonism out under the oak tree at Zion's Park Lodge. I had a wonderful visit in their home with them and their children.

How I admired this young man for resolving that he would never marry other than in the Temple. Had this young lady not responded to the teachings of the church, I am sure he would not have married her.

Is He a Member?

At the close of a Conference session in West Florida, a recent convert, a lovely young woman school teacher, came up to me and said, "President Richards, I am going to get married. What do you think of that?" I replied, "Wonderful, do I know him?" She answered, "No." Then I said, "Is he a member of the church?" She answered, "No." Then I said, "Well, you are a beautiful, clean young woman, and you could no more find happiness with an unclean man than you could mix oil and water. In your courtship with him you will know whether he is motivated by clean and holy desires, or whether he would take advantage of you if he could." Then I added, And he must be a prayerful man with faith in God, for as wicked as the world is, I would not trust any man to be true to his wife and children who does not believe there is a God and that some day he will have to answer to him for what he does here on earth. Also, he must be willing to let you raise your children in the Church, for knowing as you do that the Lord has restored His truth to the earth, you would be a very unhappy woman if you could not teach your children the truths of the gospel." Then I added, "Let me know when he joins the church." I didn't dare tell her not to marry a non-member of the church, for I didn't know where she could find a young man in the church, except our missionaries, and we had "hands-off" signs hanging all over them.

I didn't hear anything more from her until the next conference about four months later. Her train was late so she came into the morning meeting late. After the meeting she came up to shake hands with me. As she put out her hand, I said, "Name, please." She replied, "Oh, I am still Miss so and so." I said, "What became of your anticipated marriage?" Her answer was, "He did not come up to your specifications."

I told that story in a conference in Alabama a few months after that. At the close of the meeting a young seventeen year old Mormon girl came up to me and said, "If I had heard that story six months ago, I would have been an unmarried woman today." It did not take that young Mormon girl long to find that a sweet, clean Mormon girl couldn't find happiness with an unclean man.

Nip Trouble Early

L.D.S. parents have a solemn responsibility to teach their children the doctrines of the gospel, including eternal marriage, so they will desire Temple marriage. The time to start is when they are young.

President Grant recognized the importance of parents keeping in touch with their children's dating activities. When he was President of the European Mission and

was visiting the Netherlands Mission where I was secretary, I wrote many letters for him. His girls were
just at the mating age and President Grant would write
to Bishops, Stake Presidents, and ex-Mission presidents
inquiring about the boys they seemed interested in. He
would say, "I don't ask for anything but they have a
testimony of the gospel, and that they are honest and
energetic." And then he said this to me, "Elder Richards,
I have learned that the time to stop trouble is to nip it
in the bud." I think that is wonderful counsel.

Just to Make Sure

At one time one of my own sons was going to go out
with a non-member of the Church. My wife said, "Do you
know who your son is taking out tonight?" I said, "No."
She said, "Well, she is not a member of the church."
I spoke to my son and he said, "Well, Dad, she is a good
girl and I don't intend to marry her." Then I said, "Well,
that's wonderful, and just to make sure that you don't
marry her, don't take her out again because if you do,
you will get to thinking more of her and she will get to
thinking more of you and then there will be broken hearts
if you do not marry her." He never took her out again.

Broken-Hearted Man

One of the young men who labored under me in the
Southern States, entered the service following his mission
and was an officer. He met a beautiful young southern
girl and fell in love with her. I advised him not to marry
her unless she would first join the church. I cautioned
him that promises that they will join later are seldom
fulfilled. His mother, having married out of the Church
and having been successful in bringing his father into
the Church, thought it would be alright. So he married
this beautiful southern girl. Now she smokes in the home
and takes the children off to her church, while he goes

to his own church all alone, almost a broken-hearted man.

As contrasted to this, his brother married a faithful, intelligent Mormon girl and they have a wonderful home life. Their children take part in church activities and they are united in all things.

Duty of Parents

I have always advised the young people in the Church that the Church is the most wonderful thing in all this world. If any boy or girl not a member of the church is worthy to marry one of our girls or boys, they will join the Church before marriage if someone will take time to teach them what the gospel is. If they are not willing to join the Church, then I think our young people should not marry them. I am a great believer that while not all of the good young people in the world are in the Church, Catholics should marry Catholics, Baptists should marry Baptists, Presbyterians should marry Presbyterians, Methodists should marry Methodists, and so forth. I think that parents owe it to their children to raise them in a home united in spiritual matters since spiritual leadership is the most powerful influence to produce fine men and fine women, and happy homes.

Authority

Endless Priesthood

I love this gospel with all my heart. I just wish everyone in the world could share the wonderful truths that have been restored to earth in these latter-days. I know we have the truth. I know that Joseph Smith was and is a Prophet of God, and that he was an instrument in the hands of the Lord to bring forth this marvelous work and a wonder. I know that God has restored his authority to the earth through the Holy Priesthood, and that this authority is the greatest thing we possess next to life itself.

Just to illustrate — When our son, Alden, was ordained a deacon in Atlanta, Georgia, he came into my office and said, "Father, I have more authority than the President of the United States, haven't I?" It took my breath away, and after composing my thoughts, I replied, "Well, yes, you have. The President of the United States gets his authority from the people. When his term of office ends, his authority ends with it. But your authority comes from the Lord, and if you will live for it, it will be yours forever and forever."

Power from God

Isn't it wonderful when you think of it! Our chosen leaders have the power and authority from God to direct his kingdom here on the earth. We can never go astray if we will follow the counsel of our leaders, for they are inspired and instructed by God in matters pertaining to our welfare. We need never have the quarrels and disputes over position and eminence in our Church that are so prevalent in other churches, for God has stated that only one man on the earth at a time would have all the keys and authority necessary to guide this great work.

The President of our Church may have his counselors to help him see all sides of a problem, but the final decision is his. He is entitled to inspiration from God and must act as he feels inspired. I was impressed as to the truth of this by a statement President Clark once made in a meeting of the First Presidency and the Bishopric. He said, "I can argue with President Grant about policies and important matters until President Grant says, 'I feel that it ought to be so and so.' Then I can argue no more. I have seen his judgment vindicated so many times when he felt the right or the wrong of a certain proposition."

A Vast Difference

The churches of the world do not have this sure guidance and authority. Just to illustrate — In the Netherlands Mission, a man came up to me at the close of a conference meeting and asked if I would come to his home for an hour or so. I asked if I might bring one of the missionaries with me and he consented. When we arrived, there sat three men. Our host explained that they were the council of their own church in that town. Then he asked us, "What are you really here for?" We explained to him that what we had said in the conference was the truth, and that we were there for one reason and one reason alone — that we had a testimony that God had spoken again from the heavens, had raised up a Prophet, and had established his Kingdom in the earth, never to be thrown down or given to another people. Our host said, "Now, we are the church council of our church. We know the Lord isn't running our church; we run it. We hire the ministers and we fire them. We hire the best we can find for the money we can afford to pay. If the minister doesn't preach what we want him to, we ask him to look for another field and we replace him." What a difference between the work of the Lord and the work of man!

Position of Reorganized Church

Some churches are not so frank. They claim to have authority, but a little good missionary work on our part can soon convince the honest in heart of the truth. Brother Robert I. Burton, whose wife is my cousin, and who served as a counselor in the Salt Lake Temple Presidency for years, told me this little story. Since it has to do with a missionary who labored under me in the Netherlands Mission, I want to give it here.

During the war, the missionaries were brought out of Europe and reassigned to the missions in the United States. Elder Lyle Larkin of Ogden had labored with us in Holland and was assigned to the Eastern States to complete his mission. While out tracting one day, he came to the home of an officer in the Reorganized Church. This man invited him in and said, "Tell me your story." Brother Larkin told him his story until he got to Brigham Young, then the man said, "That's where our roads part." But Brother Larkin was a very friendly man and he made a friend out of this officer of the Reorganized Church. After his mission was completed and he returned home, he lived at the home of his Grandfather, Patriarch Larkin in Ogden. The officer of the Reorganized Church wrote to Elder Larkin that he had an appointment in California and if Brother Larkin desired to have him do so, he would stop over and spend a night with him in Ogden. Brother Larkin asked his grandfather, Patriarch Larkin, for permission to invite him to the home and this was done. After supper Patriarch Larkin said to this man, "Now we don't want any argument or quarreling going on in this home. I suggest that you tell me anything you would like to about your church, and I will not interrupt you. When you are through, I want the same privilege." So when this man had completed his statement, Brother Larkin said, "Now are you through?" He said, "Well, I am for the present, but after you get through, I might want to add something." Then Brother Larkin started out like this: He said, "When the Savior came upon the earth, whom did he choose to carry on his work?" This man answered, "The Twelve Apostles." Then Brother Larkin added, "And when the Savior no longer could be with his people, whom did he leave in charge of the Church and his followers?" This man replied, "The Twelve Apostles." Then Brother Larkin said, "When he visited the Nephites, whom did he call to represent him among the Nephites?" This man replied, "The Twelve Disciples." "And when he left them, whom did he leave in charge of his work?" "The Twelve Disciples." Then Brother Larkin said, "And when the Lord called the Prophet Joseph to establish His Church in this dispensation, whom did He instruct him to call to assist him?" This man said, "The Twelve Apostles." Then Brother Larkin added, "And when the Prophet Joseph was martyred, whom then should carry on the work of the Kingdom?" The man sat and thought for a few minutes. He said, "You floor me."

A short time after he had filled his assignment in California and returned to the East, he joined our Church through this one argument of Patriarch Larkin's.

How grateful we ought to be for the sure knowledge we have that this is the true Church and is directed by God through his chosen servants! How grateful we should be for the glorious priesthood of power and authority!

Bible As A Guide

A Threat

Millions of people accept the Bible as the word of God, but how many believe it and are willing to follow it? When we called at the home of one investigator, his friend was there. I asked him if he would be willing to read some of our literature. He agreed that he would. I handed him tracts discussing the apostasy and restoration of the Gospel. I did not see him again for a few weeks. Then, on another occasion when we called at this same home, there he sat as we entered. Turning to him, I asked if he had read the tracts I had given him. He replied that he had. I asked him what he thought of them. His reply was: "Well, if those tracts tell the truth, you have the truth," so right then I made an appointment to visit him at his home. He and his wife were lovely people. They had no children.

While they were investigating our message and attending our meetings, President Joseph F. Smith and Bishop Charles W. Nibley visited Rotterdam and spoke in our meeting. Upon their return to the United States, President Smith was arrested for the birth of his last child, from a plural wife. This was announced by the Associated Press and carried in the newspapers over the world. It also appeared in the Rotterdam Newspaper, where this investigator read it. He met one of the saints on the street during the week, and said: "When Mr. Richards comes to our home next Sunday for dinner, if he admits that the newspaper report is true, I will throw him down the stairs." (Their apartment was on the second floor.) This threat was conveyed to me by the member to whom it was told.

What Good Is It?

Sunday came and my companion and I went to his

home according to our invitation for Sunday dinner. When we arrived, the man seemed a little reserved. I put on all the smiles I could to try and warm him up. Finally, as if he were dropping a heavy burden off his shoulders, he said: "Well, I am glad you have come." I replied, "We are always happy when we can make other people happy." We sat up to the dinner table, and after a short conversation, he said, "Do you read the Dutch newspapers?" I answered, "Not very often, but if there is ever anything in the papers about our people, the saints usually call our attention to it." I didn't want him to think I was trying to evade anything. Then he said, "They have printed something terrible about your Prophet—did you read it?" My reply was, "Yes, I did read it." Then he said, "But, it isn't true, is it?" I answered, "Yes, I guess it is." He turned pale, and I reached in my pocket for my Bible, pushing my plate from me at the table. He said, "Never mind, let's finish our dinner first." When we had finished, I asked him to get his Bible and I discussed the principle of plural marriage from the Bible. Then I asked, "How much of your Bible do you believe, and how much are you willing to accept? If only a portion, what good is it as a guide anyway?" He sat and thought for a few minutes and then replied, "Come on, let's go to Church." Soon thereafter he and his wife were baptized, came to Utah, and were faithful members to the time of their death. I have had the honor of speaking at the funeral service of each of them. I thank the Lord for the privilege that was mine of bringing the gospel to them.

I heard a Missionary tell about being asked by an investigator about the principle of Polygamy, and his reply was that he was proud to be the product of polygamy on both his father's and mother's side. Then he added: "What was good enough for the Savior of the world is good enough for me."

Blessings

A Handicap

One of the important functions of the Priesthood is the bestowing of personal blessings, according to the direction and inspiration of the Lord.

When I received my first mission call, I was boarding with my brother and his family and working at the C.W. & M. Company in Salt Lake City.

I took my call and went to the President's Office in the old building connecting the Lion and Beehive Houses. I was on crutches with a floating kneecap. When Brother George Reynolds saw me he said, "What do you want?" I replied that I had come to answer a call for a mission. His answer was, "It looks to me as if you ought to go home and take care of yourself." This was in February 1905. He asked me when I wanted to go and I told him I wanted to accompany my cousin who was called to leave the forepart of April. He agreed to book me for that time, but added, "If you are not over your lameness by that time, let us know and we will defer your mission. I assured him that I would be ready.

My parents were then living in Tooele and my father was the Stake Patriarch and a member of the Stake Presidency. I asked him to give me a blessing so I would be able to leave on my mission at the appointed time. He did so bless me in these words: "I bless you with strength of body and limbs, that you may not become lame and be overtaken with sickness." I threw my crutches away a few days before the time I was to report for my mission, and never lost a day through lameness during nearly three years away from home.

Security in a Storm

When I returned from my first mission in Holland, a terrific storm arose, as we neared the coast of Portland,

Maine. The newspapers reported it was the worst they had had on that coast for thirty years. People walking along the streets had to hold to the fence to keep from being blown away. Houses were blown from their foundations. Ships were destroyed on the rocks. We had to put back to sea to avoid being dashed upon the rocks. The waves would roll right over our ship. Everything that was loose was rolling around in the rooms. They couldn't serve meals. Many of the passengers were frantic. One man came up to me and said, "Why don't you missionaries pray?" I said, "We have already taken care of that." He said, "If I ever get back to Scotland, I will never leave it again. I want to be where, when trouble comes in the front door, I can run out the back." One of the L.D.S. Sisters who had been visiting her relatives in one of the Scandinavian countries with her daughter came up to me and said, "You don't seem a bit worried. Aren't you really worried?" I said, "No, sister. I had a promise of the Lord, that if I would fill an honorable mission, I would return to my loved ones in safety." I said, "I don't know what is going to become of this ship and the rest of you, but I feel just as much at ease as if I were sitting in my mother's parlor."

Though I had prayed for the safety of the ship and its passengers, I had no positive assurance of their safety. But I had a perfect assurance that I would be safe because by authority of the Priesthood a special blessing for my protection had been pronounced on me. How grateful I am for that Priesthood of power!

A Sure Promise

A member of the Stake Presidency told me this wonderful experience. He said he was drafted during the first world war and he felt *bad* about going. He wanted to get married and have a family. He had a feeling that if he went into action he would never come back. He went

to the Patriarch who came in from the field and laid his
hands upon his head. While he wrote the words of blessing as they fell from the lips of the Patriarch, the Patriarch promised him "That inasmuch as you have been
called to go to the defense of your country, I promise
you that if you will be humble and faithful and prayerful,
that if your life is ever brought into danger, the way
will be opened for your escape, and you shall yet be
given in marriage and have sons and daughters of good
repute and be the means of doing much missionary work
in the world."

This brother said that within ninety days of the time
he left home, he was going over the top with the infantry
in France. They started out with two hundred and fifty
men and received thirty replacements. At 10:00 o'clock
on the day of the armistice they were ordered to cease
firing, knowing that the armistice was to be signed at
11:00 o'clock. They then had eighty men left of their
two hundred and eighty. The soldiers gathered in a
group. He and two companions were in the same fox-hole
together. They had had no supper or breakfast, and
he saw an army kitchen about two hundred yards away
feeding their men. He suggested to his buddies that they
go and get something to eat. They would not go, so he
left them and went alone. Just as he was receiving his
stack of pancakes, a bomb was thrown into the midst
of his company of eighty, and thirty were killed, leaving
only fifty of the two hundred and eighty. He found his
two buddies with the tops of their heads blown off.
That he was unhurt, was a marvelous fulfillment of the
promise of the Patriarch.

He lived to marry, as the Patriarch had promised,
and has raised three sons and three daughters of good
repute, who have done missionary work and have filled
other positions of responsibility in the Church.

Power of Healing

In the Netherlands Mission we had been out performing a baptism one evening, and had gone to the home of a new convert. One of the brethren came and said that his wife was in great distress and wanted us to come and administer to her. She had been serving a lady who had a contagious disease and she had acquired it on her hands. The doctor had bound them up and they were in bandages when we called. We administered to her. She said she knew she could be healed if we would perform the administration. The next day was fast day. She stood up in the Fast Meeting with her hands unwrapped and bore her testimony that through the administration of the Priesthood, the Lord had completely healed her of this affliction.

Very often the person administering the blessing will have assurance from the Lord as to the outcome of the blessing. When I had a severe heart attack and lay at death's door, Elder Harold B. Lee and the late Bishop Marvin O. Ashton drove up to Idaho to visit and administer to me. Elder Lee testified that as soon as he laid his hands upon my head he knew with certainty that the Lord would spare me for further work on this earth. I was later sustained as a member of the Quorum of the Twelve.

Body And Spirit

Worldly Confusion

The greatest confusion in the churches of the world exists in their beliefs concerning the body and the spirit. When the clear, simple truths of the gospel are presented, these erroneous beliefs are exposed as illogical and absurd. Just to illustrate . . .

The Seventh Day Adventists do not believe that the soul or the spirit of man exists from the time of death until the time of resurrection. In attending a missionary convention in Los Angeles, Brother Pearson, the Institute Director, told of a discussion he had had with a Seventh Day Adventist Minister, who said that the spirit did not exist between death and the resurrection. Brother Pearson asked this question, "Didn't Moses die?" The minister answered, "Yes." "How then did he appear upon the mount at the transfiguration?" The minister answered "He was resurrected." Then Brother Pearson asked, "Wasn't Christ the first fruits of the resurrection?" The minister had no answer.

Simple Logic

In Massachusetts I met a retired minister and at Easter time, I asked this minister what he really meant by Easter. "Well," he said, "we are celebrating the resurrection of Christ." Then I led him on, "Do you actually believe that Jesus was resurrected, that he took up from the tomb the very body that was laid away?" He agreed that he did. I asked him if he believed that the Savior in that body appeared to his disciples as is recorded; that he showed them the prints in his hands, and the wound in his side, telling them to feel him, for said he, "A spirit hath not flesh and bones as ye see me have." The minister agreed to that. Then I said, "Do you believe that he ascended into heaven in the presence of many of the brethren, when two men in white apparel stood saying "Ye men of Galilee, why stand ye gazing up into heaven? This same Jesus, which is taken up from you into heaven, shall so come in like manner as ye have seen him go into heaven." I said, "Do you believe that?" He said, "Yes, I do." Then I said, "Will you kindly explain to me what he did with His body? Did He die again the second time that he could be a spirit everywhere present so large that he filled the universe and yet so small that he could dwell in our hearts?" His reply was, "I have never thought of it in that way before."

Truth is consistent. The scriptures are consistent. But men leaning on their own learning and understanding reach absurd and inconsistent conclusions because they will not seek for revelation from God. The spirit of revelation enlightens the mind and helps us understand the plain and glorious truths of the gospel, the true nature of God and man.

Brotherhood

Friendly Spirit

It would be hard to say what the most wonderful thing about our Church is, but I think the brotherhood that exists in the Church is one of the most wonderful things in life. We can travel anywhere in the world and meet our own people, members of the Church, and feel as much at home with them as we would practically with our own families.

Some years ago I attended the Teton Stake Conference. It was the first time they had ever had a visit from a Presiding Bishop, so they met me with a school band and we marched to the Stake President's home where they serenaded us. A young Deacon made a speech of welcome that was wonderful. He was just like a senator. Then we took a ride up into the Jackson Hole country and there, by Jenny's Lake, was a large automobile from Illinois. A man stood with his foot on the front bumper. I said to him, "I'll bet you haven't seen anything as beautiful as this since you left Chicago." He didn't answer me; he said, "Where are you from?" I said, "Well, I'm from Salt Lake; these other men are from Driggs, Idaho." "Well," he said, "Driggs. I know a man back in Chicago by the name of Driggs. He is a Bishop in the Mormon Church. You don't happen to know him, do you?" I said, "Yes, I stayed in his home not long ago." Then he mentioned a Dr. Williams and said, "He is a Mormon; you don't know him, do you?" I said, "Yes," and then he started to mention someone else and I said, "Wait just a minute; if I were a betting man, I would bet that you are a Mormon yourself." He replied, "I am." Then he said, "I have been traveling from Chicago with my wife and two Catholic girls." He pointed them out. The girls were smoking; his wife wasn't. He said, "We have just been taking it leisurely. Everywhere we have stopped enroute, and have met someone from the West, I have either known them, their relatives, their neighbors, or their friends. The Catholic girls say, 'Do you know *everybody* out West? Why, we don't even know the people who live on the same floor with us in the flat we live in.' "

That's what membership in this church does.

Samoan Farewell

No matter where we travel, if we come to one of our branches or wards we soon feel at home, for the love of the gospel binds us together with a love stronger than any other power. When Elder Huntsman and I visited Samoa a few years ago and were about to leave, a group of approximately one hundred and fifty came down to bid us farewell as we took a boat to take us to our seaplane. It was hard for them to get there; they had to rent a bus to come. When we landed in Suva in the Fiji Islands and went to the hotel, a man came up and introduced himself as a newspaper man from the State of Washington. He said, "I have never seen a farewell like that in my life. Did you notice that every man and woman was wiping the tears out of their eyes?" I said, "Yes, but did you see what we were doing? We were wiping the tears out of our eyes." We had only been with them a few days, but such was the love of brotherhood we felt. While I was there, I think I gave over two hundred and fifty blessings The people were not sick; they just wanted a blessing from one of the Lord's servants.

A Friend in Need

During a railroad strike, in order to fulfill an appointment in Oakland, California, the presidency invited me to drive my car. So Sister Richards and I went together. When we reached Winnemucca, Nevada where we intended to stay overnight, all the hotels and motels were filled. No one seemed to know where we could find a place to stay. We phoned ahead to the next city and found the same conditions were there. Because the trains were not running, other people were doing what we were. I said to my wife, "Well, I'm sure we can solve our problem all right." I got out my Church directory, looked up the name of the Bishop, called him up and said, "Bishop is there anyone in Winnemucca, Nevada who would be willing to put up a Mormon Bishop overnight?" He answered, "I'll say there is! Where is he?" He wouldn't let us come to his home; he had us wait at the drug store where I was phoning until he came.

He had company so he took us to the home of his mother and father. They treated us grand and sent us on our way the next day and wouldn't let us pay anything. They tried to get us to promise as pay that we would stop with them on our way home. That is the type friendship we find everywhere we go in this Church.

The Greatest Union

What missionary has not felt the depth of this brotherhood and love among the people he has labored with! When my son was in the mission field, he wrote a letter, a portion of which reads as follows: "My! Father, these saints are wonderful. They do us all kinds of favors. They make my Fraternity brothers look sick. I would never ask to join a fraternity again. The Priesthood of God is the greatest union in the world, isn't it?" And I was happy to know that he had reached that decision.

In times of distress we can count on the spirit of love and brotherhood that exists in the Church. When the first World War broke out, the Saints of Europe suffered greatly. So the Saints here in Zion held a special fast to raise funds to alleviate their suffering. Some of the Saints who were allowed to leave Germany inquired about the Saints in Belgium, knowing their country had been overrun by the German army, and left part of their hard-earned savings to help the suffering Belgian saints.

Brotherhood Amid War

The love of the Saints for each, regardless of what country they belong to, is wonderful to see. They will risk their lives to help each other. Just to illustrate . . . One of our missionaries in Germany was drafted into the German army much to his consternation. Though he had been born in Germany, he was a naturalized American citizen but the German government refused to recognize this. During a furlough given for reasons of ill health, he was visited by one of the Saints, a German soldier guarding the border between Holland and Germany. This L.D.S. German soldier told him if he would come to visit him at the border he would turn his back and let him escape. In this way the missionary was able to get out of Germany. But if the German saint had not been willing to risk the consequences he could never have done so, and might have been killed in the fighting.

One of the most touching incidents, showing that the love of the gospel knows no bounds, occurred in an army hospital. One of our L. D. S. boys was very sick and wanted an elder to administer to him, but none could be found among the American soldiers. So the sick soldier asked if they would see if they could locate an elder among the German prisoners they had taken. This they were able to do. The German prisoner had carried with him a small bottle of oil, and administered to him. Although they were enemies as far as uniform went, they were brothers in the holy priesthood of God.

Building Program

Efforts Blessed

The spirit of brotherhood and cooperation that exists in our Church is responsible for the beautiful chapels we enjoy free and clear from debt. I doubt if any church group in the world can even begin to approach the success we have had in our building program.

Some of the interesting experiences of my life occurred when I was a bishop and we were building a meeting house here in Salt Lake City. The better-to-do people had moved out of the ward and had either sold their homes or rented them to widows and poor people. One of the members of the high council who lived in our ward said that we just couldn't build a building, that our people were too poor. My reply was, "Well, we will build the building or die in the attempt, because if we do not the ward will die."

Just to illustrate, I would ask my daughters if they were going to bring their friends to one of our parties. They would reply, "Well, Daddy, you wouldn't expect us to bring them to this old rattle-trap, would you?"

Our stake president promised us that if we would go to with all our might and build that building, that none of us would feel any poorer after it was erected and paid for because of any contributions we had made toward its construction. I am sure this was true. The effort brought us together and made us love each other more as we worked and saved and paid on the building. Our attendance at Sacrament Meeting increased. Even the tithing increased while we were building the building!

The Widow's Share

One of the widows came to me and said, I haven't received my allotment for the meeting house. My reply was, "Well, you are not going to receive an allotment. If you will take care of those children your husband left you with, we will build the meeting house." At that time, she was going out working each day. Her reply was, "No, Bishop, I must be able to point to that building and tell my children that we have done our part." "Then," I said, "You will have to indicate what your part is." She paid us a substantial contribution. I have met her children as I have traveled through the Church and they are all active in the Church. One of her daughters, also a widow, has since filled a mission.

When the widow insisted that she wanted to pay, I thought of the experience of the widow of the Patriarch Hyrum Smith who was martyred with his brother Joseph. She came West with the saints, her young son, Joseph F. Smith, driving the ox team most of the way. She settled in Millcreek. One day she took a load of potatoes to the old tithing office back of where the Church Offices now stands. When the brother in charge of the tithing office saw it, he said, "Widow Smith, it's a shame that you should have to pay tithing." She rebuked the brother, saying, "William, you ought to be ashamed of yourself. Would you deny me a blessing?" Widow Smith paid her tithing all her life, and her family never had it as hard as many others who did not pay their tenth to the Lord. Her son later became the President of the Church.

As I thought of experiences like this, I thought of the words of the ancient Prophet, "*Cast your bread upon the water and after many days, it shall return.*"

A Poor Man's Share

We had another brother living in our ward, a foreigner. He lived in a very cheap little frame house that had never been plastered inside or out except with magazine pictures. He offered us $200.00 to help build the meeting house when money was really worth something.

I told him to take it home and fix up his own house for his children. He said, "Bishop, is there a law in this Church that a man can't give what he wants to help build up the kingdom?" I said, "Well, if you put it that way, I can't refuse to take your money." I have seen the children of that man achieve greatness. I met one of his sons in San Diego in the uniform of his country—as fine a specimen of young Mormon manhood as I have ever seen. I met another in the East who was a Professor. If I remember correctly one of his daughter's husband became the President of a Stake. Again I remembered the words of the Prophet, *"Cast your bread upon the water and after many days, it shall return."*

A Non-Member's Share

I went into the store of one of our brethren while we were building our chapel. He was not a member of the Church, but his wife and children were, and he had promised to pay $200.00. I told him I didn't know how his finances were, but that we had gone about as far as we could with the chapel unless we could get some more money. He stood for a moment and said, "Wait a minute, Bishop." He went in his office and wrote me a check for $200.00. I never knew just what that meant to that Brother at that time, until years later I went to visit him. He said, "Bishop, do you remember when you came to my store for money to help build the meeting house?" I said, "That's why I am here today, to thank you again for the wonderful support you gave us." Then he said, "When I gave you that $200.00 check I didn't know how I was going to meet my monthly bills, but I figured that if it was the work of the Lord, the Lord would help me through some way. Now," he said, "you can believe it or not, but before that day ended a man came into my store and paid me $200.00 on an old account that I had long since charged off my books and never expected to receive." When this good brother told me that, I knew that he knew who sent that man in, because the tears were rolling down his cheeks when he told me of the experience.

First Payment Hardest

We had many other wonderful experiences. We started our building the same week that one of the wards, supposed to be one of the rich wards, started their building. When our building was complete and paid for, they still owed $30,000 on their building. That was a lot of money in those days. I know, because I moved into the ward just in time to help raise the $30,000.

As Presiding Bishop, I used to tell the bishops never to promise the people that if they would pay so much, they would not be asked to pay more. I said, "The last $100 will be easier to pay than the first."

Just to illustrate ... When I was going into the dedicatory service of a chapel in Idaho, I said to a young couple coming up the walk, "I'll bet you are proud of this building aren't you?" The wife replied, "Yes." "Did you find it hard to pay for?" She said, "Only the first payment; after that, it was easy." I remembered the words that President Grant so often repeated to us. "That which we persist in doing becomes easy, not that the nature of the thing has changed, but that our power to do has increased."

President's Share

One of our good Bishops who presided in a section of the city where most of the people are tenants told me this story. He said he went to the First Presidency to get an appropriation to build a ward meeting house. At that time, they got permission direct from the First Presidency. President Grant asked, "How can you ever raise enough money among the members of your ward to build that meeting house?" The Bishop said there were two or three mining men living in his ward and he was going to ask them each for $1,000. That was when money was really money. Then he named the men. When he named one man, and I know that man well and his family, President Grant said, "When you get the first contribution from him, will you let me know?" President Grant followed this Bishop out into the hall and gave him his personal check for a substantial amount to help build that building.

The Miner's Dividend

The wife and children of this mining man belonged to the Church but he did not. When he would get a dividend on his mining stocks the mother or the daughter would call the Bishop and tell him he had better see the father. This man finally paid his $1,000 to help build the meeting house. Then when they furnished it, the man was disappointed because the Bishop didn't ask for an additional contribution. The Bishop just felt that he did not have the courage to do that.

The result was that this man who was one of the highest ranking Masons in Salt Lake applied for baptism. The Bishop said that he would arrange a special baptismal service so he wouldn't have to go along with the little children. The man replied, "No, Bishop, I should have been baptized when I was a young boy. I will go right along with the children." He lived long enough to take his family to the Temple and all were sealed together. Surely his dividend on the investment he made in that chapel was great.

Competition

Sometimes we do not make as fast progress as we would like in getting our chapels finished. In such cases, a little friendly competition between the members doing the work really speeds things up. Just to illustrate . . .

A Bishop in Ogden was erecting a new building and had lights strung so that his men could come and work at night. After the trenches were dug, he assigned the Elders to pour cement for the foundation the first night, the Seventies the second, the High Priests the third, and then to rotate. The first night the Elders poured twenty-four sacks of cement; but the seventies were checking up on them, and they came the second night and poured thirty-six sacks of cement. The High Priests in turn were checking on them, and they came and poured forty sacks of cement. By that time, the Elders had rounded up every Elder they could find and they returned and poured fifty-six sacks of cement. The only difference between the twenty-four the first night and fifty-six the second night being a little enthusiasm. The Seventies returned their second night and poured sixty sacks of cement. The High Priests returned and poured sixty sacks of cement and ran out of cement. It is marvelous what a little enthusiasm can do.

Worth of a Soul

Down South I was trying to impress the Saints with the need for some new buildings, for we had only two recreation halls in the entire mission. I told them I was sure that the souls of our young people were more valuable in the sight of the Lord than the cost of some new buildings. A short time later in the upper room of the Temple, President Clawson of the Quorum of the Twelve spoke to us on the marvelous creations of the Lord. Holding out his finger toward us mission presidents, he said: "But I say unto you, that the soul of one of his children is more precious in the sight of God than all things else he has created—with the earth thrown in as good measure." It was just as though President Clawson were speaking to me, and I said to him in my heart, "Thank you; I have made a mistake."

I went back to the South and told the people that I had told them that the souls of our young people were more valuable than the cost of a few buildings. "But," I said, "If President Clawson is a prophet, the soul of one of God's children is more precious in his sight than all the buildings the Church owns, including the temples, and all other buildings in the world, and the earth thrown in for good measure."

We need attractive, wholesome places for our people to meet, and adequate recreation halls for our young people. Their welfare far outweighs the sacrifices we make to build new chapels, and if we do our part, the Lord will bless us in our building program as in all other things.

Calling Missionaries

Give Each a Chance

Calling young men to fill missions is one of the many important responsibilities of a bishop.

I tell the bishops that if I had my way (I always add that I don't expect to get it) every young man in Israel who grows to manhood would be invited to go on a mission. Even if he does not go, he will feel drawn closer to the Church by virtue of the fact that his bishop has invited him. Otherwise, he will say, "I guess the bishop doesn't think much of me; he has called Frank and John and Harry on missions, but he has never asked me to go." I ran on to a case like this only recently, where one of our Salt Lake boys left home and went to Idaho because his bishop had called all his buddies on missions but had not asked him to go. He felt that the people would think he was not worthy or else the bishop would have called him.

Ready and Able

I tell the bishops that they cannot sit in their offices and determine whether a boy is willing to go or not, or whether he is financially able to go. I give this illustration: One of my friends aims to keep a missionary in the field at all times. Recently, he went to a bishop on the west side. He asked him if he had a young man in his ward whom he would like to send on a mission, but whom he had never asked because he did not think the boy nor the family could take care of the financial obligation. The bishop replied, "We have just such a boy— we have wanted to send him on a mission but we just didn't feel that he would be able to meet the financial requirements." So my friend said, "Well, interview him and his family and see what they can do. I will furnish whatever they are short." When the bishop told this young man the purpose of his call, his face lighted up, and he replied, "Bishop, I have the money in the savings bank for my mission—I have been waiting for two years for you to tell me that you would like to have me represent your ward in the mission field."

Then my friend inquired if there were someone else in the ward. The bishop said, "We have a boy whose father is not a member of the Church, and we haven't dared ask him." My friend said, "Well, talk with him and see what he and his family can do, and I will pay the balance." When the bishop went to the boy and his father, the father said, "I am willing to pay $25.00 per month for my son's mission, and I will be his first convert —I will let him baptize me before he goes on his mission."

It is my feeling that many a man's life would have been greatly enriched had his bishop invited him to go on a mission. In addition thereto, think of the lives of others whose lives would have been enriched through their missionary labors.

A "Must" Item

I tell the parents at our stake conference that if I had my way, every parent in Israel who is blessed of the Lord to be the parent of a male child would raise that child from the days of his youth with a "must" item in his life to go on a mission. I tell them that the proof of the pudding is in the eating of it, and that I have had the privilege of filling four missions and presiding over two. I wouldn't want to raise a boy in this day and generation and not have him go on a mission, for his own good, and because I think we owe so much to the world to share with them the glorious truths of the gospel. I always add, "If this universal military training is here to stay, we, and our boys, are going to have to broaden our views to include a mission even if the boys do have to serve their country, or we will fall down miserably on discharging our great responsibility of carrying the gospel to all nations, kindred, tongues and people."

The Last Straw

I used to enjoy very much hearing President Grant tell of the Scandinavian Brother who came over to Utah. He had not been taught much about the gospel; all he knew was that it was true. The bishop went to him and taught him the law of tithing. He paid his tithing. He taught him about fast offering. He paid his fast offering. He taught him about ward maintenance and he paid that. Then the bishop went to him to get a donation to help build the meeting house. The man felt that ought to come out of the tithing, but before the bishop was through with him, he paid his contribution toward the meeting house. Then the bishop went to him to get his son to go on a mission. The good brother said, "That is the straw that breaks the camel's back. He is the only child we have, and his mother can't miss him." Then the bishop countered, "Brother so and so, who do you love in this world more than anyone outside of your immediate family?" He thought a few minutes and said he guessed he loved that Mormon Elder who came up to the land of the midnight sun and taught him the Gospel of Jesus Christ. Then the Bishop countered, "Brother so and so, how would you like someone to love your boy just like you love that young Mormon Elder?" The brother said, "Bishop, you win again. Take him. I will be glad to support him in the mission field."

They Were Being Cheated

When I took the mission over, we had one full-time missionary out of that mission with eighteen thousand members of record; when we took a census however, we only found twelve thousand. I told the good saints of the

South that they were being cheated; that their boys and girls were as much entitled to missionary training as our boys and girls from the West; that if they would live for it, pray for it, work for it, and save for it, their boys and girls could go on missions as well as the boys and girls from the West. It was only a short time until we had fifty-six fulltime missionaries out of that mission. Everywhere I would go parents would say to me, "We will soon have a missionary for you." We would call them for three months or longer. Many who would go for three months would remain six. Those who went six months would remain a year. We trained those young people, and when they returned to branches we had something to build the work on in the various branches and districts. Some of these young people have become presidents of stakes and held other important positions.

If in our interviews with young men for their missions, we find that they are not fully worthy, that doesn't mean that we should dismiss the idea. We should work with them to help them to become worthy. Just to illustrate . . .

A Smoker

When I was a Bishop in California, we had a young man who played on our basketball team. He had acquired the habit of using tobacco. My boy used to say, "Isn't he a wonderful boy, if he would just quit his tobacco?" So I called him into the office one day. I don't believe in doing it on the run. Calling him by name, I said, "Would you be willing to give up your tobacco to prepare yourself to go on a mission." He said, "I don't believe I could do it." I said, "Would you try? Would you ask the Lord to help you?" Right after that he was transferred to San Francisco and was gone for six months. When he returned, he couldn't wait to see me at Sacrament Meeting. He came up to my home. When he put out his hand to shake hands with me, he didn't say, "How are you, Bishop?" He said, "Bishop, I haven't touched it since I left you." Then I said, "You are ready for your mission, aren't you?" He said, "That is what I came to tell you."

I later visited his stake of Zion, and we had our preliminary meeting with the stake presidency and the stake clerk, there he sat as the clerk of that great stake of Zion. I said to myself, "I wonder where he would be today if I hadn't said, 'Do you love the Lord and His Church enough to give up your tobacco to go on a mission?'"

A Matter of Leadership

Again, I emphasize the importance of every young man being given the opportunity of serving the Lord in the mission field. There are many wards and stakes that maintain at least one percent or more of their stake population in the mission field all the time. The last time I checked with my own stake, they had a stake population of sixty-five hundred with one hundred and five missionaries in the field. If each stake would maintain one percent or better, we would have over twelve thousand missionaries in the field, whereas, we only have about eight thousand. I am sure the difference is only a matter of leadership.

Recently, I attended a stake conference in a prosperous section of Idaho. They had a population of four thousand five hundred with only fourteen in the mission field. The next Sunday, I attended a conference in the older section of Provo, where most of their young people had married and moved away. They had a stake population of four thousand five hundred with forty-five in the mission field, and I interviewed two more missionaries while attending the conference. They were getting the experience and the blessings, while the other stake was missing out in part.

A Two-Edged Sword

In calling missionaries it is good to remember that a mission is like a two-edged sword—it blesses the families at home and the people in the mission field. In a missionary report meeting, one missionary bore his testimony that since his arrival in the mission field six months before, his father had started attending Sunday School and Priesthood Meeting. He said that he had received a letter from his Bishop stating that the attendance at Sacrament Meeting had increased and attributing it to the fact that they now had a missionary in the field. Another young man arose and said that during his six months in the mission field, his father had mastered the habit of tobacco to which he had been addicted for forty years.

My counselor and I once called on the parents of a certain young man in the ward to see if they would consent to our recommending their son for a mission. We did not think the father was a member of the Church. He said he did not want his son to go on a mission because he was the youngest child and the only one at home and his mother could not get along without him. We told him we had not come for his answer, but that we had come to tell him what we desired. We asked him to think and pray about it, and we would be in touch with him for his answer. The following week his son took sick. His illness was so severe that they sent for us to come and administer to him. This we did, and he had a speedy recovery, so his father said, "I guess we better let him go on his mission."

A Father Re-activiated

The boy was a fine missionary. As a bishopric we called at the home to visit the parents from time to time. We would often find the father sitting with his son's letter, looking up the references in the Bible and Book of Mormon his son had referred him to in his letter.

Finally, one day, the father came to my office and said, "Bishop, how can a man get back into the Church when he has once left it?" I said, "You mean to tell me that you were once a member of the Church?" "I was once an Elder in the Church," he replied. I asked him why he discontinued his activity. His reply was that when his sainted mother died, he couldn't believe there was a God who would let such a good woman suffer as she had.

Well, to make the story short, we looked up his membership, and he died a faithful member of the Church, all through the call of his son into the mission field.

The President of the West Canadian Mission reported in a meeting in the Temple that he had eighteen missionaries who came out of inactive Latter-day Saints homes, and that in fifteen of these homes the parents had become active while their sons were in the mission field.

I could understand fully what he had experienced, for I had had similar experiences in the Southern States mission. I shed many a tear in my office as I read letters from our missionaries reading something like this: "I have just received a letter from mother and she said father has quit his tobacco and has commenced attending his Priesthood meetings, and is getting himself ready so we can all go to the Temple together when you get home."

Children

Quick to Imitate

We hear again and again that children are our most valuable possession. Yet, it is amazing how little care sometimes goes into their training. A short time ago I heard this little anecdote: Peggy had been to the circus and her mother sought to impress a lesson. "When dogs, ponies, and monkeys obey so well, don't you think a little girl ought to obey even more quickly?" asked her mother. "So I should, Mommy," was the instant reply, "if I had been as well trained as they have."

It does seem that when dogs, and ponies, and monkeys can be made to obey so well, that with the same effort we can achieve most any desired result with our children, who are so much more intelligent, if we will give the proper attention and patience to training them. Like monkeys, children are quick to imitate—and perhaps that is part of our trouble. I would like to quote from an article that appeared in *The Kiwanis Magazine* entitled "Children are Dumb" by Roe Fulkerson:

"There is a general opinion that children are bright. In my opinion, there is no greater fallacy. They are so dumb it is a wonder we ever make really useful citizens out of them.

Wayward Fathers

"I want to illustrate. I know a fellow, a Kiwanian by the way, who has two small boys. He is a well-educated, cultured gentleman with a lovely wife and a nice home. Those two boys have been reared with every advantage. This man takes his golf clubs and hikes out to the golf course every Sunday morning of his life. Can you imagine those two boys are so dumb that they can't understand why they should be made to go to Sunday School?

They think they should be permitted to go fishing or swimming Sunday morning instead of going to church! Nothing their father says to them seems to convince the dumb little creatures that they should spend two hours in church on Sunday morning.

"I have a friend who has a boy of six. This friend rates very high in his profession and in the town, but if he mashes his finger with a hammer, or walks across the backyard and gets hooked under the chin with a wire clothesline, he makes the air a dark cerulean. He can swear longer without repeating himself than any other white-collar man I have known. Alas, his little boy is dumb. The family kitten jumped on the dining room table the other night at dinner and the boy exclaimed, 'Well, would you look at that . . . . cat!' His father spanked him promptly and thoroughly, washed his mouth out with soap, but do you know that he was never able to make that dumb kid understand that it is wrong to swear?

Perfect Example!

"I know a woman who doesn't like to go places she doesn't like to go and doesn't like to do things she doesn't like to do. So, when an unwelcome caller comes to the door, she has the maid say that she is out. If she is asked over the phone to do something she doesn't want to do, she blandly explains that she has house guests and can't do it. Do you know that woman has a dumb little daughter who is like Ananias. She has done all she can to break her of it, but the child is just a natural-born liar!

"Children are so doggoned dumb that they think their parents are perfect. Your son thinks you could lick Jack Dempsey without half trying. My daughter thinks that I am the smartest man in the world, and that anything I say or do is exactly right.

"Of course, if your son was not dumb, he wouldn't believe you could lick Jack Dempsey, because of course you can't. If my child was not so dumb, she would know that there must be three or four men in the world smarter than I am.

The Only Solution

"It looks to me like the mistake we make is overestimating the intelligence of our children. We are just going to have to act down to their dumb level. If we want them to go to church on Sunday morning, we are going to have to stop playing golf and go to church ourselves. If we want them to talk nice, we are going to have to stop swearing. If we want them to tell the truth, we are going to have to stop lying. If we want them to be orderly, we are going to have to stop throwing our own things all over the house. The same goes for all those other things which are all right for us, but all wrong for our children. Since our children are so dumb we are just going to have to show them plainly the way they should act, whether we like it or not."

Choice Seer

A Wonderful Promise

Joseph who was sold into Egypt received a promise from the Lord that in the latter days God would raise up a prophet from among his descendants. God promised that this prophet would be a choice seer like unto Moses. ". . . unto him will I give power to bring forth my word . . . and not to the bringing forth my word only, saith the Lord, but to the convincing them of my word, which shall have already gone forth among them."

In fulfillment of this promise, God raised up the Prophet Joseph Smith, and gave him power to bring forth his word, as it is recorded in the marvelous scriptures of the Book of Mormon, Doctrine and Covenants, and Pearl of Great Price. He further gave him power to convince the people of his word — the Bible — which had already gone forth among them.

Joseph Smith, the choice seer, was empowered by God to make the scriptures of the Bible plain and precious to men, so they believed their Bibles more fully and firmly than they ever had before.

There is not a church on the face of the earth which believes the Bible more wholeheartedly and completely than do the Latter-day Saints, even with their reservation to its correct translation — and all because God gave power to his choice servant to make its meaning clear to us.

The Bible Class

Building on the foundation Joseph Smith laid, we can make the scriptures of the Bible plain and precious and meaningful to others. Just to illustrate . . . While I was on my mission in Holland I was invited to talk to a Bible class in The Hague. This group met weekly to study the Bible, for the people of Holland are great Bible students. As I recall there were about twenty present the evening I met with them, and each had his own Bible. I was given an hour and a half to discuss the subject of universal salvation which includes our understanding of the preaching of the gospel in the spirit world, and baptism for the dead.

As near as I can recall, not a question was asked me during that discussion. When I had finished I closed my Bible and laid it on the table and folded my arms and waited for a comment. The first comment came from the daughter of the house. She said, "Father, I just cannot understand! I have never attended one of these Bible classes in my life that you have not had the last word to say on everything, and tonight you haven't said a word."

The father replied: "My daughter, there isn't anything to say. This man has been teaching us things we have never heard of, and he has been teaching them to us out of our own Bibles."

Scriptures Made Clear

On another occasion my missionary companion and I had been visiting in the home of a man and his family in Amsterdam once weekly for several months. After one of our visits the man of the house exclaimed, "I have learned more about the scripture and religion through your visits than in all the rest of my life!" Though his family had been accustomed to read a chapter from the Bible following each meal, without the light of the restored gospel they could not comprehend many of the scriptures they read. It took a choice seer raised up by God to convince men of the truth of their own Bible.

I once spent the night at the home of a Deacon of the Baptist Church and we sat up until two o'clock in

the morning discussing religion. The next day we baptized his wife, and that evening he drove me out into
the country to hold a meeting. The following night he
drove me over a hundred miles to Montgomery where
we held a meeting. All the time I was teaching him the
truth as fast as I felt he could absorb it. At the close of
the meeting he was standing with a group of members
and non-members and remarked to them: "I have learned
more about the Bible and religion in the last forty-eight
hours than in all the rest of my life put together!"

Isn't it wonderful. We have the truth — the fulness
of the gospel — and we can share it with others. And
all because God blessed us by raising up a choice seer
to bring forth his word and to convince men of his word
which had already gone forth among them. So great
was Joseph Smith's power to convince men of the truth
of the Bible, that many will admit the truth of his teachings even though they are not willing to make the
sacrifice to live up to them.

Church Attendance

Vitality of Mormonism

In 1956 I interviewed a young man from Toquerville for his mission. He had just returned from serving eighteen months in the army in Germany. He said the L. D. S. boys went to the chief chaplain and asked permission to hold their own meeting in the army chapel. The chaplain replied, "We would like to accommodate you, but the chapel is in such constant use, we just cannot do it." Then he added, "There is a classroom in the basement you can use."

When the L.D.S. boys handed him the report of their first meeting, the chaplain exclaimed, "My, you must have a lot of Mormon boys at this base!" He was told that there were thirty-five, to which he replied, "I just can't believe it! How do you do it? You have more boys attending your meetings than I have attending mine, and I have five thousand Protestant boys under my direction." Then he added, "I'll tell you what we will do. We will take the classroom in the basement—you can have the chapel."

When thirty-five Mormon boys far away from home and loved ones can make a better record of attending their meetings than five thousand Protestant boys, it certainly tells the story as to the vitality of Mormonism.

I told this story in a meeting in Glendale West Ward in California. At the close of the meeting a member of the bishopric came up to me and said he was raised in the Episcopal Church in San Francisco where they had a beautiful building with ten thousand members of record. He said their average attendance at Sunday service was less than one hundred. On the basis of our average attendance at Sacrament meeting, our attendance from a membership of ten thousand would have been three thousand seven hundred instead of a mere one hundred. Doesn't this show that we have a living religion? Church attendance is one measure of the vitality of a religion.

Church Membership

High Honors

Sometimes it takes a new convert to really appreciate what a wondeful blessing membership in the Church is. We get so used to it we take it for granted. But the teaching and training we receive as members make our lives rich and full, and help us to excel. Mormon men, women and young folk stand out in whatever group they happen to be in. Just to illustrate . . .

I was invited to attend "Religion in Life Week" at the University of Arizona in the forepart of 1957. There were four other ministers there. I spoke twenty-eight times during the four days.

I was informed that although our church members represented only three percent of the student body, they had taken twenty percent of the honors during the past year. The main exercises of the week were conducted by an L.D.S. girl. The president of the College presented her with an award in a Faculty Banquet, which all of the guest speakers attended, for the outstanding work she had done and for her leadership.

While I was meeting with a Sorority and Fraternity group one evening at 10:30 p.m., the young lady sitting next to me said that she was from Phoenix, Arizona, and that the Mormon young people in the schools of Phoenix were always outstanding.

Something Special

While I was in the Eastern States, one of the lady missionaries had to go to the hospital, so her mother came out to be with her. In visiting, the mother told me this experience:

She said she was traveling on the train between Salt Lake and Los Angeles. As she was reading the Book of

Mormon, a young man passed in the aisle and noticed what she was reading. He stopped and introduced himself and asked if she were a Mormon. When she informed him that she was he told her this experience.

He said he was a graduate from Harvard University. He said that when he graduated, he felt that he could meet any person and be prepared to converse without embarrassment. Then he said he was sent overseas during the first world war, and he was thrown in with two companions who had filled missions for the Mormon Church. He said he hadn't been with these young men for long before he felt inferior in their presence. He said he didn't know what it was, but decided that it must be their church. "So," he said, "When I obtained an assignment to do some engineering work in Arizona, I decided I would route myself via Salt Lake City so I could learn something about their church." He told her that he had spent three interesting days in Salt Lake. Then he opened his traveling bag and showed her the church books he had purchased, saying: "I am going down to Arizona and I am going to read these books and see if I can find in them that which made me feel inferior in the presence of those young men."

Capable Women

My wife's mother was born in North Carolina and came West with her parents when she was a young woman. While serving as President of the Southern States Mission, I took her back with me after a General Conference. On Mother's Day we visited the place of her birth in North Carolina and met many of her relatives and found them to be honorable people. They lived in good homes. They had their oil paintings and their colored maids. It was one of the most interesting experiences I have had. In one home a little woman in her nineties would rap her cane on the floor and her colored

maid would come. She looked up at grandma and said,
"Why, Cora, it is just like the dead coming back to life
again."

Grandma had not been back for some fifty to sixty
years since she left there. We tried to hunt up her old
sweetheart who threatened to kill the Mormon Elders
if they ever came around for having taken his sweetheart
from him. We found that he had passed away.

One evening we were in quite a group and there was
a woman there, not a member of the Church who had
taught school for a year in Utah. She made a statement
like this, "You can't keep up with those Mormon women.
They raise large families; they do their own house work;
they put up their fruit for winter; they work in their
Church organizations, and in civic organizations. Then
they go to school to get an education while they are doing
all that." She said, "It made me tired to watch them.
I decided I would come back to the South where I could
live a peaceful life."

The training we gain through activity in our Church,
and the standards we are required to live up to (if we are
good members) are a real asset to us.

Positions of Responsibility

When in Washington some time ago, I was told
that there were more Mormons in positions of responsibility in Washington per capita than members of any
other church, and that our young people were consistently sought after.

Brother Widtsoe used to tell the story about a business firm in Los Angeles that advertised for a book-
keeper. They received many applications. After sorting
them out, they invited some applicants to call at the office
for interviews. When one boy called, the manager said,
"I note from your application that you were born in
Utah." The answer was, "Yes, Sir." "Are you a member

of the Mormon Church?" "Yes, Sir." "Have you filled
a mission for the Mormon Church?" "Yes, Sir." "Do
you keep their Word of Wisdom?" "Yes, Sir." "Do you
pay your tithing?" "Yes, Sir." "Do you have your daily
prayers?" "Yes, Sir." The manager then replied, "You
may have the job." He didn't ask him how many years he
had spent in school.

Youthful Testimony

Early in 1957 I took my grandson with me to a conference in Spanish Fork. The Stake President called him
to speak. He told of attending a speech class in the high
school in Glendale. One day the teacher asked each
member of the class to either write a report, or be prepared to speak for twenty minutes, on some book they
had read or on some show they had seen. After the class
the teacher spoke to our grandson and said he would like
him to talk on the Book of Mormon. Our grandson
replied that he would be glad to do it, but that he could
not do it in twenty minutes. His teacher asked him how
much time he would need. He said, "Three hours." The
teacher said he would give him three hours. Before he
had finished discussing the Book of Mormon covering
speech class periods for several days, he had many of the
teachers come in to listen to him and students from other
classes. When he had finished, his teacher, called him
by name, said, "I believe you believe what you have told
us." His reply was, "I don't believe it . . . I know it."

The Bishop of his ward told me that the Principal of
the High School had attended several of their ward
meetings giving as the reason for his interest the fact
that he had noticed for years that the Mormon young
people seemed better adjusted than any students in his
school.

He further said, "If I were to select any boy I have
ever known to pattern my life after, were I a young man

again, I would select the young man from the speech class who talked on the Book of Mormon."

Our entire Church program is geared to help us develop as individuals. Take the matter of speaking, for instance. I doubt that my grandson could have talked to his class and the visiting teachers for three hours intelligently if he had not had the training that begins with our two and one half minute talks in Sunday School. Youth of other churches are not so lucky.

Competition Unwelcome

My son-in-law living in Los Angeles told me of an interesting talk he had with the Clerk of the Court. The Clerk told him that his wife had been appointed on a committee to investigate the churches of Los Angeles, to see which one was doing the most for its young people. After visiting the Wilshire Ward in Los Angeles, this lady went to her minister and said, "Why can't our young people take part in our church like the Mormon young people? Why can't they preach and pray from our pulpit, and conduct their own exercises?" The minister's reply was, "I don't propose to develop any competition in my church. If our young people want to preach in church, let them go and get it like I got mine. It cost me a lot of money to learn to preach."

Practice Makes Perfect

While our speakers may not always be the best, they learn by doing, and it's up to us to help them by patience and encouragement. That's how we got all the fine speakers we have in the church. As an illustration of what I mean, let me relate this little experience.

While presiding in the Netherlands Mission, we called a local brother to speak at one of our meetings. He unwisely took all of the time. At the close of the meeting, one of our new converts from a little higher social strata than the average, came to me and complained because I sat on the stand all through the meeting and let that man take all of the time. "Well," I said, calling her by name, "Sister so and so, you don't seem to understand the philosophy of Mormonism. We don't have a preacher in our Church who hasn't practiced on someone. I don't know that you are any better than the rest of the saints that this man should not practice on you. Someday he may be one of the best speakers among the Dutch people." He has, I think, filled three full-term missions, and is one of the best speakers we have produced among our Holland people. Then I told her how grateful I was to the good Dutch saints who put up with me when I could not speak their language and yet made every effort to try and make them understand.

Converts In Amsterdam

A "Ripe" Group

Elder Martin Dalebout, who was President of a Branch in Amsterdam Holland, had contacted a group of people who had withdrawn from their church because they did not feel that their church had the truth. One of them had dropped in to one of our meetings a few years before when Brother Dalebout was on his first mission. He had heard him preach and had gone home and told his wife what he had heard, for his heart had been touched. She forbade him to go there again, but he did not forget the impression that had come to him. Finally he dropped into the same little church, and listened to Brother Dalebout again, who had now returned on his second mission. This opened the door to an invitation to visit these people. After the first visit, Elder Dalebout invited me to join him. As I recall, there were over thirty present, including one minister. Before the meeting closed, one good woman stood up and thanked God that there was still water so she could be baptized as was her Savior. As near as I can recall, we baptized over thirty from this group within about six weeks time. We told them all about tithing and polygamy — everything that we felt might make them want to leave us after baptism. Out of that group have come many wonderful saints who came to Zion. They have filled positions of responsibility, and have furnished many, many years of missionary service to their native land.

Predestination

I had another family of investigators in Amsterdam. They believed strongly in the doctrine of predestination. They had a friend well versed in the scriptures who would visit them every time after I had been to their home, and would try to undo all the good I had done. I invited the man of the house to invite his friend to come when we were at his home so we could have an opportunity to meet all his arguments, but the friend refused to meet us.

He attended our meeting one night. At the close of the meeting, the missionaries engaged him in conversation at the door. I stepped up and listened a few minutes, not knowing who the man was. When I found that the missionaries were taking good care of themselves, I walked away to attend other matters. This man visited my investigators again, and told them that he had been to our meeting, but that Mr. Richards was afraid to talk to him. On hearing this, I renewed my invitation to meet him at any hour of the day or night that would meet his convenience, but he would not agree to meet me.

One evening, a few weeks later, when I called to see this family, there this man sat. After I had been introduced to him, I drew my chair up near to him, and offered him my Bible with an invitation to show me just one passage of scripture therein that would justify his teaching the doctrine of predestination. He refused. Finally the man of the house said, "You have come into our home for years to discuss the word of God with us, but from now on, you will be welcome but I never want you to attempt to discuss the word of God again in our home."

These people joined the Church, but never came to America; however, their son did and has filled a mission for the Church.

Council Meetings

The Big Difference

I tell this story on the importance of council meetings. The Church allowed us to purchase a new Ford for the Southern States Mission, the first it had owned. Our first conference thereafter was at Jacksonville, Florida. I drove this new car and parked it by the oldest Model "T" I could find. At the close of the meeting, I invited the missionaries to come and see their new auto. I said, "It belongs to the mission." Then pointing to the two autos, I asked, "What is the difference between these two autos?" I got all kinds of answers to which I kept saying, "No." Then I asked them if they would like to have me tell them what I felt was the difference. They agreed that they would, so I said, "The only difference is council meetings. If Henry and his engineers had thought the Model "T" was good enough, they would still be making it. But they held some Council Meetings, and decided that they could make it look a little better, and they did; that they could make it ride a little easier, and they did; that they could take some of the rattles out, and they did. Now when you see the two autos standing side by side, you wouldn't even think they were related, and here they are, full brothers." I have since been informed that when Henry's engineers wanted to build a better auto, they had a hard time to convert Henry that the Model "T" was not good enough.

When you go into an auto showroom today and examine any new model, you say to yourself: "What in the world will they add next time to make the next model better than this one?" But when the next model is produced, it is better and has some new gadgets. That would not be true if they didn't continue to hold council meetings.

The same is true with our church work. It makes the constant holding of Council Meetings necessary to enable us to keep out of the ruts and lift our work to new heights.

Courage

Choose the Right

When people hear the gospel they have to make a choice — whether to accept it along with the persecution or loss it brings, or to reject it and keep their worldly station and friends. A right decision takes courage.

Some people love the truth enough to be willing to make the sacrifice, like the minister who gave up his position as head of a congregation and took a menial job. But some people, though they recognize the truth, do not have the courage to live it.

In New Bedford, I called to see a lady who had been visited formerly by the missionaries. She told me that she would be glad to join the church if it were more popular in New England, but that her husband was in business and they were sure he would lose his business were they to join the church. She said they just didn't have faith enough to make this sacrifice.

Then she told me of a visit to her home by her minister. He saw a copy of the Book of Mormon in her book case and said, "What are you doing with that thing in your book case?" To which she replied, "Don't call that a thing — as far as I am concerned it is the word of God." To which he replied, "Well, I wouldn't call it that." Her reply was, "But I would."

Now, I know that if that woman and her husband had had enough faith to join the Church, their blessings would have outweighed their business success many times. We have to be willing to sacrifice to get the blessings!

Fear of Prejudice

I imagine we would have twice as many people in our Church if everybody who believed our message had courage to accept it. Just to illustrate. . .

I visited the home of the treasurer in the Presbyterian Church in New Bedford, Massachusetts. He paid the minister, and had to substitute for him at times when he was not able to attend his meetings. He and his wife attended one of our conferences in Boston at which President B. H. Roberts and President Heber J. Grant were present. After he had read most of the Book of Mormon, I asked him if he felt impressed as he read that book that it had been written by Joseph Smith, or any other person, for the purpose of leading men away from God; or if he felt it had a "familiar spirit." His reply was: "As I have read the Book of Mormon I have felt the same spirit that I feel when I read the New Testament. That book was not written to deceive men or lead them away from faith in God — it is the word of God."

I later received a letter from this man thanking me for bringing him the truth, but admitting that he was too much of a coward to accept it until he could get his family and friends to feeling more kindly toward the Mormon people, because of the terrible prejudice in the minds of the people of New England toward the Mormon Church.

Fear of Ostracism

The agent of the Holland American Steamship Line from Rotterdam called to see President Heber J. Grant with a letter of introduction from our mission president in Holland. President Grant invited me to his office to help entertain this gentleman because I had filled two missions in Holland. After President Grant had taken us to lunch, and autographed some books for this gentleman, he turned him over to me to entertain. After showing him around the city, I asked him what he would like to do for the evening. I said, "I can take you to a show, or I can drive you out to the Bingham Copper Mines, or to the Saltair Beach, or if you would like to see the Mor-

mons in action, I can take you to a Mormon Bazaar."
His reply was that he could see shows anywhere, and
he could see country, but that he might never be able
to see the Mormons again in action.

I took him to the Granite Stake House at 33rd South
and State Street. In the basement were all kinds of
booths operated by the Relief Society and other auxil-
iaries and Priesthood Quorums — Deacons polishing
shoes; girls selling candy, and so forth. I introduced
him to quite a number of our Holland Saints who had
come to Utah for the gospel's sake. He bought more
homemade candy than anyone else and treated the
people.

Then they announced that there would be an Oper-
etta in the chapel upstairs, so we went up there and it
was beautiful — so refined and cultural.

Then they announced a dance in the recreation hall
in the basement. Calling him by name, I said, "Mr. so
and so, I don't want to tire you — if you prefer I will
now take you to the hotel." He replied, "Couldn't I see
the dance first?" When he saw several hundred couples
of our young people dancing and having such a good
time, he said something like this, "If I hadn't seen it,
I would not believe that you could bring so many young
people together in a dance with no evidence that anyone
had an evil thought, with no smoking or drinking, and
everybody seems so happy."

On our way to the hotel, he said, "If I were a young
man, I would like to cast my lot with you Mormons,
but my son in Holland is a doctor and my daughter is
married to a professor, and you know what the people
of Holland think of the Mormons — I would be ostra-
cized by my own family."

A Glass of Milk

Some of our young people haven't the courage to live
their religion when they are away from home. They

seem to feel it will be a detriment to them. But I know that almost without exception the world admires us when we live up to our convictions.

During the war one of our L.D.S. boys was attending officers' training school in the East. A new commanding officer came into the camp and they gave a reception for him. Since all the boys were potential officers, there was a cocktail glass placed at each plate at the banquet. At the proper time each boy raised his glass to toast the new commanding officer — all except one boy, and he raised a glass of milk. The officer noted it, and at the close of the banquet he went right to the boy and said, "Why did you toast me with a glass of milk?" The boy replied, "Officer, I have never touched liquor in my life — I don't want to touch it — my parents would not want me to touch it, and I didn't think you would, so I toasted you with what I am accustomed to drink."

"You report at headquarters tomorrow morning," he said, indicating the time. The boy, of course, spent a restless night, but when he reported to the commanding officer next morning he had a pleasant surprise. He was assigned a place on the officer's staff, with this explanation from the officer: "I want to surround myself with men like you who have the courage to do what they think is right regardless of what anyone else may think about it."

Courage! what a wonderful virtue.

Divide Opportunities

Personal Sermons

I was a stranger in Sugarhouse Ward when I became Bishop. My counselors and I spent night after night going over the Priesthood rolls acquainting ourselves with various brethren who held the Priesthood. One of my counselors had lived in the ward all of his life so he knew them well. I suggested to my counselors that we ask our stake president not to send any home missionaries to us for months, but to permit us to call each man holding the Priesthood to speak in a Sacrament meeting. I always felt that that would do them more good than anything I know of to help re-kindle the spirit of the gospel in their hearts. The stake president approved of our recommendation, so we would have three or four speakers in every Sacrament Meeting. We would invite them a couple of weeks in advance so they could preach to themselves for that period of time, figuring that that would do them more good than all the sermons they had heard for years. We told them what we wanted them to preach about. We said, "We don't just want a gospel sermon; we want to know what the Church means to you and your families, and what it meant to your pioneer ancestors when they crossed the plains." We had men stand up and with tears in their eyes testify that they had been home from their mission some twenty, some twenty five, some thirty years, and it was the first time they had been asked to speak from the pulpit of their church since they had reported their missions. I have always felt that it is a shame for the leadership of the Church to permit our missionaries to return home and then let their spirits wither because we fail to give them an opportunity to bear witness of the truth before the people.

Changes Necessary

It is good for the members also to have a change of the usual run of speakers. They may see the same faces so often and hear the same messages so often that they just don't pay attention anymore. We become blind and deaf to the everyday condition of things. Just to illustrate. . . .

While attending a Stake Conference some years ago, I stood looking at the Stake Tabernacle grounds with a member of the Stake Presidency during the interval before the afternoon session. There was an iron fence around the grounds with dagger-shaped pickets. Each picket was bent, one inward, the next outward, alternating around the entire corner.

The man to whom I was speaking was a blacksmith. I said, "President, how long would it take you to straighten those pickets." He looked at the fence and turned to me and said, "I surely owe you an apology. I come here at least three times every week of the world, and this is the first time I knew the pickets were bent."

I use this illustration to point out to the leadership of the Church how we have to change stale patterns. There is a great difference in the Church in one location and another because the people have lived with their conditions so long they do not recognize their actual conditions and weak spots.

In some stakes all of our young men want to go on missions as soon as they are old enough. In other stakes, they all want to join the army. In other stakes, they all want to get married. So, it is a great labor and responsibility of leaders to help to change patterns, where such changes are necessary.

Dr. Hugh Nibley's Testimony

Book of Mormon Scholar

Hugh Nibley grew up with our children. We were always Uncle LeGrand and Aunt Ina to him.

His mother told me that he read the Book of Mormon eleven times by the time he was twelve years old, and then commenced studying it. He says it is the greatest book in the world.

While he was teaching at the Brigham Young University, I asked President Wilkinson how he got along with the other faculty members. His reply was: "Oh, they never bother Dr, Nibley; he knows too much."

His mother told us that when he went to Berkeley to get his Doctorate, one of the Professors asked the Doctor who was examining him, what he was going to do with the young man Nibley. His reply was: "I am going to let him go right through without any argument. I am not going to let him make a fool out of me."

While visiting with Dr. Hugh's mother July 3, 1957, she permitted me to copy a paragraph from his Christmas letter to her for Xmas 1956. He was telling of his work in writing the Priesthood manual for the Melchizedek Priesthood. I quote:

"This is a strange state of things — always thinking of you but never writing! The same things happen day after day, and the same thoughts night after night. It has been a steady diet of Book of Mormon, and no other food is so invigorating — it is the bread of life in the most digestible form."

Test of Time

Dr. Nibley gave a series of radio talks over K.S.L. entitled, "Time Vindicates The Prophets." I quote from his address of September 5, 1954. After discussing the

Philosophers, and how they can go only so far and then
they have to turn to the Prophets, he said:

"This is not the case with the Book of Mormon.
What do we find in it? A wealth of doctrine embedded in
large amounts of what is put forth as genuine historical
material, not devotional or speculative or interpretive or
creative writing but genuine historical fact, stuff that
touches upon reality—geographical, ethnological, lin-
guistic, cultural, etc.—at a thousand places. On all these
points the book could sooner or later be tested, as Joseph
Smith knew. We cannot possibly deny his good faith in
placing it before the whole world without any reservation.
Aside from all other considerations it is a staggering
work; its mass and complexity alone would defy the talent
of any living man or body of men to duplicate today.
Its histories are full and circumstantial; yet sober, simple,
straightforward—there is nothing clever in the whole
book. For a century and a quarter it has undergone the
closest scrutiny at the hands of its friends and enemies,
and today it stands up better than ever."

Dreams And Visions

Tithing Funds Saved

The Lord has many ways of communicating with his children. Some people are more receptive to spiritual promptings than others but there is no doubt that the Lord instructs and directs all his righteous children for their benefit.

While in the Netherlands Mission, our Mission Secretary and the District President spent an evening visiting investigators. Afterwards, the Mission Secretary invited the District President to stay with him at the Mission office. He accepted the invitation, and as missionaries always do, they had their prayers together and went to bed. The District President was restless and could not go to sleep. Finally, he told the Secretary that he felt that he should return to the District office, which was at the chapel in Rotterdam, St. Jan Straat 15. The Secretary said, "Well, if you feel so impressed, I think you had better go." The District President got up, dressed himself, and went to the District office. He arrived there just in time to find two men carrying his trunk down the front steps of the building, which trunk contained the Tithing funds of the District in quite a substantial sum.

If the District President had not hearkened to the promptings of the spirit, the tithing funds would have been stolen, but the Lord wanted those funds put to good use so he warned the one in charge of their safe-keeping.

A Timely Rescue

The Lord has to have instruments through whom he can answer the prayers of his faithful children. Sometimes he sends angels, and sometimes he just moves upon the hearts of some of his children by the power of His Holy Spirit to do the things he wants done.

The missionaries and saints from the Southern States Mission, particularly from the State of Florida, all know the Jenkins family in Jacksonville. They have built up a chain of jewelry stores all over the State of Florida. They were some of the first converts in Jacksonville and did much to help establish the Church in that city.

While in the south, I received a letter from Brother Jenkins relating an experience he had when he went in swimming at the beach with his two sons. He said that the undertow started carrying them out and he could not control the situation. It looked as if it was going to cost him and his boys their lives and he prayed to the Lord for help. There were two scouts on their way to a resort along the beach some distance away. When they were half way there, one of the boys said to his companion, "Let's turn around and go back; I don't feel like going to the resort." So they turned around and came back just in time to hear the cries of Brother Jenkins for help. They went in and rescued him and his sons. Brother Jenkins bore his testimony in the letter to me of his gratitude to the Lord, and of his acknowledgment that it was the Lord that put it in the hearts of those boys to turn around and come back just in time to rescue him and his sons.

Power of Prayer

I was once invited to speak at a stake High Priests meeting in Salt Lake. The President of the Quorum insisted that he would like to pick me up at my home and take me to the meeting, so I agreed. On the way to the meeting he told me this experience.

He worked for the city. One evening as he was driving up Main Street in his auto, he saw a young man in uniform in the clutches of a wicked woman. He said,

"Something seemed to say to me 'You rescue that young man.'" So he parked his car and went back and took him by the arm and said, "You come with me." The woman said, "Oh, no you don't—he belongs to me." This brother pointed to a policeman at the corner and said, "That policeman will take care of you," so she made no further protest. He drove the boy around until he had sobered up. Then he took him to a hotel and paid for his room for the night, and left him his calling card inviting him to let him know if he could ever be of any further assistance.

In a few weeks he received a letter from this boy's mother from the East thanking him for what he did for her son. She said he had never used liquor before nor had he had anything to do with wicked women before. Then she added, "I don't know why you rescued my boy, unless it was that I prayed for him that night as I had never prayed before." You see, the Lord had to have an instrument to help answer her prayer.

Seekers After Truth

Many persons have testified to having been prepared for the missionaries by a dream or vision.

While visiting the Central American Mission, I heard one of the lady missionaries giving her report. She said she and her companion were walking along the street in Guatemala one day when a man came up to them and said, "I know you women—I have seen you in a dream—you have the truth. I would like you to come to my home and teach me and my family."

At mission headquarters I received a letter one day from a Brother Bathune in South Carolina reading about as follows:

"I understand there is a son of Brother Arthur A. T. Shurtliff laboring in this mission. If there is, would you please let him attend our next District Conference, and spend a few days in my home? I would like to put my arms around the son of the man the Lord let me see in an open vision of the day as I was sitting in my home, a year before he and Elder Turner called at my home and brought me the Gospel of the Lord Jesus Christ."

I visited Brother Bathune the next time I was in South Carolina. He told me that he was sitting in his front room one day before the fireplace. His spiritual eyes were opened and he saw Brother Shurtliff and his companion, Elder Turner, call at his door and inform him that they were sent to teach him regarding the restored gospel of Jesus Christ. He said it was a year later that these two Elders called at his home He recognized them as soon as he saw them at his door. He invited them in and they taught him the gospel.

After a successful street meeting in which we had been challenged about our "Golden Bible," I met a woman who became one of our strongest members. I asked her if she would like a copy of the Book of Mormon. She indicated that she would but that she didn't have any money with her. I persuaded her to take a copy, explaining that she could give me the money some other time if convenient.

The next week she was at our meeting, paid me for the book, and accepted my invitation to visit her at her home. She had joined a number of churches seeking the truth, but in each case had been disappointed. She told us of a dream she had in which she was being chased by a man. She either had to run into a slough or barricade herself in a little shanty at the side of the road. She chose the latter course. While she was there, a man called and offered her a new volume of scripture.

He made her promises of how she would become a blessing to her family and loved-ones.

All we had to do was to teach her the truth. She joined the Church, and was the means of bringing many of her people into the church. I had the privilege of baptizing her before returning home.

Divine Manifestation

I baptized the brother of Sister Ruby McCall of Lisman, Alabama, at his request, together with his two sons. President Melvin J. Ballard confirmed him a member of the Church. Sister McCall, a wonderful woman, had written me telling me of his conversion and informing me that it was his desire that I should baptize him. I later misplaced her letter, so while touring the mission in December, 1956, I met Sister McCall at Montgomery, Alabama, and asked her if she would write me again and relate the experience as she could remember it, although it had been twenty years since he joined the church. I quote from her letter of December 12, 1956 as follows:

"It has been around twenty years since this manifestation occurred. The letter that I wrote you at the time contained more details than I can remember now.

"I had tried to interest my brother, Emmet LeRoy Coker, in the gospel by giving him tracts and a Book of Mormon, but he had never been to conference, nor had he ever seen or met you.

"You were to hold conference in Mobile, Alabama. The girls and I were going. I invited my brother and family to come with us and they did. It was a wonderful day—so many good speakers. You the most wonderful of all.

"I watched my brother during the meeting, saw he was very quiet and interested. Knew you had made an impression on him. He had very little to say on our drive to Lisman. That night after arriving home, he said to his wife, 'Honey, I saw something today no one else did.' 'What was it?' she asked. 'While President Richards was up speaking I saw a bright light shining above his head. I know the Church is true and I want to join, and I want President Richards to baptize me.' "

A Worthy Soul

No doubt this manifestation came to Brother Coker because of his worthiness and wonderful character. His sister, commenting on him and his life, made this statement:

"My brother, Emmet LeRoy Coker, and I say this without prejudice, in his early manhood was 6 feet, 2 inches, weighing one hundred eighty pounds, the handsomest man I have ever seen, with brown curly hair, brown eyes, and dark skin. He was kind and considerate to everyone and everything. He was honest and truthful in all things. He feared neither man nor the Devil. All his life, as a boy in school, he fought the bullies who picked on the underpriviledged kids, defending colored or white people that he knew were being abused in any way. Once in a court trial of a negro that he saw being mistreated or about to be, he stood up and stopped the proceedings. He was above the average in intelligence.

"After his death, his niece Lillian said, 'Mama, if Uncle Emmet had been born in a gutter, he would have been a gentleman.' Maybe that sums up what I have been trying to say. We, his family, know what I write you is true."

Such experiences are but testimonies that the Lord has not forgotten his promise made when he sent his Apostles into the world to preach the gospel unto all people following his resurrection: "And, lo, I will be with you always, even unto the end of the world."

Increased Understanding

When I arrived in Holland on my first mission I was very disappointed at being assigned to serve as secretary of the Mission. I had looked forward for years to the time I would be a missionary, and I had a strong desire to preach the gospel. Whenever the other missionaries went out I chafed at the restraint of having to stay in and do secretarial work. I wanted to be out actively bearing witness to the truth. It bothered me so much that the Lord blessed me with a dream which made me feel satisfied to do the work I had been assigned.

I dreamed that I was keeping books for my father in his implement and lumber business. I kept pleading with my father to let me leave because I wanted to go outside and work as a regular laborer. Finally, Father gave his consent and I took the train for Salt Lake. Upon my arrival I was met by a friend who took me and introduced me to the foreman of a section gang. In those days these section hands would drive their truck along the railroad track to keep it in repair. The foreman gave me a job and four of us left the station, two on each side, operating that truck by hand. We had gone but a short distance when one of the men asked me what I had been doing. When I told him I had been keeping books, he asked me how much I had been earning. When I told him, he replied, "You are foolish. If I could keep books, I wouldn't be out here. Anyone can do this, but not everyone can keep books."

With that I awakened with this thought, "Anyone can do regular missionary work, but not everyone can keep books, and both are necessary."

This satisfied me so that I was content to keep the books, realizing I was doing what I was needed to do. Later, when I was given the responsibility of presiding over that Mission, I understood all the office procedures which was a great help to me in my work.

Joyous Intimation

Shortly before my release from presiding over the Southern States Mission, I dreamed that I met President Grant on the street in Salt Lake. He invited me to his office telling me that he had a special blessing for me. Accordingly, I went to his office and he gave me a blessing. When I awakened I could not remember what he had said. All I could remember was how thrilled I was at receiving his blessing.

Within a year from that time, in the Salt Lake Temple, President Grant placed his hands upon my head and set me apart as the Presiding Bishop of the Church. I realized that this was the special blessing I had dreamed he had for me, but it would not have been proper for me to be able to remember what it was until it actually found its fulfillment.

Called Home

Bishop John Wells, a member of the Presiding Bishopric related to me an experience of one of the Brethren who worked at the Presiding Bishop's office. The Brother said that one morning while he and his wife were sitting at the breakfast table with their son, their son made a statement like this, "I had a peculiar dream last night. I dreamed that I had died and went to the other side. I was met by a guide who showed me around. We came to a group of Brethren and stopped and listened while the roll was called. To my great surprise, my name was the last name on the list of a Quorum of Elders of 96 members." He said, "I had the ability to hear my name called, but I had no ability to make known my presence. The man in charge turned to the secretary and said, 'Where is Brother so and so?'

He was told that I was still upon the earth. Then he said, 'See that he is here to answer the roll call next Wednesday.' "

Naturally, when Wednesday came the parents were very much concerned. They tried to get their son not to leave the house. He was working in a grocery store and he said, "Nothing can hurt me there." So he went to work and a woman came in for an article—that was up on one of the high shelves. When he got up to get the article—the shelves caved in and it cost him his life. According to Brother Well's story of this incident, he went on Wednesday to answer the roll call according to the requirement of the Brother who was conducting this meeting with the Elders Quorum in the spirit world.

A Grandmother's Request

Occasionally departed spirits are permitted to return to convey a message of importance, or to comfort loved ones. Just to illustrate . . .

After we had lost our son, LeGrand, in an accident at the beach in California, Bishop Wells, representing the Presiding Bishopric, attended our Stake Conference. In trying to comfort us, he told us these two experiences he and his wife had. She seemed to have had a gift of enjoying spiritual experiences.

He told us that when they were preparing to leave England to immigrate to America, they had sold all of their furniture. They went to spend the night with his wife's mother. During the night, his wife's grandmother appeared to his wife, Sister Wells, and told her that when she was a girl, she heard the Mormon Elders preach and she went to one of their meetings. When she told her parents, they had forbidden her ever to go there again, so she never did. "But," she said, "Since I have been dead, the Elders have taught me the gospel and I have accepted it. Now I am waiting for my Temple work to be done for me." She asked them if they would go to the Temple and do her work for her when they reached Zion. Then she said to Sister Wells, "Now you look at me and then you describe me in the morning to your mother. She will tell you that I am her mother," and she did.

When the Wells arrived in Salt Lake, they hired a horse and buggy and drove to Manti, the Salt Lake Temple was then not in use, and did the work for Sister Wells' Grandmother according to her request.

A Comforting Visit

Sister Wells had another wonderful spiritual experience when her son was killed in an accident in Emigration Canyon. She felt so broken up about it that one night he appeared to her and explained some things she was eager to know. He said that when his spirit left his body that he went to the Presiding Bishop's office where his father, Bishop John Wells, was talking to a certain sister, and he named her. Afterwards Brother Wells checked his desk calendar and found that was correct. Then he said he came up to the home and he told his mother that she had been baking pies. He even told her the song that she had been singing. Then he told her not to worry anymore about him because he was happy, but that he felt a little strange because he was not so well acquainted there. Sister Wells asked him how he happened to get killed. He explained to her that while he was working with the switching of the train he caught his foot in a root which threw him under the train, and the train ran over him and killed him.

Then she worried about him because he had expressed the thought that he felt strange where he was. So he came to her again and told her that he had now been assigned to work in his Priesthood and that he was very happy. He told her not to worry about him anymore, because he would not be permitted to come back to see her again. I am sure that persons must live close to the Lord to enjoy spiritual blessings like this.

In response to great faith or patience the Lord may give special blessings. In Rotterdam I heard a good sister, who had waited eight years for permission from her husband to join the Church, bear testimony that the Lord had made it known to her that she was going to be baptized before our next fast day. After meeting she asked what I thought of her testimony. I said, "It is wonderful if the Lord has revealed this to you after all the years you have waited. But remember, it will have to be with the consent of your husband." Well, before the next fast day we baptized her and her daughter with her husband's consent. The foreknowledge she was given, though not necessary, was a special comforting reward from the Lord for her long patient wait.

Effects Of Sin

Permanent Scars

When I was a boy, a good brother in our ward was asked to speak in the Sacrament Meeting one evening. He brought a 2 x 12 plank with a sack of ten penny nails and a hammer. He drove all those nails in that plank right in the presence of us young people. Then he pulled them all out. Then he commented, "You see, they were there, but they are not there anymore; but the holes are there." Then he preached a sermon on the holes and how we could mar our lives and how it would take time to overcome the scars if we did not keep the commandments of the Lord and keep our lives sweet and clean.

In speaking of how we should behave during our years of courtship, he said, we should not kiss the girls until we were sure we were going to marry them. He used this little homely expression which made quite an impression upon me as a boy. He said, "Which one of you boys would like to eat a sandwich where one of your friends had licked all the butter off?" Right there I resolved that no friend of mine would ever be able to accuse me of licking the butter off of his sandwich for him.

Entanglements

Some years ago, I was invited to speak to the inmates at the Utah State Penitentiary. When speaking to young people I always add, of course, I got a round trip ticket, so I could get out after I once got in. We had a good attendance. Apparently, there was nowhere else for the inmates to go. At the close of the meeting quite a group surrounded me to ask questions. One young man had been a district president in one of the missions, another had been a ward clerk, another was a nephew of one of the Presidents of the Church, another a nephew of a former presiding bishop. These men were there because they had entangled themselves in sin.

I was invited to return again to talk to the Alcoholics Anonymous group at the prison, which I did. When I turned to the man in charge of that group and said, "I would like to hear from you. I would like to know something about you men and what your aims and your ambitions are." The man stood up and said something like this, " I thank God for the privilege of being in this institution." Then he proceeded to explain: He said, "Before I came here, I was no good to my family, to my church, to my country. I was just no good period. Now I have hopes that when I leave here, I will be worth something to somebody." I couldn't help but think, "Isn't it pitiful when a man becomes a slave to strong drink to the point that he can thank God for the privilege of being behind prison bars for the help he can get!"

A few years ago a newspaper here in Salt Lake reported a boy who killed himself. The paper said he was discouraged. His father told me that his body was being wasted away because of immoral living and that was why he committed suicide. The good book says that the way of the transgressor is hard.

In visiting in the city of Brussels, I went into the Wiertz Museum. There I saw an oil painting showing a man who shot his head off. As he did that, an angel of light stood at one side and an angel of darkness at the other. The angel of light wept. The angel of darkness laughed with a laugh of triumph. That impressed me as being typical of our lives—each one of us individually. Constantly, we are having to make decisions as to which we will please, the angel of light, our guardian angel, or the angel of darkness, who seeks to destroy our souls.

Evil Spirits

A Widow Afflicted

We know that there are good spirits and evil spirits, and neither are to be trifled with for the sake of curiosity or sign-seeking, or we will have cause to regret it.

My companion and I had an unusual experience with evil spirits in the City of Amsterdam. We had held our morning meetings and had gone home to have lunch with a widow and her daughter and son. The daughter and son were members of the Church. The widow was not. After eating we tried to talk to her to see if we could not encourage her to become a member of the Church. She explained that she thought the Word of Wisdom was so hard to live. I explained to her that the Lord gave us the Word of Wisdom to free us from bad habits so that our bodies would be strong and healthy. Right at that time the evil spirits came upon her. From the sweet lovely woman that she was she twisted her face and addressing me in the most sneering manner I had ever experienced, she said, "Who are you?" I answered, "I am a servant of the Lord." She replied, "So, you are a servant of the Lord." Then she turned to her daughter and said, "Who are you?" She replied, "I am the daughter of the house." "So," she replied, "You are the daughter of the house." Then turning to me again, she said "And who are you?" I replied that I was a servant of the Lord. Then she said, "Well, if you are a servant of the Lord, then I have nothing to do here." With that I called my two companions. We administered to her and rebuked the evil spirits. She fell limp and we carried her to the bedroom, put her on the bed and gave her cold water. In a short time she was the same sweet woman she had been before these spirits had entered her body.

Her daughter explained that years earlier, before her father died, that her father and mother had come to America and had become interested in spiritualism. Since that time the spirits would not leave her mother alone. They would come and rap on the walls at night and disturb her. This was truly an unusual experience for us, and the first we had had of its character.

Family Influence

Special Time

If we can maintain a spirit of love and cooperation in the home, it will have a powerful and lasting influence for good on our children when they are away from home.

An article appeared in the *Reader's Digest* during the war that told of a Utah boy in the armed forces. He was carrying his watch set at Utah time. Some of his buddies noticed that and kidded him about it. They asked him why he didn't set his watch so that he would know what was going on in the world. Holding the watch out, he said something like this, "That watch tells me what time father is getting out in the morning to look after the cattle, what time mother is getting the hotcakes ready for breakfast, what time they are kneeling in family prayer, and when they are getting ready to go to Church."

This little experience impressed me greatly and I have told it a number of times showing what the influence of the home can do to keep our young people from evil when they are away from home. By telling it, I learned who this boy was and who his parents were. I have a great respect for them.

On Their Own

I once heard of a mother who requested her husband to talk to their son before he left for the armed forces. The father replied, "I will see." When the boy left, the father said, "God bless you, my son." The mother was disappointed, but the father said, "Mother, it is too late now to talk to our boy; he goes away as he is. We can do nothing more now." Certainly a word of caution is always appropriate, but as far as the boy is concerned, the die is cast. His deep-rooted convictions

are what they are. Parents must not wait until an emer-
gency to teach their children, but should train them from
early childhood to walk in righteousness.

When one of our sons who was serving in the Navy
was stationed on Treasure Island, just out of San Francisco, he and his companion with approval rented a room
on the mainland. The reason they gave was that they
could not stand to listen to the foul language they were
subject to all day long.

While he was there, I attended a conference in San
Francisco. Remembering how my father used to come
into the city and sleep with me while I was attending
business college, I decided to go and spend a night
with my son. My father used to say to me, "I never
worry a moment about you; I would trust you anywhere
I would go myself."

When my son went back to the Island in the morning,
I went upstairs and talked to the landlady. I asked her
what kind of boys they were rooming in her home. Her
reply was, "I have raised eight children and there isn't
one as good as that boy of yours. What I can't understand is how you could raise such a good boy in such
a wicked world." That made me appreciate more than
ever before the influence of the gospel in helping us to
raise our children.

When this son returned from his service in the Navy,
I said to him, "My son, I don't know whether your
mother and I have been duly appreciative of the fact
that you came home clean, that you did not take up the
habits of the men with whom you were associated." He
replied, "Well, Father, you don't need to thank me.
All I needed to do was think of you and Mother and
my brother and sisters, and I want to be like you."

100 JUST TO ILLUSTRATE

Offspring

I have a daughter who says to me often, "Daddy, what did I do in the spirit world to entitle me to be your daughter?" Then, I always answer, "What did I do to entitle me to be your father?"

I read a letter written to one of my dear relatives by his daughter who was away attending school. He had been sending her a substantial amount each month, but she would keep wiring for an extra $100.00 for this and an extra $100.00 for that. The letter I read contained a statement like this: "If you didn't want to take care of me, what did you bring me into the world for?" Some contrast in the matter of appreciating parents! No wonder the Lord included in the Ten Commandments, "Honor thy Father and thy Mother, that thy days may be long upon the land which the Lord thy God giveth thee."

During the war my son, LaMont, was serving as a missionary in Great Britain, when the missionaries were all brought out of Europe because of the war. He was reassigned to complete his mission in the Southern States where I had presided as President of the Mission.

One day I received a letter from President Wallace McBride of the South Carolina Stake, whom I knew well during my term of Presidency in that Mission before the stake was organized. His letter read like this, "LeGrand, you will have to get your boots on or this son of yours will be a better preacher than you are." I wrote back and said, "Wallace, I can't think of anything I would rather do than take a back seat to one of my sons."

I can't think of anything that would bring greater joy to a father than to see one of his sons excel him particularly in activities in the Church.

A Father's Footsteps

The importance of the role of the father in the family cannot be overemphasized. Boys get to a certain age and they want to be just like Dad. Girls get to a certain age and Dad in their eyes is a model of what they will seek in a husband.

Just to illustrate the first point . . .

The Aaronic Priesthood Pageant that was produced two different seasons to more than capacity houses several nights in succession in the Salt Lake Tabernacle was built around the theme that we lived in the spirit world before coming to this earth, and that we were told that upon the earth we would have our parents and the Priesthood to show us the way.

In one of the scenes was shown a group of boys discussing their problems together. One young boy said: "My father does not go to Priesthood meeting, and I want to be like my father."

A short time after this, in a Relief Society Meeting held in the Southeastern part of the city, one sister reported her experience in connection with her attendance at the pageant. She said that she took her husband, and that when that young boy turned over and said: "My father does not go to Priesthood Meeting, and I want to be like my father," that she felt her husband cringe as though he had been hit with an electric shock. The next Sunday morning when his son was about to leave for his Priesthood meeting, the father said, "Wait a minute, my son; I am going with you." The son replied, "You don't mean it, do you Dad?" But the mother got his eye and he waited and took his father with him to Priesthood Meeting.

A man who had traveled around the world was in Salt Lake and attended the Aaronic Priesthood Pageant.

He made a statement that it was the most impressive thing he had ever witnessed.

A man who was passing through Salt Lake returning to his home in California attended the Aaronic Priesthood Pageant. He was so favorably impressed that he went to California, got his wife and mother, and drove back to Salt Lake with the explanation that he wanted to know more about a people who could present such a pageant.

Fit The Man To The Job

Try Again

I am a great believer in fitting round men in round holes and square men in square holes. In some of our wards people are appointed to positions as they come into the ward, and then the Bishops are afraid to move them around. Sometimes they remain in a position for which they are not best fitted. When I was serving as a ward bishop and I would suggest to my counselors that we try Brother so and so in such and such a position, one of the counselors would say, "We tried him in another position and he failed, didn't he?" Then I would always reply, "Probably that was our fault rather than his. Perhaps we asked him to do something for which he was not qualified and in which he had no particular interest."

A Happy Change

To illustrate my point: We had a chorister who would do anything for his choir. He would have been willing to go out and haul the members in for practice, but somehow or other his members did not respond to him. Our choir was not outstanding. We never got invited to sing in stake conference or outside of our own ward. The brother of this man was a choir leader in an adjoining ward, and they sang in the tabernacle, the assembly hall, and at stake conferences. So I said to my counselors, "Let's ask our chorister if he would be willing to let us transfer him to another assignment." One of my counselors said, "You will break his heart." I said, "No, I don't think so." So we talked to him. I asked him if he had enough confidence in his Bishopric that if he knew we were united in feeling that the ward could be blessed by transferring him to another assignment, would he be willing to sustain us. He said he would. So we put him in charge of our youth program before the mutuals had the full responsibility. He did a grand job. We called another man to be our chorister. In a few weeks he had a waiting list wanting to join the choir. We sang at the next stake conference. People would say, "What in the world has happened to that ward?" Nothing in the world happened except we took a round man out of a square hole and put a square man in it and put the round man in a round hole. Now each was where he fit and the ward was blessed.

Fulness Of The Gospel

Eternal Marriage

Our message to the world is that we have the fulness of the everlasting gospel. We know that they have a part of it, but we have the fulness and we want to share it with them. Because of this fulness, we understand and teach principles of truth which other churches do not have or are afraid to teach. Just to illustrate . . .

I preached a sermon at Quitman, Georgia on the eternal duration of the marriage covenant and the family unit. I quoted from Rulon Howell's book: *Do Men Believe What Their Churches Prescribe?* showing that none of the churches believe in the eternal duration of the marriage tie and family unit. At the close of the meeting, I stood at the door to shake hands with the people. A man came up to me and introduced himself as a Baptist Minister. I asked, "Did I misquote you tonight?" His reply was, "No, but it is just as you say; we do not all believe the things our churches prescribe." I said, "You do not believe either—why don't you go back to your people and teach them the truth? They will take it from you though they are not yet willing to accept it from the Mormon Elders."

While in the South, I visited one day in the study of Dr. Peter Marshall. Most people have heard of this man because his wife wrote about him in the book, *"The Man Peter,"* and his life was portrayed in a movie. He had had many contacts with the Elders. He and President Callis preached at a funeral together. He boarded at the home of one of the members of his church, but she and her children attended our church more than they did his. Our missionaries used to play ball with him. He sent over to our office at times for our handbooks on our youth program. Those who saw the movie will remember that he almost lost his position as a minister in Washington because of his youth program, most of which he got from our church. The talk that his wife gave in the movie before she was his wife was one of our talks on the Word of Wisdom. At the time of his death, Dr. Marshall was the chaplain of the United States Senate.

In our discussion in his study, I asked him what his feelings were with respect to the principle of eternal marriage and the eternal duration of the marriage covenant. His reply was, "Well, we are not allowed to preach that doctrine in our church, but in my own heart I have some stubborn objections." Then he proceeded to make this explanation: "When you take the kitten away from the cat, in a few days the cat has forgotten all about the kitten; when you take the calf away from the cow, in a few days the cow has forgotten all about the calf; but when you take a child away from its mother, though she live to be one hundred years old, she never forgets the child of her bosom. I find it difficult to believe that God created love like that to perish in the grave."

True principles have a natural attraction to the human mind. People want to believe in eternal family life—it is natural to the affections. But the churches of the world do not understand the scriptures sufficiently to be able to offer hope or comfort to their members concerning it, but teach man-made doctrines instead.

Salvation of Children

In California, I attended the funeral service for a little three-year-old girl, the only child of one of my business associates. I listened to the preacher deliver his sermon. Not once did he hold out any hope to these parents that they would ever see their little daughter again. All he did was to tell them how grateful they should be that they had had the privilege of being her parents for these few years.

After this service I talked with this man and told him that the Lord had something better than that in store for him, if he just wanted to live for it. Well, you can imagine my joy when here just a few weeks ago I received a long letter from him, telling me that he had just joined the Church. So I wrote him and reminded him what I had said to him following the funeral of his little daughter. I told him he could look forward to receiving her in the morning of the first resurrection and raising her to full stature of womanhood.

Sister Richards and I met a new convert from Tampa, Florida who was in Atlanta attending her daughter who was under the doctor's care. She told us this story:

She was raised a Baptist, and lost a twenty-one year old son who had died without baptism. According to the teachings of her church, he had forfeited all chances of salvation. She was very much concerned and worried. One morning while doing her house work she went into her bedroom, got down on her knees, and asked the Lord that if there was anything she could do for her son who had died without baptism, would he please let her know. While she was still praying, a knock came at the door. When she went to the door there stood two lady missionaries from our church, the one holding in her hand a tract entitled "Baptism for the Dead." This lady read this heading and said, "Come in—tell me all about that—that is just what I want to know." After a few visits from the missionaries, she joined the Church.

Kingdom of God

At a meeting in Florida, one of our Elders spoke on the Dream of Nebuchadnezzar and its interpretation, showing the rise and fall of the kingdoms of this world until the latter days (Daniel 2:28), when the God of Heaven would set up a Kingdom which would never be destroyed nor left to other people, but it would break in pieces and consume all other kingdoms and it would stand forever. (Daniel 2:44).

I stood at the door at the close of the meeting. A minister came up to me and said, "You don't mean to say that you think the Mormon Church is that kingdom, do you?" My answer was "Certainly, Why not?" His reply was, "It couldn't be." My answer was, "Why not?" His answer was, "You can't have a kingdom without a king, and you haven't a king, so you haven't a kingdom." "Oh," I replied, "You did not read quite far enough. Read the seventh chapter of Daniel, and you will see where Daniel saw . . . 'one like the Son of man came with the clouds of heaven and came to the Ancient of days, and they brought him near before him, and there was given him dominion and glory, and a kingdom, that all people, nations and languages, should serve him; his dominion is an everlasting dominion, which shall not pass away, and his kingdom that which shall not be destroyed.' " (Daniel 7:18, 27).

Then I asked, "Tell me how can the Kingdom be given to him when he comes in the clouds of heaven if no Kingdom has been prepared for him?"

In 1956 a man sat in my office who had spent thirty years as a minister of the gospel. He made this statement to me: "When I think of how little I had to offer my people as a Methodist Minister compared with what I now have in the fulness of the gospel as it has been revealed through the Prophet Joseph Smith, I want to go back and tell all my friends what I have found, but now they will not listen to me—they regard me as an apostate from their church."

This man gave up his ministry and took a menial job here in Salt Lake because of his conviction that Joseph Smith was a Prophet. He told me that when he joined the Church he didn't feel that he could say he knew that Joseph Smith was a Prophet, but he believed with all his heart that he was, "But," he said "when an Elder laid his hands on my head and ordained me to the office of a Priest in the Aaronic Priesthood, I felt a thrill go through me until my whole body tingled from my head to my feet and I knew that no man could give me such a feeling."

Yes, we have the fulness of the gospel with authority from God to act in his name through the Holy Priesthood. What a wonderful blessing!

Fund Raising

Enthusiasm

I always explain to the Bishops that it is enthusiasm on the part of the members which makes it possible to raise funds. Then I give them these two little illustrations. Sister Richards and I attended a banquet here in Salt Lake Valley where they were raising funds for their church. As I recall they charged $5.00 a plate. There were four long tables. At the close of the banquet they auctioned off four plants that were on the tables. The first plant sold for $2.50 and I think the florist would not have sold it for that small amount. The second one sold for $10.00. The third one sold for $11.00. The fourth one for $19.50. By that time the man who bought the first one for $2.50 felt ashamed of himself and so he gave his plant back to the Bishop and they auctioned it off again and it brought $22.50. The new buyer gave it back and they auctioned it again and it brought $50.00 and they auctioned it again and it brought $27.50 or a total of $143.00 for the four plants as against $2.50 for the first one. The only difference being a little enthusiasm.

While I was the Presiding Bishop we often had inquiries from Bishops for suggestions for raising funds to erect their new meeting houses.

Calendar Party

In visiting in a stake in Idaho some years ago, the Stake President's wife had been made chairman of the finance committee for raising funds to build a ward meeting house. They raised most all of their funds by having luncheons and she explained to me the nature of these luncheons as follows:

She held what she called a calendar party. She invited twelve ladies into her home, one for each month of the year, and served them a meal for $1.00 each. That brought in $12.00. She asked each of the twelve to invite four ladies into their homes and charge them each $1.00, representing the four weeks of the month. That brought $48.00. Then they were asked to invite seven ladies into each of their homes representing the seven days of the week. That was thus seven times forty-eight or $336.00 making a total of $396.00 for that one calendar party.

Revolving Party

Then she explained that they held a revolving party where she invited thirty-six ladies into her home for lunch and charged them each $1.00, that was $36.00. She asked each of them to invite four so that four times thirty-six was $144.00. She asked each of those to invite four and that was just four times one hundred and forty-four or $576.00 or a total of $756.00.

In holding parties like this, they can invite friends who do not live in their ward, although the Church does not recommend that we go from one ward to another or one stake to another to raise finances; nevertheless, in such a case that would be permissible.

When they had finished their building and paid for it, there was a non-sectarian lady minister in their town whose house badly needed painting and she needed a garage. So they put on another party and built her a garage and painted her house. There is no trick to fund raising if you divide the responsibility. Divide and conquer, I say.

God Hath Chosen The
Weak Things Of The World

A Humble Convert

On several occasions I have heard President Heber J. Grant say that it was a miracle in his sight what the Lord had been able to accomplish with the material available, referring particularly to the work of the missionaries. The Apostle Paul said:

"For ye see your calling, brethren, how that not many wise men after the flesh, not many mighty, not many noble are called:

"But God hath chosen the foolish things of the world to confound the wise: and God hath chosen the weak things of the world to confound the things which are mighty." (1 Cor. 1:26-27).

The following illustrations seem to sustain this thought:

In Holland, I had an investigator who applied for baptism. I hardly felt that he would be an asset to the Church—he had but a meager education, could hardly read or write, and he looked more like an escaped convict than a saint—so I advised him to wait awhile and study the Gospel more and we would talk about baptism later. I kept on visiting him, and a few weeks later he said: "Brother Richards, what am I waiting for? I have quit drinking liquor and tea and coffee; I have quit using tobacco; I have quit swearing, except when a word slips out before I can catch it, but I catch most of them; I am willing to pay my tithing and fast offerings, and attend Church. What lack I yet?" My reply was that I felt that we should baptize him, so we took him and his wife out to the North Sea Canal and baptized them at midnight. The reason we went at midnight was because it was against the law to enter public waters, so we had to wait until the law had gone to sleep. We figured that what the law didn't know in this case wouldn't hurt it, since we had no other place where we could baptize people.

As impossible as he seemed to me at the time that he first applied for baptism, I lived to see him and his wife emigrate to the United States. I saw him learn the English language well enough to fill a full-time mission in the United States. I saw him and his wife fill full-time missions in Holland. Sometime thereafter he passed away and left me as sole administrator of his estate with provision that I was to take care of his wife and the balance of his estate was to go to the Primary Children's Hospital. The estate was settled and I was able to turn over to the Hospital about $5,000. And to think I wasn't anxious to let him join the Church!

The Spirit Giveth Utterance

In South Georgia we had a brother who could neither read nor write when he joined the Church. One day his daughter saw him looking in the geography and asked "What are you looking for, Father?" He answered, "I am looking for the meaning of the word 'utmost.'" She replied, "You have the wrong book," and she gave him the dictionary. Well, I heard that man preach a sermon in the Courthouse in South Georgia on the subject of "In the utmost bounds of the everlasting hills," when he held his audience spellbound.

In Mississippi we had a brother who could neither read nor write when he joined the Church. I heard that man deliver a sermon one day in South Mississippi. At the close of the meeting, I went up to him and, calling him by name, said, "Brother So and So, I would have been proud to have heard that sermon delivered in the Salt Lake Tabernacle." It was very choice.

Another illustration . . .

In Mississippi, we had a young man whose mother died and left him in young manhood without an education. He had a great love for the Church and admired the missionaries, and always felt that he would like to be like them. One day he went up town. In front of the barber shop he saw a signboard inviting young men to join the U. S. Navy with the promise of an education. He could not read it, so he called to one of the men in the barber shop to read the sign to him. He then went home and asked his father for approval to join the Navy. When his father inquired as to why he desired to join the Navy, his answer was that he wanted to get an education so he could learn the gospel to be able to preach it. We had no Elders from the West who could preach a better sermon than this young man after his return.

Simple Testimony Converts

I think I might add one of my own experiences. Before I left on my first mission, President Anthon H. Lund of the First Presidency instructed us missionaries. Among other things he said that if we ever lacked for something to say when called upon to speak, that if we would bear our testimonies that we knew that Joseph Smith was a Prophet of God and that the Book of Mormon was true that the Lord would give us something to say.

I had only been in the Mission field a few months when we held a conference in Rotterdam with President Heber J. Grant, then President of the European Mission, present. I was Secretary of the Mission, and my Mission President had promised me that if I would take President Grant's talk in shorthand I would not be called to speak in the evening meeting in the "NUT ZAAL," one of the largest halls, if not the largest, in Rotterdam.

We must have had 1,500 people present—many came wearing their stove-pipe hats and carrying their walking sticks—a real congregation of representative people.

Along about the middle of the meeting, my Mission President announced that Le Grand Richards, the Mission Secretary, would be the next speaker. You see, there was one there higher in authority than the Mission President, and he had asked that I be called. As I walked from the body of the hall to the platform, I thought of the promise of President Lund, and I bore my testimony. I felt that the Lord surely lifted me above my natural ability upon that occasion—I felt that were the floor to pass from under my feet, I would still be standing there bearing my testimony.

I didn't know whether I had done any good or not— all I knew was that the spirit of the Lord had rested upon me as I had never felt it before. A few weeks later, I attended a baptism service in Rotterdam. As I introduced myself to the man and his wife who were being baptized, he said: "You do not know us, but we know you. We heard your testimony in the 'NUT ZAAL,' and that caused us to investigate the message you brought." They came to Utah and were faithful members.

Surely "God hath chosen the weak things of the world" to declare his truth to the nations. God started with a humble, uneducated boy of fourteen, and by revelation and inspiration enabled him to lay the foundation for this marvelous latter-day work, and to bring forth glorious new scripture. Yet in the eyes of the worldly wise, this humble boy was despised. But God knew he was teachable, and obedient, and though with little formal education he became a choice instrument in the hands of God.

Unschooled Prophet

It is interesting to note that in the Special Historical Section commemorating the One Hundred and Fiftieth Anniversary of the entry of the independent Republic of Vermont into the Union of States, Joseph Smith was given recognition, and the beautiful memorial marking his birthplace was described as follows: "SHARON (Vermont)—enters the hall of fame by being the birthplace of one of the immortals of American History, Joseph Smith, who founded the Mormon religion. Today a monument weighing forty tons, the largest polished monolith in America, stands on the crest of a hill in commemoration of his birth. The monument bears this inscription: 'Sacred to the memory of Joseph Smith, the prophet, born here 23 Dec., 1805, Martyred Carthage, Illinois, 27 June 1844.'"

I once read the first section of the Doctrine and Covenants to a well-educated woman who attended many lectures in Boston by prominent men. When I finished reading I asked her, "Does that sound as if it had been written by a young man who had scarcely seen the inside of a school room?" She answered, "I would think that any College Professor would be proud to attach his name to that article." While she had not comprehended the power or significance of that marvelous chapter, yet she had clearly seen that it took refined intelligence to produce it. Joseph Smith possessed that refined intelligence, for in his weakness and humility he had been taught by the spirit of God. Why does God choose the weak things of the world to accomplish his purposes? Because he knows that the wise and mighty depend on their own power, but the weak depend on the power and help of God and are strengthened thereby. The more a man recognizes his dependence on God, the stronger he grows.

God's Blueprint

Ministers Convention

In June of 1959 the ministers and leaders of two of the churches of this western part of the United States were holding a convention here in Salt Lake. They came from California, Oregon, Washington, Idaho, Nevada, Utah and I think Arizona. They wrote a letter in advance to President McKay asking if he would appoint one of the general authorities to attend the morning session of their convention and to speak for two hours on Mormonism, remain for lunch as their guest, and then remain for one hour and a half in the afternoon and let them ask questions. President McKay assigned me to attend this convention.

I asked the ministers if they wanted me to be frank and to tell them exactly how we got the Church, what it stood for, and what our teachings were. That was what they wanted. They changed the program a little because some of the men wanted to get away on earlier planes. So they gave me two hours and a half in the morning, deferring the luncheon for a brief period. I was undisturbed, and I had an opportunity in that length of time to lay a foundation that I thought they could not help but be impressed with, as to how we got the Church, our authority, our organization, and our operation. Then they asked some questions. One of the questions was, "Now Mr. Richards, you have told us that you believe that God is a personal God." I replied, "That is right." Then he added, "We have heard it said that you believe that God has a wife; would you explain that to us." I think he felt that that might be a very difficult thing to explain. So rather facetiously I said, "Well, I don't see how in the world he could have a son without a wife, do you?" That seemed to answer that question.

At the close of my remarks, I used this little illustration. I told them that while I was the Presiding Bishop
of the Church we had the plans prepared for the Los
Angeles Temple of the Church. One day we presented
those plans to the First Presidency. While we did not
have the plumbing and electrical plans complete, there
were eighty-five pages about four feet long and about
two and one half feet wide. I said, "There was that
Temple built spiritually before there was a hole in the
ground. You could take those plans and go all over
this world and try to fit them to every building in the
world. There is only one building they will fit, and
that is the Los Angeles Temple of the Mormon Church.
"Oh," I said, "of course you can find materials such
as are in the Temple in other buildings, but you cannot
find another building that those plans will fit."

Bible Blueprint

Then I held up the Bible. I said, "This is the Lord's
blueprint. Isaiah advises us that the Lord had declared
the end from the beginning, and he said, 'The grass
withereth, the flowers fadeth, but the word of our God
shall stand forever.' " I quoted them many other references to show that the Lord had intended that the
scriptures should point the way. "Now," I said "you
can take that Bible, the Lord's blueprint, and try to fit
it to every Church in this world, and there is only one
Church that it will fit. Oh," I said, "of course, you
can find things that are in that Bible, the Lord's blueprint, in each of the Churches, but you cannot find a
church in all the world that it will fit, except the Mormon
Church." I proceeded to point out to them why it would
not fit any other church.

I indicated that in a book written on the life of
Christ by a prominent non-Mormon writer, the author
made the statement that there were two passages in the

new testament for which he could find no excuse. The
first was from John 10:16: "Other sheep I have, which
are not of this fold: them also I must bring, and they
shall hear my voice; and there shall be one fold, and
one shepherd." Then I asked, "Do any of you men
know anything about those other sheep?—who they are?
or where they are? or have you any knowledge of a
record of his having visited them according to his promise? Do any of you know why that scripture is in the
Bible?"

I said, "We know all about it." Then I tied it into
what I had told them about the Book of Mormon and
the visit of the Savior to the people on the American
Continent when he told them that they were the other
sheep of whom he spoke.

The second passage that the author of the book could
not understand why it was in the Bible was I Cor. 15:29
where Paul said, "Else what shall they do which are
baptized for the dead, if the dead rise not at all? why
are they then baptized for the dead?" Then I asked:
"Do any of you know why this scripture is in the Bible?
Do any of you know any Church that understands and
teaches the principle of baptism of the living for the
dead." I tied this into Peter's account of how Jesus
while in the spirit went and preached the gospel to those
who were disobedient in the days of Noah, that they
might live according to God in the spirit but be judged
according to men in the flesh. Since spirits cannot be
baptized in water, the Lord had to provide this glorious
principle for the benefit of the dead. I explained that
we were the only Church in the world that understands
and teaches this wonderful principle.

Another Angel Flying

Then I quoted Revelations 4:1 and 14:6-7, where
John, banished on the Isle of Patmos, was invited by the

angel to come up hither, and I will show thee things
which must be hereafter." Then he adds, "and I saw
another angel flying in the midst of heaven, having the
everlasting Gospel to preach unto them that dwell on
the earth, and to every nation, and kindred, and tongue,
and people, saying with a loud voice, Fear God, and
give glory to Him; for the hour of His judgment is come;
and worship Him that made Heaven, and earth, and the
sea and the fountains of water." And then I asked,
"Have any of you ever heard of the coming of this
angel having the everlasting Gospel to preach to every
nation, kindred and tongue, and people that dwell on
the earth? Do any of you know of any Church that
claims that he has come?" Then I explained that this
is our message to the world. Then I asked, "Why do
you suppose this promise is in the Bible, if we should
not look for its fulfillment? Remember," I said, "the
Bible is the Lord's blueprint and this promise will only
fit his Church."

Times of Restitution

Then I quoted the words of the apostle Peter from
Acts 3:19-21 where he said to those who had crucified
the Lord, Repent ye therefore, and be converted, that
your sins may be blotted out, when the times of refresh-
ing shall come from the presence of the Lord; and he
shall send Jesus Christ, which before was preached unto
you; whom the heaven must receive until the time of
restitution of all things, which God hath spoken by the
mouth of all his holy prophets since the world began."
I asked, "Do you believe that Jesus Christ will come
again as Peter promised? If so, you must believe his
words—that he shall not come until the times of restitution of all things which God has spoken by the mouth
of all His holy prophets since the world began." Then
I asked, "Have any of you ever heard of such a resti-

tution of all things spoken by the mouths of all the holy prophets? Do you know of any church that claims such a restitution?" I added, "This is a part of the Lord's blueprint, and it is our message to the world."

The Latter Days

Then I referred to Daniel's interpretation of King Nebuchadnezzar's dream. After explaining the rise and fall of the Kingdoms of this world, Daniel said, "There is a God in heaven that revealeth secrets, and maketh known to the King Nebuchadnezzar what shall be in the latter days. Thy dream, and the visions upon thy bed are these. Thou sawest till that a stone was cut out without hands, which smote the image upon his feet that were of iron and clay, and brake them to pieces. Then was the iron, the clay, the brass, the silver, and the gold broken to pieces together, and became like the chaff of the summer threshing floors; and the wind carried them away, that no place was found for them, and the stone that smote the image became a great mountain and filled the whole earth. In the days of these kings shall the God of heaven set up a kingdom, which shall never be destroyed; and the kingdom shall not be left to another people, but it shall break in pieces and consume all these kingdoms, and it shall stand forever." (Daniel 2:27-28, 34-35, 44). Then I asked, "have any of you ever heard of a church that claims that the God of Heaven has set up his kingdom in the latter days as Daniel herein promised?" I added, "Again, this is a part of God's blueprint. We are the only church that claims its fulfillment." I asked, "Why do you suppose this is in the Bible if it were not a part of God's blueprint and plan for the latter days as Daniel said?"

Messenger of God

Then I quoted Malachi 3:1 as follows: "Behold, I will send my messenger, and he shall prepare the way

before me: and the Lord, whom ye seek, shall suddenly
come to His Temple, even the messenger of the covenant,
whom ye delight in: behold, he shall come, saith the
Lord of Hosts." I pointed out that this had no reference
to preparing the way for his first coming, but his second
coming. Then I said, "have any of you ever heard of
a messenger sent of God to prepare the way for his
second coming? I pointed out that when such a messenger was sent by God, he could be none other than a
prophet, quoting the words of Amos 3:7, "Surely, the
Lord God will do nothing but he revealeth his secret unto
his servants the prophets." Then I added, "Nor could
any of the other prophecies I have referred to find their
fulfillment without a prophet called and directed by the
Lord." I bore my testimony that God had raised up a
prophet for the purpose of the fulfillment of these promises. All a part of his blueprint. Then I added. "That
prophet was Joseph Smith."

Then I quoted Malachi 4:5-6, "Behold, I will send
you Elijah the Prophet before the coming of the great
and dreadful day of the Lord: and he shall turn the
hearts of the fathers to the children, and the heart of
the children to their fathers, lest I come and smite the
earth with a curse." Then I asked, "Have any of you
ever heard of the coming of Elijah, as promised by the
Lord, through his prophet Malachi? Apparently his
coming had great significance, for the Lord said, 'Lest
I come and smite the earth with a curse.' We are happy
to announce," I said, "that Elijah has come and fulfilled his promised mission. Why do you suppose this
promise is in the Lord's blueprint if we should not look
for its fulfillment. At their feasts, the Jews set an extra
plate at the table so if Elijah comes he can occupy
that place."

The Temple

Then I referred them to Isaiah 2:2-3 where Isaiah said: "And it shall come to pass in the last days, that the mountain of the Lord's house shall be established in the tops of the mountains, and shall be exalted above the hills; and all nations shall flow unto it. And many people shall go and say, Come ye, and let us go up to the mountain of the Lord, to the house of the God of Jacob; and he will teach us of his ways, and we will walk in his paths; for out of Zion shall go forth the law, and the word of the Lord from Jerusalem." Then I said, "Have any of you ever heard of the house of the God of Jacob that Isaiah saw would be established in the top of the mountains in the last days, to which all nations would flow to learn of the ways of the Lord that they might walk in his paths? Well," I said, "this church has built that house of the God of Jacob which is none other than the Temple of the Lord established here in the top of Ephraim's mountains, and people have gathered here from all nations to learn of the blessings to be received in that house of the God of Jacob." Then I asked, "Do any of you know why this promise is in the Bible as a part of God's blueprint if he did not intend that it should be fulfilled."

Do Not Err

I reminded them of the words of Jesus to the Pharisees when he said, "Do ye not therefore err, because ye know not the scriptures, neither the power of God?" (St. Mark 12:24). And his further statement to his disciples on the way to Emmaus when he said, "Oh, fools, and slow of heart to believe all that the prophets have spoken. . . .then opened he their understanding, that they might understand the scriptures." (St. Luke 24:25, 45). I asked, "Why do you suppose this promise by

Isaiah is in the Bible if the Lord did not intend to fulfill the promise."

Then I referred them again to the commandment of the Lord to Ezekiel 37:15-20, which I had already discussed with them, where the Lord commanded that two records should be kept, one of Judah and one of Joseph, and then I said, "Have any of you ever heard of the stick or record of Joseph? Do you know of any people who do know about it except the Latter-day Saints. I am sure you could all agree that the Bible is the record of the Jews; but where is the record of Joseph? Why do you suppose the Lord gave this commandment that this record of Joseph should be kept and promised that he would bring it forth and join it with the record of the Jews, if he did not intend to do so?" I explained that that record of Joseph was none other than the Book of Mormon, which I had already explained to them previously.

Perfect Fit

I explained that there were many, many other promises in the Lord's blueprint that had been fulfilled through the restoration of the gospel in this dispensation through the instrumentality of the Prophet Joseph Smith. Then I added: "The Bible is the Lord's blueprint and it will fit no other church in this world."

When I went to leave that group that day, following the luncheon, the man in charge turned to me and said, "This has been one of the most interesting experiences of my entire life." They had no arguments. I always tell the missionaries that there is no need to argue if we just learn how to tell our story. We tell people things they have never heard of before.

Go Not From House To House

Peace of Heaven

I have always felt that many of our missionaries run away from their work because they do not remain with a family long enough to tell our story. To illustrate, a woman wrote into the mission office from Savannah, Georgia, and asked if we would send our missionaries to her home with this comment: "They have been leaving gospel tracts at my door for years, but they always get away before I can get an opportunity to talk with them."

When the Savior sent His Seventy forth to preach His gospel he said, among other instructions: "And into whatsoever house ye enter, first say peace be to this house. And if the son of peace be there, your peace shall rest upon it: if not, it shall turn to you again. And in the same house remain, eating and drinking such things as they give: for the labourer is worthy of his hire. Go not from house to house." (Luke 10:5-7).

I have always interpreted this to mean that when a missionary has been in a home where he could feel that the peace of heaven had rested, that it was his responsibility to keep closely in touch with that family until they should join the Church—that if the missionary failed to bring them into the Church, it would be because the devil was a better salesman.

Resourcefulness

To illustrate my point: My missionary companion and I spent a Sunday evening in a home of lovely people in Amsterdam, an appointment arranged by one of the members of the branch. We had a wonderful evening. I knew the peace of heaven was there that evening, so I explained to the family that if their minister found that

we had been there he would warn them that we were
the most wicked people in all the world, and that if
they believed him, they would not want us to return.
Well, that is just what happened. He did learn that
we had been there and he warned them against us, so
they decided that they would not permit us to return.
We had made an appointment to return a week from the
following Tuesday. During the week, one of the girls
from this family met one of our members—a young girl—
on the street and said "When your missionaries come
next Tuesday evening, Mother and Father are not going
to be home." Well, we knew the peace of heaven had
been in that home the Sunday evening we were there,
and we felt that the Lord would hold us responsible to
see that they were taught the gospel, so what did we
do? We made an appointment with another investigator
for Tuesday evening, and then we called at this home
on Monday evening. When the man came to the door,
we put on all the smiles we could and said, "Pardon
us. We know that our appointment with you was for
tomorrow evening, but something has come up that we
couldn't possibly come tomorrow evening. Knowing that
you spend most all your evenings at home, we didn't
think it would make any difference to you whether it
was Monday evening or Tuesday evening, so if you
don't mind, we will come in." By that time we were in.
Well, the whole family joined the Church and came
to Zion. One son filled a mission and served in a Bishopric, and held other important positions.

   How easy it would have been for us to have gone
back Tuesday evening and found no one at home, and
then have scratched them off our list. But the peace
of heaven had been there at our first visit, and we had
a responsibility. We didn't want to admit that the devil
was a better salesman than we, when we had such a
wonderful message to deliver.

Follow Through

Members of the Church all over the world pray that the Lord will lead the missionaries to the honest in heart. Sometimes I think that the missionaries cannot be led; the Lord almost has to force them to go and give their message. At a report meeting one of the missionaries told of sitting in the park reading his Bible and having a man come and sit down by him. Upon becoming acquainted he learned that this man had been a friend of his father in school when they were boys. This man invited him to his home. I made a mental note of that, and at the next missionary conference I asked this missionary, "How did you get along with that friend of your father whom you met in the park?" "Oh," he said, "I haven't been there yet." You see, three months had elapsed and, though the Lord almost put this man in his lap, the missionary had not followed through.

Another missionary called at a certain door but had not courage to leave a tract. He returned three times before he had courage to give the people a tract. The Lord almost had to force him to do his work after he had been led to that particular door. As a result the couple joined the Church. They were of a higher social strata than most of our converts and the husband looked like a prophet or patriarch if ever a man did. They became some of our finest and strongest members. I wonder what would have happened if the missionary had just gone on to another house and never given them a tract.

Gospel Influence

Happy Homes

One of the fruits of the gospel is happiness. A good Latter-day Saint is too busy to be bored with life, too informed to feel self-pity over problems and trials, too trusting to be bitterly distressed with death, too full of peace and knowledge of the purposes of the Lord to be disturbed about the threat of atomic annihilation, and too concerned with correcting his own faults (or should be) to be angry, fault-finding, or gossipy with his neighbor. People who visit us notice the happy spirit that pervades our meetings, our homes, and our cities.

One woman from Orlando, Florida who had been traveling all around the country was so favorably impressed with what she had found in Salt Lake City that she wanted to ask many questions. She said she couldn't understand the difference in the spirit she felt among the people. She said she felt it as she met the people on the streets and in the stores, and she compared it with what she had found in other places. She just couldn't say enough good things about the difference she had found. She had just returned from Los Angeles and her comparison between the two places was great.

In answer to her inquiry as to the reason for the difference, it was my great privilege to explain to her what the Lord had done in restoring His truth to the earth in this, the dispensation of the fullness of times.

On another occasion, Mr. Van Pelt of Metro Golden Mayer brought little Margaret O'Brien and her mother to my office for a visit. Before she left, Mrs. O'Brien turned to me and said, "Mr. Richards, there is one thing I just cannot understand—your men all look so happy."

My reply was, "Well, Mrs. O'Brien, we really have something to be happy about."

Favorable Impressions

In 1956 Brother Robert D. Young, the receptionist at that time at the Church Office Building, told me that a Doctor Polian from Iran had recently visited the Church Office Building, and had made this statement:

"I have been in the United States eleven months as a representative from my government to study the American people, and I have obtained a more favorable impression of them in the two days I have spent in Salt Lake City than in all the rest of the eleven months."

While I was in the real estate business, I attended, with some of my salesmen, a real estate convention in Detroit. In talking to all of the representatives present, the president of the national organization, who was just being released, said that during the term of his presidency he had been in every important city of the United States. He explained that cities were like individuals, that they had individuality. He said, "Most of the cities I have visited, I forgot as soon as I left the city, but there were some that I should always want to go back to again." We, from Salt Lake City, thrilled when he named Salt Lake about the third of all the cities of the nation that he felt he would like to return to again.

The gospel influence with its spirit of good will helps to break down prejudice that has been built up by our enemies. In New York we were honked off the road by a gentleman who wanted to assist us in finding our way. He said that he had been treated with such kindness in Utah, that when he saw our Utah license he wanted to try to return some of that kindness. He asked us where we were going, led us directly to our hotel, and waved goodbye. All because he had felt the friendly spirit of the gospel in his visit to Utah.

Gospel Is A Pearl Of Great Price

If You Have Hunted

While I was in Los Angeles, a very prominent attorney joined the Church. At one of our Stake Conferences shortly thereafter, I asked him if he would like to say a few words in the morning session of the Conference, and tell the people what he found in Mormonism that appealed to him.

He arose, and in a rich, deep voice that just seemed to pierce to the soul, he said, "If you have hunted for something all your life until you decided that it did not exist, and then you just happened to stumble on it, you do not need anyone to tell you what you have found. That is what I did when I found Mormonism, and the most wonderful thing about it to me is the fact that the more I learn about it the more wonderful it becomes."

A Stake President told me of a Jewish boy who was in the armed forces and met and married a Mormon girl. She converted him and brought him into the Church. He then went back East to visit his people and they disinherited him. He said, "You can't disinherit me — what I have found out in Utah among the Mormons is worth more than all the wealth this family ever owned." Then he said to his Stake President upon his return, "How long must I wait to get a recommend to the Temple so I can take my wife there and be sure she is mine for eternity?"

While Sister Richards and I were touring the Danish Mission in the summer of 1959, we met a young couple in Copenhagen who had just returned from a trip to the Temple in Switzerland. They had three children, and her comment was, "We have been members of the Church only six years. We figure we are only six years old, that we did not know how to live or what life was for, until the gospel was brought to us."

The gospel can change a person's life completely from a dreary existence to vital joy.

In the Netherlands Mission, I had several conversations with a young man who had experienced all the bright lights that Paris had to offer until he had become disgusted with life. I got him to read the Bible and the Book of Mormon and to attend Church. It completely changed his life and attitude toward life. I recall his making a statement like this. "The trees look greener, the flowers are more beautiful, the songs of the birds are more enchanting, in fact this is like a different world." Joy and happiness come only when one finds the truth and lives the truth.

Love of Converts

Before I left on my first mission, President Anthon H. Lund of the First Presidency instructed us. Among other things he told us that the people would love us, and then he added, "Now don't get lifted up in the pride of your hearts and think they love you because you are better than other people—they will love you because of your callings and the message you bring to them, the precious gospel. I little realized at the time just what he meant, but I found in Holland many wonderful people, fathers and mothers who treated us with every kindness, as if we were their own children. They would go without to be able to feed us food such as they seldom ate, and they did our washing for us, and our mending. They were wonderful.

The climax came when I was released to return home, and made the rounds to bid them farewell. I shed a thousand tears as I left them compared with the tears I shed as I left my loved ones at the station in Salt Lake as I left for Holland. I wept all the way from Amsterdam to Rotterdam, with a realization that I might never see many of my dear Dutch friends again. I called at one home where the oldest daughter had left for America a few weeks before. As I told this good Dutch mother goodbye, with tears streaming down her cheeks, she said, "It was hard to see my daughter leave for America, but it is much harder to see you leave." Then I realized what President Lund meant when he told us that the people would love us for the message we would bring, for I had brought the gospel of the Lord, Jesus Christ into this home.

I went to tell a man goodbye who was old enough to be my father. He had served many years in the uniform of his country. He got down on his knees and took my hand in his and bathed it with his tears and kissed it. Then I realized what President Lund meant when he said they would love us missionaries for the glad tidings we brought.

When I returned from my first mission and sat down at my mother's table and saw what she had prepared for me to eat, I couldn't keep the tears back. Mother asked, "What is the matter, my son?" My answer was, "I was just thinking of what many of our Dutch Saints in Holland have to live on, and what they have to eat."

Happiness

Discouraged Young Wife

One of the most important lessons for everyone to learn is how to find happiness. A person can never find true happiness for himself until he learns how to make others happy. Just to illustrate . . .

Some years ago I attended a Stake Conference in which the daughter of the Stake President gave a talk, and a returned missionary reported his mission. After that they commenced keeping company together, and married. He was attending the Brigham Young University and was not able to give her the comforts she had been accustomed to. She became discouraged. She wrote me a letter expressing her discouragement and unhappiness. I wrote back and told her that I could tell her how she could find happiness, if she would follow my counsel and my advice. I said, "First of all, quit pitying yourself and realize that your husband married you to be his help-meet, to help him to make a success of his life. Figure out anything and everything you can do to help him to complete his school work so he will be prepared to give you the comforts to which you have been accustomed. Then look around you and see who else you can help, and you will find happiness." To make the story short, she did that. Now they live in a beautiful home he has built her, and have a lovely little family. They are very happy together.

Point of View

A young lady called at my office by appointment one day. She was terribly frustrated. She felt like life was hardly worth living. All of the young men were being called into the service, and it left the girls without proper companionship. I listened to her tale of woe. Then I said, "Have you ever thought of the other side of the story? Think of the history of the world from the beginning up to the present time. There has never been a period when people have enjoyed such comforts and blessings as we now enjoy. The average family of today lives better than kings and queens of the earth did a hundred years ago." I reminded her that when John on the Isle of Patmos saw the restoration of the gospel, through the coming of an angel in the latter days, to be preached in all the world as a witness to all nations, that he also declared that this should be in the hour of God's judgments. "So," I said, "we must expect the good and the bad, but we will get mostly what we look for." I reminded her of the little story of the two buckets in the well. As the one bucket came up it said, 'This is surely a cold and dreary world; no matter how many times I come up full, I always have to go down empty!' The other bucket laughed and said, 'With me it is different; no matter how many times I go down empty, I always come up full.' I said, "Attitude has so much to do with the happiness we get out of our lives."

The Happiest Time

Perhaps no one in the world enjoys quite as much happiness as a missionary, for sharing the gospel is the most perfect way to bring happiness to others. An Elder who had just given a powerful sermon on the Dream of Nebuchadnezzar came to me and said, "When we won the Intermountain championship (he played on the B.Y.U. Basketball team), our companions and friends literally carried us around on their shoulders. That was the happiest time of my life until I came into the mission field, but I wouldn't trade a night like this bearing witness of the restoration of the gospel for all the basketball games I have ever played."

We permitted a young Elder who had been in the

field only a few months to baptize five people in the North Sea Canal one evening. Returning, he came up and put his arms around me and said, "When I was home I worked and earned good money. Since my parents did not require me to pay board, I could go to shows, dances and parties whenever I felt like it; but I wouldn't trade the experience of this evening for all the shows, parties and dances I have ever attended." His spirit was stirred and he experienced the deep joy that comes only through sharing the gospel and serving the Lord.

If Ye Bring Save One Soul Unto Me

Cumulative Effort

While in the Southern States Mission, I received a letter from a brother from Phoenix, Arizona. He stated that his father was one of the first converts to the Church from the State of Mississippi back in 1840. Since his father's conversion, the father and his descendants had given over a hundred years of missionary service to the Church. There were at that time fifteen in the mission field, and we had three of them in our mission.

I told that story in a missionary conference held by the First Council of Seventy in the Barratt Hall in Salt Lake City in connection with a General Conference, in 1940, one hundred years after this man had accepted the Gospel. His son who had written me was present, but I did not know it. At the close of the meeting he came up to me and said, "It is now one hundred and sixty years of missionary service. You see, when you add ten or fifteen years each year from ten or fifteen missionaries in the field, it does not take long to add another hundred years."

This helped me to understand better than I had ever done before what the Lord meant when, in answer to the inquiry of one of the early converts to the Church, as to what he could do that would be most worth while, the Lord told him that the thing that would be most worth while to him would be to thrust in his sickle and reap, for the harvest was white already to be garnered. Then the Lord added, "And if it is so be that you should labor all your days in crying repentance unto this people and bring save one soul unto me, how great shall be your joy with him in the kingdom of my Father!"

The missionary who brought that man into the church back in 1840 might not have felt that he had accomplished much, especially if he were his only convert. Yet in a hundred years there was one hundred and sixty years of missionary work from that one man and his descendants. Add to that all the converts made by their converts and their descendants, and you would almost have a nation of men, all as the result of that one conversion.

The sacrifices made by our young and old alike to carry the gospel to the nations of the earth are tremendous, and would be hard for the world to understand. I give a couple of illustrations that have recently come to my attention:

Wives Help Husbands

I interviewed a young man for his mission in Kanab, Utah recently. In questioning him, I learned that he was a young married man. I asked if his wife wanted him to go on a mission, and he replied that she did. Then I said, "Well, I will have to interview her also, and have her tell me that she wants you to go." He replied that she was in the hospital, having given birth to a baby during the night. So we went to the hospital, and I asked this young wife and mother if she wanted her husband to go on a mission. Her reply was, "Yes, when we married we agreed that our marriage would not stand in the way of his filling his mission. I want him to go—I can go and live with my parents while he is gone." He went on his mission, and this young woman and her mother called at my office and reported that he was doing a fine work and enjoying his mission very much. But as she talked of him and how much she missed him, one couldn't help but realize what a sacrifice they were both making that they might share the truths of the gospel with others.

I had another similar experience. Recently I interviewed a young man for his mission in Provo, Utah. When I inquired as to the attitude of his wife, he said she was expecting to leave for the hospital any moment to give birth to her first child. So we went to the little apartment where this young couple were living, and the wife assured me that she wanted her husband to go on his mission. She was the daughter of a Stake President in Idaho. While her husband was in the mission field, I attended a conference in the stake where her father presided and I stayed at their home. This young wife and mother was there with her little child while her husband was in the mission field. I learned from her that her child was born within twenty-four hours from the time I called at their apartment to ascertain her wishes with respect to my recommending her husband for his mission. Surely, our young people are wonderful.

Supporting the Missionaries

We have many wonderful members in the Church who are contributing toward the support of missionaries in the field when they do not have sons and daughters of their own to send. Many have also contributed to the missionary fund at the office of the First Presidency to help young people in the foreign fields who are not financially able so that they can fill missions as well as our boys and girls here in the West.

Speaking of helping to keep missionaries in the field, I have quite a few friends whom I know are doing that consistently. One good sister, a widow, has kept many missionaries in the field. I have a relative who aims to keep ten in the mission field all the time, but he daren't tell his wife about it. I have always felt badly because she should be able to share that great joy with him. I talked along this line sometime ago in a conference. Following the conference I received a letter from a school teacher enclosing sufficient money for a month's keep of a missionary, and indicating that she would send a like amount each month for two years to keep a missionary in the field.

I was thrilled recently in interviewing a young man for his mission in California to learn that his parents were both Catholics and yet they were putting up the money for their son's mission. I always add that when we can get all the Catholics doing that for their sons, we will be well on the way with our great missionary program.

Individual Responsibility

Share the Gospel

The Lord admonished us in the Doctrine and Covenants: "Let every man who is warned warn his neighbor." When we have something as precious as the restored gospel, will not the Lord hold us accountable if we fail to share it with others? Since we have been warned of the calamities and judgments to come, have we not an obligation to our families, friends, and neighbors, to help them understand the purpose of life, and the need for repentance and righteous works?

There is opportunity all around us to share the truths of the gospel with others, if we will be alert to such opportunities. We may be tongue-tied when it comes to talking about our church, but if we really love others we will make a point of getting them interested in this wonderful Latter-day work.

Just to illustrate . . .

While I was the Presiding Bishop of the Church we had charge of the Church's building program. Following a conference in Wyoming, I went to the home of the Bishop to work out a plan for a new ward meeting house. The Bishop's counselor turned to me and said, "Our Bishop was formerly a Catholic, and since he joined the Church, he has filled a mission." I said, "Bishop, how did we happen to get you?" He said he was working in the railroad yards and one day his companion raised up and said, "Where did you live before you were born?" He replied, "I didn't live anywhere." Then his companion said, "Oh, you don't believe the Bible, do you?" He said, "We spent all our noon hour while my companion was showing me where I lived before I was born." And that caused him to study the gospel further and he joined the Church.

If his companion had not desired to share the gospel with him, they might have worked together for a lifetime and the Catholic never hear of the precious truths of the restored gospel.

There are countless examples of servicemen bringing their buddies into the Church. In October, 1956, my daughter received a letter from a neighbor's son in the armed forces. Written from Albuquerque, the letter reported that he and his associates had brought one hundred converts into the church during that year up to date. They had been giving all their spare time to missionary work.

Book Gains Converts

I try never to miss an opportunity to teach others the gospel.

I received a letter once from a woman from California, enclosing a check for One Hundred Dollars for her missionary son laboring in Holland. On the letter there was a postscript reading as follows: "Neither my husband nor I are members of your Church."

I sent an acknowledgment of the remittance. I assured her that I thought her son would enjoy his mission in Holland—that I had filled two missions there and had found the people very kind and hospitable. Then I added, "Since neither your husband or you are members of our church, I am taking the liberty of sending you a copy of a book I have written which tells the story your son has gone to tell that people. I suggest that you and your husband read it. Then forward it to your son; it will help him in his missionary work."

A few weeks later, I received a letter from this lady in which she said, "I received your book, and the best compliment I can pay you is the fact that I cannot leave it alone—I read every minute I can spare—I am to page 167." A few weeks later, I was near her home dedicating a chapel. She was there, and was then a member of the Church.

Now if I had merely thanked her for the check she sent for her son in the mission field and not mentioned the gospel, it might have been years before she received the truth for some people will not hearken to their own family members as well as to an outsider.

President McKay's Request

Everyone should accept the challenge of telling his neighbor about the gospel. If he does not feel capable of converting them himself, he can encourage them to let the missionaries come.

I attended a conference in New York about two years ago. In the general session of the conference, I told the members of the stake that President McKay had asked each one of us to be a missionary and try and bring someone into the Church through our efforts. Then I added, "Won't you just sit quiet now for a few moments and think of some non-Mormon friend or relative or associate or neighbor to whom you could carry the message of the restored gospel and thus fulfill President McKay's request?"

A few weeks after that I received a letter from a young man down in Texas, reading like this: "Bishop Richards, I was in your conference in New York. I was there attending a convention and I heard you ask each one of us to try and bring someone into the Church. So I wrote my wife a letter and told her that when I returned I had a proposition to make to her." Then upon his return he told her of my request and said, "There is a young man works in the office with me and he seems like a fine young fellow. I have never told him why I am a member of the Mormon Church. I would like to invite him and his wife over to our home some night for supper, and after supper we will have something to talk about."

The letter he wrote to me was to tell me the joy he had in his heart in having been privileged to lead this young man and his wife down into the waters of baptism.

On Sunday, February 13, 1961 I told that story in a conference in Houston, Texas and at the close of the meeting four young people came up and spoke to me. One of the young men was the man who had heard me in New York and his wife, the other the young man to whom he taught the gospel with his wife, both of whom were fine Latter-day Saints, and seemed very happy in their membership.

Golden Opportunities Missed

Why should we miss out on the great joy the Lord has promised us if we bring but one soul to Him? Are you passing up a chance to win eternal love and gratitude of one of your neighbors or friends by failing to share your knowledge of the gospel with him? You may be. Just to illustrate . . .

I was assigned by the First Presidency to attend the ground-breaking exercises for the Mormon Memorial Bridge at Winter Quarters. I met the District President of our mission there and learned that he had lived in Salt Lake for seventeen years without joining the Church. When he returned to Omaha, he met the missionaries. Feeling favorable as he did toward our people, he let the missionaries teach him the gospel, and he joined the Church. There he was the District President. I said, "Why didn't you join the Church out in Utah?" His reply was, "No one ever invited me to."

I was riding with a Stake President toward Farmington, New Mexico some years ago. In the auto was the Stake Mission President. I learned that he had lived in Ogden for fourteen years without joining the

Church, so I asked him the same question. His reply was the same, "No one ever invited me to join the Church."

I told of these experiences in a conference at Lyman, Wyoming some few years ago and the Stake President said that the experiences reminded him of his experience when he was a Bishop. He said: "One day a man living in my community called up and said, 'Bishop, do you think I am a good enough man to be a member of your church?'" The Bishop said, "It dawned on me that we had never invited him to be a member of the Church. So I made arrangement for his baptism Friday night and then I called a good woman living in our community and told her that this man was going to be baptized Friday evening and asked her if she wouldn't like to go along also. Her reply was, 'Bishop, for a long time I have wondered how long I would have to live in your community before you would invite me to join your Church.'"

I have often told the story of the Englishman who came to Utah, not a member of the Church, and bought a farm in Davis County. All of his neighbors were members of the Church, but they didn't want to force their religion upon this Englishman so when they would meet they would talk about current events, the weather, etc. Finally one of the neighbors was called on a mission to Great Britain. While there, his English friend decided to return to Great Britain to visit his relatives and friends. One night the friend picked up a newspaper and read an announcement of a Mormon meeting to be held, with the public invited. He said, "Well, I have been living out there among them. I don't know anything about what they believe. I guess I better go and find out." To his surprise the principal speaker that night was his neighbor from next door from out in Davis County. He had to go all the way back to Great Britain to get this neighbor to tell him about the marvelous work and wonder the Lord has set his hand to do in our day. The result was that he joined the Church and they returned to Utah together. But don't you think the new convert would regret that so much time had been wasted before he learned of the gospel? I do, for I have heard many a convert exclaim, "Why couldn't I have had this joy years ago!"

An Important Question

A doctor from California called at my office selling real estate temporarily because of a break in his health. We were not interested in what he had to sell, but in conversation with him, I found that he was a religious man. I said, "Do you really love the Lord?" His reply was, "I surely do." Then I asked, "Do you love the Lord enough that you would be willing to join the Mormon Church if you knew the Lord wanted you to?" He thought a few minutes and then replied, "Yes, I do." I then proceeded to tell him how he could know that the Lord wanted him to join the Mormon Church.

I didn't hear from him for about three years, when he called me one day by 'phone. He was in Salt Lake with his wife, and he invited Sister Richards and me to join them at lunch in the Hotel Utah. He was then the High Priest's leader in his ward in California, and this is what he said to me, "But, why couldn't I have known this thirty years ago? Why couldn't I have had the joy all these thirty years that you have had in helping to promote this work in the earth?"

A Missionary Boy

Many of our young people are doing a good missionary work by taking their friends with them to Primary, Sunday School and Mutual.

A few years ago a non-Mormon doctor and his family moved into one of our Mormon towns in Idaho.

The doctor's son made a friend of a Mormon boy who took him to Sunday School and Primary. When the Mormon boy was old enough to be ordained a Deacon, the doctor's son went to his father and asked permission to be baptized a member of the Church so he could become a Deacon. The father gave permission. The doctor's son grew up through the grades of the Priesthood, was called into the service of his country, and was ordained an Elder. When he returned on a furlough he sat up one night till the wee hours of the morning with his father teaching him the gospel. The result was that the next morning the father and the son went to the Bishop and the father asked permission to have his son baptize him a member of the Church.

The Bishop wanted to be good to this prominent man so he offered to let him attend the Elders Quorum rather than to meet with the Deacons, but the doctor said, "No, I want to learn the Gospel from the grass roots like my son. I will meet with the Deacons and pass the Sacrament with them." I have since met this doctor and he has become a very valuable asset in the community, all because one Mormon boy started by taking his friend, the doctor's son, to Primary and Sunday School with him.

Many of us could accomplish the same result if we would but invite our family and friends to our Sabbath and weekday meetings and socials. All we need is love in our hearts and a desire to share our blessings with others.

Israel, Do You Know?

Message to the Jewish People

For many years I have had a great desire to preach the gospel to the Jewish people. When I returned from presiding over the Netherlands mission, I said to my father who was then a member of the Council of the Twelve, "Father, if the Church ever starts the work with the Jewish people, I would like to have a hand in it." When President Grant called my home to see if I would serve as the Presiding Bishop, my wife said, "I thought surely that was your call to Jerusalem."

When I became the Presiding Bishop of the Church, I felt that the opportunity would never come to me. After I wrote the book *A Marvelous Work and a Wonder,* and it seemed to be so helpful in the missionary work, I said to myself: "Why don't I write our message to the Jewish people as I would like to present it to them?" Accordingly, I wrote the book, *Israel, Do You Know?* It has been helpful in bringing some of the Jewish people into the Church.

Sometime ago a Jewish friend from California wrote a letter to President McKay, calling him Prophet McKay, asking a lot of questions about the Gospel. The letter was handed to me to answer. I answered it and sent this man a copy of my book, *Israel, Do You Know?* In a few days I received a letter from him indicating that he had prayed three nights in succession for answers to his questions and they had all been answered. He testified in that letter that he knew we had the truth. I sent his name to the Stake President and suggested that they ask the Stake Missionaries to call on him. In a short time he wanted to be baptized a member of the Church, but his wife threatened to leave him if he did. He had three children and I advised him to wait until he could obtain the consent of his wife. This he did, and he is now a fine Elder in the Church.

Visitors from Jerusalem

Because of my interest, most inquiries that come to the church office building regarding the work with the Jewish people are referred to me. I have had opportunity to talk with many prominent visitors from Jerusalem who have come here out of special interest since Israel today is practically duplicating what the saints did here in Utah, subduing the wilderness to make it blossom as a rose.

When these prominent visitors come to my office, it takes only a brief conversation to convince them that there are no other people as interested in them as the Latter-day Saints. We call their attention to the fact that we are their distant cousins, since we also are descendants of Abraham, Isaac and Jacob.

I usually say in not too serious a mood so as not to offend, "What would you think if I were to tell you that you are not really Israelites?" Then they will say, "Why do you say that?" Then I call attention to the fact that Jacob, whose name Israel was bestowed upon him by the Lord, had twelve sons; that after some period of time his descendants were divided in two great kingdoms, the Kingdom of Israel and the Kingdom of Judah. Then I ask, "To which of these two kingdoms do you belong?" They of course have to admit that they belong to the Kingdom of Judah. Then I remind them that because Reuben fell, Jacob took the birthright from Reuben and bestowed it upon the sons of Joseph saying, "My name shall be named upon you." Then I ask, "And what was his name?" They have to admit that his name was Israel. Then I ask, "Then who has really the right to the name Israel, the Kingdom of Judah or the Kingdom of Israel under the leadership of Joseph and his sons?"

Two Records

Then I remind them that the Lord commanded their Prophet Ezekiel that two records should be kept, one for Judah and his posterity, and one for Joseph and his posterity; that in the days of their children (meaning coming generations) when the children should ask for the meaning of this command, the Lord would tell them that he would take the record of Joseph which would be in the hands of Ephraim and put it with the record of Judah and make them one in his hand. Then I ask, "Do you know anything about the record of Joseph?" Of course they admit that they do not. Then I tell them how grateful we are to them that we have the record of Judah, which is the Old Testament and the New Testament, and the knowledge of their prophets. I remind them that the Lord commanded one of their prophets that the Record of Joseph should be kept and that he would put it with the record of Judah and make them one in his hand. I explained that when the Lord fulfilled that promise, it would be necessary that they should accept the record of Joseph, for it would be equally as binding as the record of Judah. Then I inform them that we have the record of Joseph.

Spiritual Division

I call their attention to the fact that the Jews are divided spiritually into many groups, just as are the so-called Christians. I call their attention to the fact that the Lord stated through Amos their prophet, "Surely the Lord God will do nothing, but he revealeth his secret unto his servants the prophets." Then I say to them that they cannot expect to be united as a people until they have living prophets as did their forebears. I inform them that we have a living prophet, and have had a succession of prophets to guide us since the restoration of the gospel to the earth. I inform them that we appreciate

the record of Judah that they have given to the world;
that we appreciate the leadership and direction their
prophets gave while they lived, but that we have now
the record of Joseph with living prophets to guide us.
I testify that they cannot look for a fulfillment of the
promises of the Lord until they are willing to accept this
new record and the living prophets. In other words,
they have nothing further to give to us, but we have a
great deal to give to them. Then I call attention to the
fact that when they are willing to accept this record of
Joseph, which the Lord promised to them, there would
be no reason for their having any further doubts as to
who is their expected Messiah. I offer to give them a
copy of my book, *Israel, Do You Know?* if they will
promise to read it. All this comes as a great surprise to
them, but creates a desire and interest to know more, as
evidenced by the following statement from Brother and
Sister Earl Remington of California, who brought to my
office in January, 1961, a prominent representative from
the Government of Israel:

"Dear Brother Richards, Gratefully we acknowledge
the wonderful half hour spent in your presence last week
with our guest, Dr. Pinchas Blumenthal of Israel.

"He expressed a great respect and admiration for
you and the things he listened to. The twinkle in your
eye caught his fancy and won his heart. Several times
during the day, he remarked that nothing he had seen
in all America impressed him half so much as the things
he saw and heard that one day in Salt Lake City."

So Much to Offer

We are in a favorable position to do missionary work
with the Jewish people since we have so much to offer
them. They have nothing additional to offer to us for
we have their record, but we have everything to offer

them—our record and our inspired, ordained prophets having authority from God to act in His name.

In this connection I have in mind the preface to the Book of Mormon, indicating that the Lord had preserved it for "The convincing of the Jew and Gentile that Jesus is the Christ, the Eternal God manifesting himself to all nations."

When such visitors have time, I call their attention to the statement of the Lord through the Prophet Jeremiah as recorded in Jeremiah 31:3: "Behold the days come sayeth the Lord that I will make a new covenant with the House of Israel, and with the House of Judah." I point out to them that the Lord puts the House of Israel ahead of the House of Judah, so they must look to the House of Israel for information concerning the new covenant the Lord promised to make.

Then I quote from Jeremiah 3:18 the following: "In those days the House of Judah shall walk with the House of Israel, and they shall come together out of the land of the North to the land that I have given for an inheritance unto your fathers." I call attention to the fact that in this promise the House of Judah shall walk with the House of Israel, not the House of Israel shall walk with the House of Judah, showing that they must look to the House of Israel or our branch of Israel for leadership that will bring us together.

One Nation

I remind them that the Lord has promised to bring the two nations together and that there shall be no more two nations, but one nation. I invite them to be willing to listen to the message we of the House of Israel have to offer unto them. I quote from Ezekiel 37:21-22, "And say unto them, thus sayeth the Lord God; Behold, I will take the children of Israel from among the heathen. whither they be gone, and will gather them on every side, and bring them into their own land; And I will make them one nation in the land upon the mountains of Israel; and one king shall be king to them all; and they shall be no more two nations, neither shall they be divided into two kingdoms any more at all . . . so shall they be my people, and I will be their God."

Then I quote the words of Isaiah recorded in chapter 11: verses 10-13 which is one of the quotations given to the Prophet Joseph by Moroni when he visited him three times during one night and again the next morning. "And in that day there shall be a root of Jesse, which shall stand for an ensign of the people; to it shall the Gentiles seek: and his rest shall be glorious. And it shall come to pass in that day, that the Lord shall set his hand again the second time to recover the remnant of his people. . . . And he shall set up an ensign to the nations, and shall assemble the outcasts of Israel, and gather together the dispersed of Judah from the four corners of the earth. The envy also of Ephraim shall depart, and the adversaries of Judah shall be cut off: Ephraim shall not envy Judah, and Judah shall not vex Ephraim."

I explain that there is no envy in Ephraim of the House of Judah, the Lord was to gather these two different nations to two different gathering places. Then I invite them to become one with us as the Lord has directed.

I still have hopes that in some manner I will be able to contribute in a substantial way to the preaching of the Gospel to this chosen branch of the House of Israel, for great are the promises of the Lord unto them, when they will accept Jesus as their Savior.

Keep The Lead

A Wise Missionary

Missionaries are sent forth to teach and not be taught. They must therefore, keep the lead in their teaching or they will find themselves wasting a lot of time listening instead. I learned a very valuable lesson shortly after my arrival in the mission field, in Holland, as to the importance of the missionary holding the lead —in other words to teach rather than to be taught.

I accompanied an Elder, who was on his second mission, in making a first visit to the home of a man in Rotterdam. While passing our meetinghouse one evening this man had been attracted by the singing of the choir and dropped in. At the close of the meeting, this Elder had obtained his address at the door with permission to visit him and his family.

While my companion was explaining the importance of our message, this man, having stood it as long as he could said. "What about polygamy?" My companion's reply was, "That is a good question—if you hadn't asked us, we would have told you all about it, but, if you were building a house, you would not attempt to put the roof on before you had laid the foundation, would you?" He agreed to this. Then my companion said, "Get your little memorandum book and write 'polygamy' in it so we will not overlook it. We will promise to answer your question later." The minute he wrote "polygamy" in his memorandum book it was just like signing a contract: "I hereby agree to let you keep coming to my home until you tell me all about polygamy."

Later in the evening they offered us coffee and cookies. When we refused to drink the coffee, the man said, "That isn't against your religion, is it?" My companion explained that we were taught not to use coffee, to which he replied, "I would never join your Church then—I couldn't live without my coffee." My companion said, "Write 'coffee' in your memorandum book and we will discuss that later."

Every Question Answered

After we had visited this family for a few weeks, my companion said, "Where is your memorandum book?" When he produced same, all the questions had been answered. Of course, the family joined the Church and emigrated to Utah, and have been among our very most respected members from Holland.

The point I desire to make is this: If my companion had discussed polygamy and coffee that first night, the chances are that we would never have had the privilege of returning to that home, for there was nothing that could be said on those subjects that would have interested that family until they began to feel that the Lord had truly raised up a Prophet in this dispensation.

In other words: We were not sent forth to be taught, but to teach the children of men.

Know Your Religion

Nine-Year-Old Missionary

Parents have a responsibility to see that their children know the basic principles of the Church, and the wonderful stories from the standard works. We all have a duty to be well informed on our religion so we can share it intelligently with others when the opportunity arises. By the measure of our understanding, we can either accomplish great good or little at all. Just to illustrate . . .

In a Relief Society Meeting in a Conference I attended in Sacramento, California, a sister told this story.

She said she was living in San Francisco; while traveling on the train to visit her son in Salt Lake City, she noticed a young boy about nine years old traveling alone. She said, "He was such a cute young fellow I tried to visit with him. I asked him about his school, and he didn't seem too much interested. I tried to visit with him about the games he liked to play, and he did not seem very interested. Then he spoke up and said, 'You are going to Salt Lake aren't you?'" When I answered that I was, he said, 'Then you are a Mormon, aren't you?' I replied, 'No, I am a Catholic.' Then he said, 'Well, I am a Mormon boy. Would you like me to tell you about my Church?'" The sister continued, "Even a Catholic couldn't refuse to listen to a little boy who wanted to talk about his Church. He told me how Joseph Smith didn't know which church to join and how he went into the woods to pray. He told me of the visit of the Father and Son, and of the visit of Moroni who delivered to Joseph the plates from which the Book of Mormon was translated. Then he quoted me the Articles of Faith. When he went to bed that night in one of the upper berths, his light burned quite late so I asked him the next morning why it took him so long to settle down. He replied, 'I always have to read a chapter in the Book of Mormon before I go to sleep.' "

When this woman arrived in Salt Lake, her son met her and took her to the Hotel Temple Square. She then went through the Temple Block with a guide, purchased a Book of Mormon and read it, then met Bishop Clawson who taught her further the truths of the gospel. She was baptized a member of the Church, and returned to San Francisco, a Latter-day Saint instead of a Catholic, all because of this young Primary boy and his knowledge of his Church.

Some time ago one of our Latter-day Saint girls married and went east to live. When her neighbors found that she was a member of the Mormon Church, they all wanted to know what the Mormons believed. She was not able to give a reason for the hope that was within her, as Peter has indicated each member should be able to do, so she wrote a letter to Sister Williams who was then the editor of the 'Question and Answer' page in the *Deseret News*. She wrote, "Please write and tell me what we believe. (I got this story from Sister Williams.) She said I know that the first two principles are that you should not use tea or coffee or play cards." I doubt if anyone could create a desire in the heart of anyone to want to know much about the Mormon Church if that is all they could tell about its precepts.

Let us study and prepare ourselves and our children to do good.

Let us know our religion so we can share it with others.

Leadership

Ruts and Circles

Probably the most important thing in the world is leadership. The progress of our Church depends on effective leadership. On every side we see the need for training men to be leaders.

Bishop Ashton was constantly warning the Bishops against getting in a rut, always adding that the only difference between the grave and a rut was that one was just a little deeper than the other.

The Italian was asked what he did for a living. His reply was, "I digge de ditch, to earnie de money, to buyie de bread, to gettie de strength to digge de ditch." But he never got out of the ditch. We must be careful that we are getting somewhere with all our effort and activity.

During the Civil War, the lady of a Southern plantation asked her colored servant how the war was coming. She herself was confined to her bed. The colored servant replied, "Well, Ma'm, our soldiers am charging backwards, and the Yankees am retreating forward." I tell our leaders that we don't want any of them charging backwards.

We had a slogan in our Hollywood Stake, which went like this: "Not failure, but low aim is often our greatest sin." It isn't always that we have tried and failed as much as it is that we have not tried.

In my leadership experience in the Church, I have not found it difficult to get the support of the Church members as long as we were trying to do things finer and better than they had ever been done before. But the members do get tired when things are just done over and over again in the same manner. In other words, when you get in a rut.

"To be going nowhere is to arrive nowhere. That is where one arrives with utmost certainty without the aid of guide-posts or road signs."

Checking Up

Shortly after returning from my first mission, I heard a brother, in a Sunday School Union Meeting, make the statement that there were three requisites to successful leadership: Planning your work; assigning your work; and checking up on your assignments. This statement has helped me a very great deal in my leadership responsibilities in the Church. I have come to feel that it is the checking up that really determines whether the work will be done or not. One may plan his work, and yet it may never be done; he may assign his work, and yet it may never be done; but when he checks up on his assignments, usually the work is done.

My wife and I once planned a new home. We paid the architect several hundred dollars for his help, but when we obtained a price for the building of the home, we never built it. But the architect won a national prize for having designed it. It takes more than planning to achieve results.

I once asked one of our Sunday School Superintendents if they always had their two and one-half minute talks in Sunday School. I knew they didn't and hence my question. His reply was: "Not very often. We always assign them but the students seldom fill their assignments." I commented: "Oh, making assignments is easy; it is the checking up on the assignments that really determines whether the talks will be given or not." I offended him and he did not come to Sunday School for a few times, so I called at his home to see him. Calling him by name I said, "I have come to apologize to you—not for what I said, for what I said is just as true today as it was the day I said it, but I have come to apologize for having hurt your feelings."

I talked on this subject in a Stake Leadership Meeting a few years ago. At the close of the meeting, a new Bishop came up to me and said, "I surely got a lot out of that talk." The next day we asked him to speak in one of the general sessions of the Stake Conference. Among other things he said, "Last night I listened to Bishop Richards speak of the importance of checking up on our work, and I thought of what he had said all night, so I got up early this morning and checked up on each member of the Aaronic Priesthood in our ward. They are all here but three, and they had to come sixteen miles to get here."

Are You Making Weaklings?

I drove over two hundred miles to attend a Stake Priesthood Leadership Meeting preceding the Stake Conference. When the roll was called, half of the High Council and half of the Bishops were not present, so the stake President made wonderful excuses for them. At the close of the meeting I asked the Stake President if I could talk with him alone. We went into his office, and I said, "President, has it ever occurred to you that you might be making weaklings of your associates by making such wonderful excuses for them? They knew that they didn't need to come to their meeting for you would excuse them. Now, I will give you a little contrast. A few weeks ago I attended a Conference in Arizona. When the roll was called there was one member of the High Council missing. The Stake President turned to me and said, 'I'll know where that man is before this day ends, you can be sure of that.' "

See the difference in what the Stake Presidents expected of their stake leaders. We don't usually get more than we expect. When men and women are called to positions of responsibility in the church, I think we have a right to expect real devotion to their callings.

The Best Paymaster

Some Stake Presidents and Bishops seem afraid to expect their associates to measure up to their responsibilities because they are not handed a check each week or month for the service they render. I always say that the Lord is the best paymaster in the world, and he will adequately compensate all those who serve in His vineyard.

As a boy, my father taught me that there was no corporation, organization or institution in the world that would pay me as great dividends on the investment of my time, talents, and means as the Church. That statement came home rather forcefully to me a short time ago when one of my rich friends, a man worth several million dollars, said, "LeGrand, I would trade you all my money for your Church experience." To which I replied, "Yes, but I wouldn't trade you. You can't take your money with you when you go, but I can take my experience. Furthermore, you are always in trouble keeping your taxes paid and worrying what will happen with your estate when you die, and how the inheritance tax will be paid. I don't have anything like that to worry about!"

Recipe for Success

A successful leader was asked his recipe for success. He said it could be summed up in three words—"and then some." You do a good job "and then some." A successful leader will first acquaint himself with all the responsibilities his position entails. He will then seek for the very best men he can find to help him, and he will inspire them to be as devoted to their individual responsibilities as he is to his. He will set them an example by doing a good job "and then some." Nothing is as effective as a good example, coupled with praise and encouragement. Then, when the leader feels he has done his very best he should check up on himself to see if there are weak points he can overcome. He might ask his superiors or co-workers for suggestions, or he might find an in-direct way to get an objective look at his work. You recall the story of the darky boy who went into the Drug Store and called up his boss, saying, "I understands you wants to hire a colored boy." The boss responded that he already had one. Then he was asked if his work was satisfactory and was told that it was. Then the colored boy asked: "Perfectly satisfactory?" and the boss as-sured him that it was. As he went to leave the drug store the owner said, "Rastus, I thought you had a job." He replied: "Yes, sir. Yes, sir, I is just checking up on myself." It would be wonderful if we could all check up on ourselves occasionally.

Let Each Man Learn His Duty

Individual Responsibility

At one of our stake conferences, while I was the visiting authority, we asked the stake coordinator of Aaronic Priesthood to speak twenty minutes on what his duties were, and he had a week or two to prepare. He stood up and said something like this, "Well, I don't know what my duties are, but this is what I think they are." You have heard of the man who was called to speak in a Sacrament Meeting who said he didn't have anything to say. Then he took twenty minutes proving that he didn't have anything to say. Well, this brother took twenty minutes to prove that he did not know what his duties were. When my turn came, I asked him why he did not know his duties. I said, "Do you have a handbook?" His reply was, "No." I turned to the Stake President and asked if he couldn't get him a handbook. I said, "They don't cost you anything—all you have to do is to order one."

Here was a man with one of the major stake responsibilities who didn't think enough of his calling, even when asked in advance to discuss the same in a Stake Leadership Meeting, to get a handbook to teach him what his responsibilities were.

In a revelation to the Prophet Joseph Smith, the Lord saw fit to express Himself on this subject in these words:

"Wherefore, now let every man learn his duty, and to act in the office in which he is appointed, in all diligence.

"He that is slothful shall not be counted worthy to stand, and he that learns not his duty and shows himself not approved shall not be counted worthy to stand. Even so. Amen." (Doctrine & Covenants 107:99-100).

Team Work

Speaking of every man knowing what his duty is, years ago I had the privilege of going through an automobile assembly plant in Detroit. In those days, the chassis was first dropped onto a conveyor that ran for possibly two blocks without ever stopping. The automobile was completely assembled while traveling on this conveyor, including the filling of the gas tank, so that it ran off the conveyor into the parking lot on its own power.

It was wonderful to watch the precision with which each man performed the work assigned to him as that conveyor moved along. One would throw on a front wheel and screw the bur on; another a rear wheel, another would push the steering wheel into place; another, on his back on a little dolly underneath the auto, would ride back and forth screwing on nuts as he traveled.

While watching this operation, this thought came to me: What if when the gates swung open to let a new shift of workmen in, the men did not know what their duty was. One would run for a screwdriver, another for a monkey-wrench, etc. Wouldn't that be a great looking jalopy when it left the assembly line?

If it is necessary for men to know what their duty is for success in industry, isn't it equally essential for them to know what their duty is to successfully carry on the work of the Lord? How can His kingdom be established among men without men knowing what their duty is?

It is the duty of leaders *to lead*. A newly appointed District President of the Southern States Mission came to me and said, "President Richards, it is about time to plan our next district conference. What have you to suggest?" I looked at him and said, "Well, do you want this to be my conference or your conference?" He thought a few moments and then replied, "I want it to be my conference." I said, "I thought so. Now you plan

what you think would make a good conference. Then
if you want me to go over your plan for suggestions, I
will be glad to do so."

Set High Standards

We had just commenced our youth program in the
mission, so we planned to have each branch of his district
prepare a number for our program the night before the
conference. When the program was presented, nearly
every number proved to be a "Negro stunt," and some
of them were quite off-color. At the close of the program,
the District President came to me and said, "I dare not
ask you what you thought of the program." My reply
was, "Oh, I think it was wonderful." He said, "You
don't mean that, do you?" "Yes," I said, "It was wonderful because it showed us what our starting point is;
but if you ever have another program like it while I am
in the mission, it will not be wonderful." I told him that
next time he should censor each number on the program
before it was presented; that the people had to be taught
to discriminate between the good and bad in all things;
that while music was the voice of the angels, it could also
be found in the hell-holes and dives; that with the voice
we praise God and edify His children, but that it could
also be used to profane God and curse man; that, while
it could lift men out of this world, it could also arouse
in man every evil tendency with which man is possessed.
I told him it was up to us as leaders to train our people
to select that which would uplift and ennoble man and
help to make him more like his Father in Heaven.

Later, this same district presented a program in a
rented theatre in Atlanta, Georgia that I would have
been proud to have seen presented in the Salt Lake
Tabernacle.

Good leadership will teach people how to change
patterns.

Let Your Light Shine

The Boy in Uniform

During the war, I received a letter from a missionary laboring with his wife in Southern California, in which he said: "Brother Richards, there have been so many L.D.S. boys in uniform stationed here in this city, and they have been such outstanding, fine young men that it has literally changed the attitude of the people of the town toward the Mormon Church."

Then he told of a Women's Club that was having a luncheon at a hotel. The woman in charge had an extra plate placed at the table, and explained to the women that it was her thought to invite the first soldier who came along in uniform to occupy the extra place. Well, he happened to be an L.D.S. boy, and one that did not hide his light under a bushel.

When the coffee was passed, he would not touch the coffee. They offered to get him tea, but he did not want the tea. Then they wanted to know all about him and how he was raised and where. This gave him a wonderful opportunity to tell them about our people and our standards. At the close of the meal the women lighted their cigarettes, but he refused to smoke with them.

One woman said: "I resolved that if the Mormon Elders ever knocked at my door, I would let them in. I wanted to know more about a people who could raise a boy like the one who sat at our table." When the letter was written this woman was a very earnest investigator of the Gospel.

Sometime later, I told this story in a Conference in the Assembly Hall in Salt Lake City, and at the close of the meeting a young man came up to me and said, "Brother Richards, I am that boy," to which I replied, "No kidding! Did I tell the story correctly?" and he replied that I had done. Then I asked, "What are you doing in the Church now?" His reply was, "Oh, I am the Bishop of such and such ward."

How much good we could accomplish if all of us let our light shine like this young man!

Life Sketch

Taught to Work

My publisher has suggested that I give a little synopsis of my early life. I was born in Farmington, Utah on February 6, 1886. Shortly thereafter my father moved to Nephi for a short period to help his sister, who had lost her husband, adjust her affairs. Then we went to Tooele, where he had charge of a large ranch belonging to his brother-in-law.

In later years Father purchased a dry farm there in Tooele. I have always been grateful that I was raised on a farm because we were taught to work. I think that is a great asset in the life of any young man.

Boyhood Accidents and Affliction

While I was young, I had some experiences, as most boys do, that could have resulted very seriously. One time when I was a small child, I approached my father who was cutting wood, unobserved by him. I received a blow from the head of the ax upon my forehead. A narrow escape from death.

A few years later while standing in a wagon to which a team was attached, by a sudden start backward, I was thrown from the wagon. The wheel passed over my head. A quick forward movement of the team caused the wheel to pass over my head the second time. It was truly a miracle that I was not seriously injured.

When I was 9 years old, I was stricken with a disease of some nature in my hip bone. The doctors called it hip trouble. I wore a plaster cast on my leg from my shoe top and around my waist for about nine months, during which time I walked on crutches. I have gotten along pretty well all my life as far as that lameness was concerned, but now as I am getting older my leg stiffens up and I use a cane which is a great help to me.

While on crutches at the age of nine, I was loading hay for a friend who came to purchase hay on the ranch. In pulling away from the stack I got the lines twisted. The wagon tipped over and I was under the load of hay. The wagon ran over my arm and broke it. The doctor was called. My father was not home and I would not permit the doctor to touch me until they located my father so he could administer to me.

School and Work

After we had purchased the farm, father built one of the nicest homes in the county. We boys had some real experiences hauling lumber, lime, brick, etc. from Salt Lake and Grantsville in all kinds of weather.

We had no high school in our town at that time. In order to do our farm work, we had to stay out of school for some weeks to get our fall planting done. Then we had to stop early in the spring to do some more of the farm work, and go back for final examinations. I have always said our teacher had to advance us because our father was a member of the school board.

Graduation Talk

I had an interesting experience when I was graduated from the district school. I was asked to deliver a paper prognosticating the future of the members of our class. After nearly sixty years it's interesting to look back and see how nearly I guessed the future of the class members.

I heard a little poem written by J. W. Johnson of Chicago in the Journal of Commerce, entitled "The Way of the World," that seemed to fit in a better manner than I was able to do what I attempted to do in my prognostication of the future of our class members.

THE WAY OF THE WORLD

Oh, where are the playmates of yesterday?
    The fellows we knew at school?
Oh, what has become of the studious one?
    And where, oh where, is the fool?
Oh, what has become of the orator,
    Whose passion was to recite?

And the bashful kid who could speak no piece
    Unless he succumbed to fright?
Oh, what has become of the model boy,
    Who was always the teacher's pet?
And where, oh where, is the tough young nut,
    The one we can never forget?

The studious one, so we have been told,
    Is driving a hack these days.
While the fool owns stock in a bank or two,
    And a railroad that always pays.
The orator that we knew so well
    Is a clerk in a dry goods store;
While the bashful kid we knew has been
    In Congress ten years or more.
The model boy is behind the bars
    For stealing a neighbor's cow—
And you ask what of the tough young nut?
    Oh, he's the preacher (the Bishop) now.

Teachers

In January of 1902 I enrolled in the Salt Lake Business College and boarded with my older brother, George F. Richards, Jr. This was in the top floor of the Templeton Building at the corner of Main Street and South Temple, which building has since been torn down to make way for the Kennecott Building. President J. Reuben Clark, Jr. was my teacher in English and Mathematics. Milton H. Ross, one of my dear friends, tried to teach me penmanship. He was a better teacher than I was a student.

Joy in Church Assignment

At that time the church held a Sunday School each Sunday in the L.D.S. University for the out-of-town students. Brother Milton Bennion was the Superintendent, President J. Reuben Clark, Jr. was his first assistant, and Brother Stanley Hanks (the father of Marion D. Hanks and Lincoln Hanks) and I were assigned to take care of the administration of the Sacrament. I enjoyed this assignment very much. Brother John M. Mills taught the class on the Book of Mormon, etc. Brother James E. Talmage taught a class on the Articles of Faith which I attended. At the close of the season we had a testimony meeting. One man made the statement that Sunday after Sunday, he had felt that he had been lifted out of this world into the Celestial Kingdom as he listened to Brother Talmage teaching the Articles of Faith. I thought he expressed my feelings perfectly.

First Mission

I completed my eighteen months course at the business college in twelve months by attending night school along with day school. After a number of temporary jobs, I went to work as a secretary to the Secretary of the Consolidated Wagon and Machine Company, for which company I was working when called to go on my mission to the Netherlands in February of 1905. I had just received the appointment to serve as Sales Correspondent for the company which would have given me quite an advancement; but I left that in order to fill my mission, leaving Salt Lake on April 17, 1905 in the company of four of the sons of President Joseph F. Smith, one being my cousin, Willard R. Smith.

Disappointment Proves a Blessing

Upon my arrival in the mission field, I was appointed Secretary of the mission. In a few months thereafter, we held a missionary conference in Rotterdam of all the Elders of our mission. President Grant, who was then the President of the European Mission met with us with about a hundred of his missionaries. The missionary meeting lasted all day. When President Grant spoke, he said something like this, "Brethren, today we have feasted on the fat things of the spirit. Now go out and give it away, for the more you give away, the more you will have left."

While President Grant was in Rotterdam, I wrote quite a number of letters for him. He said, "Brother Richards, they have been taking my missionaries for the German Mission. How would you like to go to Liverpool and be my secretary?" I told him I would be thrilled, and asked if I could go. He said he would have to think it over until the next day. I was struggling with the language and felt that would be a good out. I thought it would be an honor to be the secretary to President Grant. I could hardly wait for the next day and I asked him what he had decided. His answer was that he had decided that if he took me, it would be because he had the authority to do it, but that my president needed me as much as he did. He thought I should remain. At that time I was disappointed, but after I became the president of that mission, I realized what a wonderful preparation my eighteen months as secretary of the mission had been.

Upon my return from my mission in February 1908, I spent a few months in the Presiding Bishop's office helping to audit the yearly reports. I went from there to keep books for a stock brokerage firm. In the Spring of 1909 I went to Portland, Oregon to serve as the secretary of the Portland Cement Company. I arrived in Portland at the same time as President Melvin J. Ballard arrived to preside over the Northwestern States Mission. Shortly after our arrival, he appointed me as president of the Portland Branch, when there was only one small branch in Portland in a little four square frame building.

Marriage and Family

A few weeks later I returned to Salt Lake and married Ina Jane Ashton, a daughter of Edward T. Ashton and Cora Lindsay in the Salt Lake Temple. The day after our marriage, we returned to Portland. We remained there until after the birth of our first daughter who was born on President Ballard's birthday. At that time we began thinking of the conditions under which we were raised in Utah and the conditions existing in Portland at that time. We wondered if we could answer to the Lord for raising our children in Portland, knowing of the way we had been raised in Utah. While I was visiting with one of the employees at the office, he said that of all the men he knew, both married and unmarried, he wouldn't bet that ten percent of them lived morally clean lives. My answer to this statement was: "I thank the Lord I was raised as a Mormon." I said to my wife that I was sure if other young men could make good in Salt Lake that I could, and that if she thought best we would return to Salt Lake.

When the President of the company, a man worth his millions, heard of our decision, he sent for me to come to his office, with this statement, "I feel that I owe you an apology. In common with others, and I think it is fair to say that I have had a very erroneous idea about the Mormons, but since I have met you and others of your church members working for this company, I have come to the conclusion that you Mormons have something the rest of us do not have." He gave me nearly an hour to tell him about our people and how we were raised and then he offered to let me name my own salary if I would remain with the company. But we had decided to return to Utah.

Netherlands Mission

I returned to Salt Lake with my wife and little daughter and went to work as the secretary of the George Romney Lumber Company. I continued there until called to preside over the Netherlands Mission in November of 1913.

When this call came, I had just planned on going into the lumber business with two of my friends. One was not a member of the Church and was investing $50,000 in cash in order to organize the business. We had purchased the property and were going ahead with arrangements when I received my call. While I was away, this friend went to Idaho and purchased an implement business. When I returned and he read in the paper of my announcement that I was going into the real estate business, he came to Salt Lake and offered me a half interest in his business if I would join him in Idaho. I told him that if he had made that offer before I had made public announcement of my intention to engage in the real estate business, I was sure I would have accepted it, but that success in Salt Lake would mean more to me than it would in Idaho. So, I thanked him for his wonderful offer.

I operated a real estate business from this time until 1929. During this time I filled a short-term mission for six months in the Eastern States while my brother-in-law managed my business for me.

Mission Calls

In the fall of 1929, President Grant sent my father to ask me how I would like to go to Los Angeles and preside over the Hollywood Stake. At this writing there are fifteen stakes of Zion there in the territory I presided over. I told him I hadn't been thinking of anything of that kind, that I didn't know what I would do for a living if I were to go to Los Angeles, and that my daughters were just at the mating age and I didn't like to take them away from their boy friends; but that I thought enough of the church to go anywhere the Brethren wanted me to, and he could so report to President Grant. I told my father if President Grant wanted me to do so, I would go down to Los Angeles and look around and see what I could find. Father reported back that the President asked that I go and look around. Within sixty days I had sold my business and moved my family to Glendale, California in January, 1930. We remained there for four years when I was called to preside over the Southern States Mission.

This was a wonderful experience except that it came during the depression. All the banks and building societies and loaning agencies were going broke, which made it difficult to finance real estate deals. Men were living in houses worth nearly a hundred thousand dollars who could not pay their light bills. The large new apartment houses off Wilshire Boulevard were selling for from 15c to 30c on the dollar of the first mortgage bonds, after the second mortgage bonds and the title holders had lost their equities.

Presiding Bishop

We spent three and a half years in the Southern States, from January 1934 to June 1937. Upon our return to Salt Lake, I again engaged in the real estate business. I was doing very well and had built quite a sales organization when I was called to be the Presiding Bishop of the Church in April 1938. I had to close my business again. Since that time I have devoted all my time to my Church duties.

Multiple Responsibilities

In our responsibility as the Presiding Bishopric, in addition to presiding over the Aaronic Priesthood of the Church, we had the task of directing the church hospitals; some of its ranch properties; and the building of ward and stake meeting houses and their maintenance. In representing the church's interests, I have had the privilege of serving as a Director of Zion's Securities Corporation, as chairman of its Executive Committee, and as a Director of ZCMI and the Hotel Utah.

I have also had a number of committee assignments, such as: Chairman of the Old Folks Central Committee; Chairman of the Committee directing the activities of the foreign speaking groups in Salt Lake City; member of the Church Missionary Committee; member of the Church Personnel Committee; member of the Church Board of Education; advisor to the Church Welfare Committee, etc.

Family

My sweet wife has borne me eight children, six of whom are living and married and have their families. At this writing (April 1961) we have twenty-six grandchildren and eleven great-grandchildren, of whom we are very proud. Our children and grandchildren are all active in the Church commensurate with their ages. The children have all been married in the Temple, also the grandchildren, as many as are married.

Wife's Blessing

A short time before I met my wife she obtained a blessing from Patriarch John Smith. Among other things, he said, "The time is not far distant when thou shalt be called to labor among those upon whom much responsibility rests."

A Real Partnership

From the time of our marriage over fifty-two years ago, I have held a presiding position in the Church, having served as Branch President; three times as bishop of a ward; twice as a member of a stake high council; once as a stake president; twice as mission president; fourteen years as the Presiding Bishop of the Church, and at this writing, I have served nine years as a member of the Quorum of the Twelve Apostles. My wife has stood faithfully by my side during all this time, so it would appear that the words of the Patriarch have been literally fulfilled. She has been a wonderful mother, and much of the credit is due her for raising our children. Because of my work in the Church, she has at times commented that the children belonged to her, and I belonged to the Church. Ours has been a real partnership.

Living The Gospel

Milk or Coffee

If we take upon us the name of Christ we should be willing to live up to the standards of his Church because the world judges his Church by us.

At an Oakland Stake Conference, we asked an officer of the Waves in uniform to speak. She said she worked in the Government Hospital in San Francisco, and that one day they brought in an L.D.S. officer of the Waves for treatment.

When they were ready to send her tray up, one of the girls asked, "Shall we send milk or coffee?" The girl telling us of this experience said: "Send milk; she will not drink the coffee." "Why won't she?" asked the other girl, and the answer was, "Because she is a Mormon."

"Oh, don't kid yourself," answered the girl, and the tray went up with the coffee on.

The officer telling this experience said: "I almost held my breath until the tray came back, for fear that L.D.S. officer would let me down. However, in a few minutes the tray came back—the coffee had not been touched, and there was a note, 'Please send me a glass of milk.'"

This may seem a small thing to bring up, but it is significant. It wasn't just this girl who was on trial. The Church was on trial. She held its honor in her hands but she did not fail. She showed the doubters that here was another Mormon who lived up to the standards of the Church.

Unless They Repent

As Latter-day Saints we are blessed with the fulness of the gospel, but it is not going to do us a particle of good unless we live it. In answer to the question, "Will everybody be damned, but Mormons?" the Prophet Joseph Smith answered, "Yes, and a great portion of them, unless they repent, and work righteousness." A lot of our members might just as well belong to other churches for all the good the glorious gospel restored in its fulness is doing them. Just to illustrate . . .

Between the Sunday meetings of a conference in West Florida, we were eating out under the trees. I went up to a good brother, put my arm around him and calling him by name said, "How long have you been a member of this church?" His reply was, "Forty years." I said, "Now what has the church done for you in these forty years? Do you hold the Priesthood?" His answer was "No." "Have you quit your tobacco?" His answer was "No." "Are you doing any work in the church?" His answer was "No." Then I said, "What church did you belong to?" He replied, "The Baptist Church." Then I said, "Why don't you go back? You would be a good Baptist and I don't see that Mormonism has done much for you." Then I proceeded to tell him what membership in the church meant.

Well, we had the satisfaction of knowing that we brought him and many inactive members into activity, and prepared that mission for the organization of Stakes of Zion.

Contrast this to the declaration of the Dutch convert in Rotterdam. I was sitting in my office one evening when one of the local brethren rang the bell. He said that he was just passing by on his return from branch teaching and saw my light. He wondered if I would be interested in knowing what he was thinking as he was returning home from doing his teaching. He said, "I was thinking of who I was and what I was when the Mormon Elders first found me, and what I am today. I just can't believe that I am the same person. I do not think the same thoughts! I do not have the same habits or objectives and ideals in life. I have so completely changed in every respect that I can hardly believe that I am the same person."

Isn't this truly a case of being "born again," the old man of sin having been buried with him in baptism?

Genuine Conversion

A new convert in Florida also proved that he knew what the gospel is for. When I was traveling in Florida with Brother Martell, he said, "President Richards, there is a new convert living over here a few miles who would be thrilled if we would call on him," so we did. He was a fruit broker. He would purchase the entire crop of the various citrus groves and sell the same on the New York market. He said he thought he was a pretty shrewd broker, but after joining the Church, he began thinking of the shrewd deals he had made. So he left his home one day with his check book in his pocket, and called on his neighbors with whom he had done business. Upon his return to his home, he had spent $3,000.00. He said he then felt that he could look his neighbors in the face and tell them he was a Latter-day Saint.

Another illustration along the same thought . . .

When I was President of the Hollywood Stake, we used to call on many of our young people in our Stake Conferences. I explained to my counselors that we had been pouring it into them and now it would be wonderful to take a little out, and see just what they have in their hearts when they are called to speak without previous preparation. We called a young boy over in El Segundo. He stood up and said something like this: "I work over yonder in the lumber yard. The other day my boss called me into his office and said, 'My boy, I have been watching you out there. I notice that when the men send out for beer, you don't drink with them, and that you don't smoke with them. I have never heard you swear. What is it that makes you so much different from these other boys?'" His reply was, "Well, I am a Mormon boy." That ought to be a sufficient answer for every Mormon boy.

Each of us can have an inestimable influence for good if we will truly live our religion. We are supposed to be the salt of the earth—to make the rest of the world more pleasant by our beneficient influence. If we truly live close to the Lord, we will have his sweet spirit, and others will feel it.

A Rare Spirit

Upon his return from presiding over the South African Mission, in April 1957, President Duncomb, in his report in the Temple at the meeting of Mission Presidents, stated that after President McKay's trip to South Africa, he was walking down the street one day and stopped in front of a curio shop. The proprietor came out and said, "You are a Mormon, aren't you?" President Duncomb replied that he was. Then the man made this statement: "I have had Royalty of all classes and nations in my store, but never a man with such a personality and influence as your President McKay."

A prominent business man from the East visited Salt Lake City. The Secretary of the Chamber of Commerce arranged an interview for him with President McKay who gave him about an hour of his time. He was so impressed that, while walking down the front steps of the building, he turned to the Secretary and said, "If I were asked to name the one man I have met in my entire life who comes the nearest approximating my appraisal of the Savior of the World, I would name that man."

Church Leaders

During the time that George Albert Smith was President of the Church, one of the greatest economists of the world was visiting in Salt Lake City. One of our banker friends, Orval Adams, gave a banquet for him at the Hotel Utah. There were twenty-five present, and it was my pleasure to be one of them. Following the meal, the Governor said a few words, and while not a member of the Church, he told this man that the leaders of the Mormon Church were the finest men he knew.

Following the Governor, President Smith said a few words, and this man was then invited to say what he felt like saying. He stood up and his jaw began to shake and his lips began to quiver. As soon as he could compose himself, he made a statement like this, "I have never stood in such presence in my life. I have to come out here to these valleys of the mountains to find the kind of Christianity I think can save the world." He then pointed to different ones of us commenting favorably on his impression of our personalities.

Change of Attitude

At the close of a conference session in Columbia, Mississippi, a young man came up to me and asked if he could speak in the afternoon meeting. I said, "Certainly, if you want to." "But," he replied, "I am not a member of your church." I replied, "O, that doesn't matter—you can't say anything to hurt our people." This is about what he said:

"I was raised here in Mississippi to believe that the Mormons were the most undesirable people in all the world. Then I completed my college work and went to Arizona, where my lot was thrown in with the Mormon people. When I returned to Mississippi, I became associated with the Mormon people here and have been attending their Sunday School and services. Now I no longer think of them as the most undesirable people in the world; I am wondering when I will be good enough to be a member of the Mormon Church."

A Better Man

Between the morning and afternoon meeting of the same conference, I noticed a man standing looking out of the window. I walked over to him and said, "I suppose you are a member of our church." "No," he replied, "I am not." I said, "Well, what brought you here to our conference?" He replied, "I live up here about thirty miles. My neighbor is a member of your church. For a long time I have felt that he is a better man than I am. I have wondered if it was his church that made him better, so when he told me that he was going to attend this conference, I asked him if there would be room for me to accompany him. That is why I am here."

I drove up to a gas station in West Florida. To a man sitting by one of the pumps, I said, "Are there any Mormons living around here?" (I knew there were but wanted to hear what he would have to say.) He replied, "There is a whole colony of them living out here a few miles." Then I asked, "What kind of people are they?" His reply was, "My nearest neighbor is a Mormon. He is one of the finest men I have ever met."

Unexpected Praise

While walking with the guide in a marble quarry in North Georgia, I turned to him and said, "I suppose you have no idea who you are walking with." Then I added, "Have you ever met a Mormon Elder?" Without comment, he turned around to the group of tourists, some members of the Church and many who were not, and made a statement like this:

"I lived out in Idaho for several years among the Mormons. They were the finest people I have ever met. I have read their Book of Mormon, and I want to tell you that if the Bible is true, the Mormons have the truth." We didn't expect such a statement, but it is good to know what other people think of us, especially when we live the gospel as we should.

Love At Home

An Evil Habit

I was raised in a good home where my parents did not quarrel. Then I left home as a young man and came to Salt Lake to attend business college. I left a number of boarding houses because the parents would quarrel and nag at each other until I could hardly see how they could live with each other. I got to feeling that an irritable man or woman was about as objectionable a creature as I know anything about. I think a man or a woman who has an irritable disposition ought to get down on their knees and ask the Lord to give them strength to overcome, just the same as they would to overcome the habit of liquor or tobacco or some other evil habit.

I boarded at one home with a widow and her two daughters. The older daughter was a member of the Stake Board of the MIA. One morning as the younger daughter was singing in the kitchen, this older daughter said, "I don't see what in the world is the matter with her; she is always singing." I spoke up and said, "It would certainly sound good to hear you or your mother sing one day before noon, just to prove that you could do it."

Happy Homes

As a short term missionary in the Eastern States and stationed at New Bedford, Massachusetts, I received a letter from Bishop David A. Smith, then a member of the Presiding Bishopric, asking me to visit a Reverend Bennett at Providence, Rhode Island. Reverend Bennett had been in Salt Lake and stayed in Bishop Smith's home and had taken some of our Church books with him. Our saints used to like to go to his Church and hear him preach Mormonism to his congregation. So I wrote to

Reverend Bennett and told him of the request made of me by Bishop Smith. I told him I would be glad to come if he wanted me to, and that he should let me know when it would be convenient. He suggested that I come the next Sunday afternoon. I spent several hours with him. He drove me all around the countryside. During our visit he said, "How do you find business?" (to him his calling was business.) I said, "Reverend Bennett, do you know what has impressed me most while I have been here in this part of the country?" He said, "What?" My reply was, "The lack of happy homes. I believe we have more happy homes on one block in Salt Lake than you have in the whole city of Providence." His reply was, "I wouldn't be surprised."

Children, a Blessing

I met a young mother who had two beautiful little dark-eyed girls. I said to her, "My, they must be a joy and a comfort to you." Her reply was, "They are a terrible burden now; I hope when they grow up they will be different." I saw more women leading dogs around on the streets on leashes than I did leading little children by the hand. Again I felt to thank the Lord for the influence of the gospel, for our happy homes, and for our understanding of what a great blessing children are.

I talked to another woman in New Bedford about the duration of the marriage covenant and the family unit and the beauty of home life. She said, "I have only had one son and he is dead, and I thank God he is dead." I told her that I couldn't understand such language and asked her to explain. "Well," she said, "This is such a wicked world, I think he is better off dead than alive."

A Beautiful Thought

How thankful we should be for the understanding the gospel gives us of the purpose of life and our responsibilities to our children. I contrast the worldly attitude to a beautiful thought one of my daughters expressed to me following a conference. "Father," she said, "I have been thinking that in the spirit world we might have had the right to choose whether we should bear the Priesthood or bear the children." She said, "I believe if I had to choose again, I would still choose to bear the children."

I thought that that was a lovely thought and I said to her, "Well, I think you would make a wise choice because, if you women did not bear the children, we wouldn't have any Priesthood very long."

Missionary Experiences

From an Educational Standpoint

There was a fine man and his wife in Rotterdam who had been visited a number of times by our missionaries, but each time he would send them away with the explanation that he was not interested in their message. Relatives of his wife were members of the church, so from time to time, they would ask the missionaries to visit this family. The man was a close friend of his Minister, and was Treasurer in their Sunday School.

I helped his young nephew, fourteen years old, to emigrate to America. He had walked the streets for weeks looking for work without success. I had saved money for my first mission, so I loaned him money for his transportation. When his Uncle heard of this, he said he would like to meet that man Richards. He was at the boat in Rotterdam when the boy left America, and the boy introduced me to him. He was there with his stovepipe hat, walking cane, and big cigar, as if he really was a man of importance. I visited with him for a few minutes, and then excused myself to make arrangements for his nephew on the boat. When I returned, I addressed him something like this: "Mr. so and so, have you ever attended a Mormon meeting?" His reply was: "No," as if it were preposterous to think that a man such as he would ever want to attend a Mormon meeting. "Well," I said, "The Mormons are accomplishing enough in the world that just from an educational standpoint, it wouldn't hurt for you to know a little more about them. A man of your intelligence would not need to be afraid of being deceived or misled, so you would have nothing to fear." He thought a few minutes, and then replied: "I will come." The next Sunday evening he and his wife were present in our meeting. I met them at the close of the meeting, and asked him how he had enjoyed the meeting. His answer was: "Tamelijk" meaning fairly well. Then I said to him: "I will tell you what I would like to do. I would like to come to your home a night this week. You take your Bible and I will take mine. I will show you things in your Bible you have never read before, I don't care how many times you have read your bible," for the Hollanders have the practice of reading from their bibles following each meal. He turned to his wife and said: "What do you say?" She replied: "Oh, let him come."

The Hirelings

We had a wonderful visit. At the close thereof, I told him that if his minister learned that we had been there, he would tell them how wicked the Mormons are, and do all he could to persuade them not to receive us again. Then I suggested that he put his minister to the test by inviting him to meet us at his home, then he and his wife could decide which of us had the truth. I told him I was sure his minister would refuse to meet us, although I indicated that we would be willing to come at any hour of the day or the night, to meet his convenience. Then I reminded him of the words of the Savior: "The hireling fleeth, because he is a hireling, and careth not for the sheep—the good shepherd giveth his life for the sheep." (John 10:11-13).

Well, the minister did come and when he was invited to meet us, his reply was: "I would not disgrace myself to talk with the Mormon missionaries." He thus proved that he was a hireling.

This man was a foreman in a liquor distillery, so when he went to work the next day he told the men working under him that he had met the Mormon missionaries, and had invited his minister to meet them, but that his minister was unwilling to do so. He said: "If any of you know any ministers who are not afraid of the Mormon Elders I would like to get hold of them. I don't care what church they belong to." So for the next few weeks, we had a new minister each week. Each time as they were about to leave, he would say to the departing minister: "Well, you have made me nearer a Mormon than I was before." We had some most interesting discussions. The following is typical thereof:

Predestination

One of the ministers was from the Presbyterian Church. He believed strongly in the doctrine of Predestination, as taught by Calvin. He was fumbling through his bible looking for something, and my companion said "Probably you are looking for the 9th chapter of Romans." Turning to it, the minister said: "A Bible within a Bible," and then he explained that before we were born, that the Lord had recorded in His book of life just what we would do while upon the earth, and that we could not change our lives from that which the Lord had recorded for us. I said, "If I should break that window, you mean to say that I couldn't help it—that it was so written up in my book of life, and I had to do it?" He affirmed that that was so. Then I used this illustration: "Suppose my brother and I are born, one written up to eternal salvation and the other to eternal damnation, is there nothing either of us can do to change that decree— one to be saved and the other to be damned?" His answer was that that was correct. Then I told him I thanked the Lord that the Lord had given me a free will, and that He had promised to reward me for what I did, whether I did good or evil. He began criticizing me for teaching such a damnable doctrine, to which I replied: "Now wait a minute: you just told me that I couldn't do anything that had not been written up in my book of life for me to do, so if you do not like what I am preaching, don't criticize me. Tell God, for who am I to change the decrees of the Almighty? If I were to believe what you have been telling these people, I would have to believe that God is the author of all the sin and iniquity in the world, for if he decreed what our lives are to be and we have no power to change them, He must love wickedness far more than righteousness, for there is much more wickedness than righteousness in the world."

The Choice

After several weeks of such meetings, this man in whose home we met said, as we visited him one evening: "Brother Richards, I would give all I own if I could prove that you are wrong." I replied: "I know you would—you have never wanted to prove that we are right. But I want to thank you for bearing your testimony that we have the truth, for, with all the help you have had, if you have failed to prove that we are wrong, there is but one other conclusion, you have proved that we are right. Therefore, there is but one decision for you to make: either you are going to get on the Lord's band-wagon, so to speak, and help establish his kingdom in the earth preparatory to his coming, or you are going to 'kick against the pricks,' and I remind you of the words of the Savior to Saul of Tarsus on the way to Damascus: 'It is hard for thee to kick against the pricks.' "

Shortly thereafter he was baptized a member of the Church with his wife. They and their children have been among our very finest Saints. I have often felt that had I only been successful in bringing this one family into the Church, it would fully compensate me for all the missionary work I have done.

Missionary Spirit

My First Mission

When I was a young man, hardly in my teens, I attended a Sacrament Meeting in our ward one night. Two returned missionaries reported their missions. I can remember them distinctly to this day. I don't know whether they said anything unusual or not, but if not, the Lord did something unusual for me, because I was so thrilled with what I heard that I felt that I could have walked to any mission field in the world if I but had a call. So I went home and got down on my knees and asked the Lord to help me to live worthy to go on a mission when I was old enough. When the train finally pulled out of Salt Lake as I left on my first mission, and I bid farewell to my loved ones, the last thing I said to them was, "This is the happiest day of my life." I had looked forward for years to my mission. I am pleased to be able to say that I was not in any way disappointed. It was the outstanding experience of my entire life. The friendships I there formed with missionaries, saints and new converts has greatly enriched my life, and I am sure will continue to do so throughout the eternities. I had such wonderful experiences in my mission that it almost seemed that I walked and talked with the Lord at times. I resolved at that time, because of my love of the Lord and His work, to always put the Church before anything else. In this, my wife has always given me loyal support.

Short-Term Mission

Some years ago President Grant called for one thousand experienced short-term missionaries. In a meeting in the Tabernacle with the Priesthood he stated that Bishops and Stake Presidents were not exempt. At that time I was serving as the Bishop of the Sugarhouse

Ward. My counselor was sitting next to me and when President Grant made that statement, I felt something go all through my body. My counselor turned and said, "I got it; you're going." I said, "Well, we will have to see what the Stake President has to say." So I went to my Stake President. I told him that I was as able to go as any man in the Ward and that he heard what President Grant said about Bishops and Stake Presidents not being exempt. Therefore, I was ready to go if he desired to call me. He said he would take it up with the First Presidency, which he did, and I went on that short-term mission into the Eastern States.

I left my wife and seven children home at that time, and I left my business in the hands of my brother-in-law to manage during my absence.

Spiritually Cold

I found conditions in the Eastern States very cold spiritually compared to what I had been accustomed to in my two missions in Holland. In the city of New Bedford, where I was assigned to labor, there had been two Elders and two lady missionaries laboring practically all of the time. I asked them how long it had been since they had a convert. They indicated that Sister Marchant was the last convert. I looked it up on the branch records and found that it had been five and one half years. So I resolved, that the Lord being my helper, I would try and see if it were not possible to make converts instead of just making friends. I was only there a little less than six months, and the night before leaving we baptized five adults. Two weeks later the Elders who succeeded me baptized five more, and before the end of the year the total reached twenty out of the investigators I left when I left the mission. I had missionaries come home from that mission and call at my office to

thank me for showing them that they could make converts instead of just making friends.

A Joyous Dream

While I was laboring there, we held a conference
at Boston attended by B. H. Roberts, our Mission President, and President Heber J. Grant. Their coming was
announced in the newspaper and yet there were only a
very few non-members who attended our meetings. We
held a Priesthood Meeting of the missionaries and that
night I stayed at a boarding house in Lynn, Massachusetts a short distance from Boston—the city in which our
Richards family first settled when they came to America
shortly after Boston was settled. That night I had a
dream that we were in our missionary meeting and all
unexpectedly the heavens seemed to open and the Savior
appeared in a glorious light. No one introduced Him;
we all started singing, "Hosanna, Hosanna, Hosanna
to the Lamb." I awakened from that dream with the
thought that even though the people were spiritually
cold, the promised coming of our Savior was a reality,
and that we were engaged in the greatest work in the
world to prepare the way for his coming.

Catholic Convert

When I was in Hawaii some years ago, I met a
recent convert to the Church from the Catholic Church.
She was so enthusiastic in her membership that she was
full of the missionary spirit. She did everything she
could to try and acquaint her friends of the Catholic
Church with what she had found. She worked her way
into organizations of the young people and took such
an active part that the priests did all they could to try
to stop her. Even her own family, as she was on the
way home one night stopped her auto, dragged her out
of it and stomped on her so she had to go to the hospital
for treatment.

The Catholic Church sent a Sister in to take charge of the nurses in one of their large hospitals, and she was a cousin to this convert. So her relatives had this Sister call on her to see if she could not induce her to return to the Catholic Church. Undaunted by the persecution she had endured, this convert said to her, "I will listen to you for an hour if you will listen to me for twenty minutes when you are through." The result was that the Catholic Sister left her home with a copy of the Book of Mormon, and the pamphlet "Joseph Smith Tells His Own Story." After three days she returned saying, "I know it is true." So she borrowed some clothes from her cousin, laid off her nuns' robes and went up town to buy some ordinary clothing.

She too was filled with the missionary spirit. She wrote to the Cardinal who sent her there and thanked him for sending her where she could learn the truth. She had served as a private nurse to the Pope during his illness, so she wrote to him and told him what she had found, and sent him a copy of the Book of Mormon.

At that time in her immediate family there were six priests, six nuns, eighteen brothers, one bishop, four cardinals and one soon to become a cardinal, and officers in every organization of the Catholic Church. In time I am sure she will influence the honest in heart among them to join the Church.

A Humble Missionary

I suppose we have the missionary spirit in proportion to our testimony and our gratitude to the Lord.

After the death of her husband, one of our good sisters filled a full-time mission in the United States, and then filled a full-time mission in Germany, her native land. I copied the following from a letter she wrote me from Germany under date of June 28, 1952:

"The Lord has accepted my humble effort to serve him—and guided us to the honest in heart. If it is his will, we will be blessed to bring five souls to him within a month or so.

"The very thought of it fills my heart with great joy, until I feel that it will burst. Such happiness I have never known before in my life. How wonderful are the ways of the Lord!"

A Dedicated Couple

I had a couple, converts from Holland, call at my office to discuss the advisability of their going on another mission. They had already filled one mission together. This brother said, "If we sell our home and our auto, we can finance ourselves on another mission." They were willing to give all their savings to fill another mission, and upon their return, they would have to start all over again.

I always say, "As long as the Lord keeps putting such faith in the hearts of his children, you can't stop the Kingdom from growing."

A widow brought in her son to be interviewed for a mission. I learned that she already had a daughter in the Great Lakes Mission and a son in the Swiss-Austrian Mission. She didn't look too well clad, so I asked her why she didn't wait to send this son until her other son returned from his mission. Her reply was, "If you will see that he goes on his mission now, I will see that he gets the money for his keep." Such wonderful faith and love for the truth!

The Test

While I was attending a conference in Oregon, a young returned missionary reporting his mission, came down with his fist upon the pulpit and said, "I wouldn't take a check for a million dollars for the experience of my mission."

He was a twin, and while he was in the mission field, his twin brother was in the armed forces. He had just been discharged, so I interviewed him for his mission, and his brother, the returned missionary, took his place in the armed forces. Our young people are wonderful.

At a conference in Idaho, we sustained a former Bishop as a member of the Stake High Council, and called him to speak. He related this experience. He said that when he was a young man he was athletically inclined. Some agents came out from the East and offered him a contract that would pay him an enormous amount each year if he would go East. He said he would want to talk the matter over with his parents, and asked if he might take the contract with him.

When he told his parents of the offer he had received, his father said, "Wait a minute, my son." After going into the other room he brought him a letter that had come that day, calling him on a mission. So with a contract in one hand that would pay him an enormous yearly salary and a call from the Lord through His Prophet in the other hand, he accepted the call to the mission. He said he had never related that experience in public before.

This is the kind of faith that is building the kingdom.

Enthusiastic Missionaries

While I was touring the Northwestern States Mission, I heard a young missionary bear his testimony. He had just returned from serving several years in the armed forces, and he said, "There isn't a company or institution in the world that could pay me enough money to get me to leave my mission." And I am sure that almost one hundred percent of the missionaries feel the same way about their mission when they have the spirit of their work. They hardly want to be released.

While touring the Danish Mission in the summer of 1959, I interviewed the Missionary Counselor to the

Mission President. He said, "Elder Richards, I almost worship my Mission President, for it was he who brought the gospel to my father. There are now fifty-seven of us in the Church as the result of that one conversion." He then asked the privilege of remaining an additional six months in the mission field. I understood that he was the seventh son in the family all of whom had filled missions, so I told him he had better go home and get his schooling and military training back of him so he could get married and raise some sons and send them on missions as his father had done. He was a wonderful young man.

To Teach the World

In a city near Atlanta, Georgia, where there was much bitterness against the Mormons, the mayor restricted our Elders from tracting. The Elders were boarding at the home of a lovely woman of good standing in the community. She took the two Elders with her to her Sunday School class, introduced them to the members and said, "Which one of you would be willing to do for your Church what these young men are doing for their Church—spend two years of your life at your own expense to teach the world the principles that you believe in?" Not one of the class answered favorably. The fact that our missionaries are not paid, but pay their own expenses, is proof of the wonderful missionary spirit motivating them to share the restored gospel with the world.

One young missionary who labored with us in the Southern States, said that his mother died when he was a very small boy. Before she passed away she called him to her bedside. She said, "My boy, I will never leave you." He bore witness that he was convinced that his mother had been with him during all his missionary labors. He said, "The greatest hope I have in my life," and tears flowed freely from his eyes as he said it, "is that I might return home and have my father put his arms around me and say, 'Well done.'"

Another missionary said that all his life he had wanted to go on a mission. His father also had wanted him to go, but had recently died. He said when he received his call, he had a dream in which he saw his father who said, "My son, I will share this mission with you."

Treasures in Heaven

The testimonies of the missionaries in the mission field are a great inspiration. Following one testimony report meeting, a missionary drew from his pocket a picture of a man sitting in a wheel chair, a cripple. Then he told this story. Being from a large family he could see no opportunity of going into the mission field as he desired. One day this brother, whose picture he held, approached him and asked him if he would be willing to go on a mission if the Bishopric called him, if he would pay the expenses. This man was earning his living as a tailor and chose this course of laying up treasures in heaven where neither moth nor rust doth corrupt nor thieves break through and steal. The missionary said, "This man will never know the feeling of gratitude I have in my heart toward him for making it possible for me to have this wonderful experience."

Another missionary related this experience. A good Scandinavian sister in his home town wanted to send a missionary into the mission field. She came to him and asked him if he would be willing to go and represent her. After he arrived in the mission field this good sister passed away, but before doing so, she left enough money in the bank for him to complete his mission. He filled a wonderful mission. When I heard him bear witness to the saints that his missionary work had been the very happiest time of all his life, I could not help but wonder if this good sister might not be aware of the wonderful contribution she had made in making this great experience possible for him.

One of our lady missionaries bore testimony that when she was called to go into the mission field, she was in the beauty parlor business with her sister. They owed two thousand dollars. The sister, filled with the missionary spirit said, "You go." She said that her sister had not only been able to keep her, but had also been blessed to pay off the two thousand dollar debt while she had been in the mission field.

Moral Cleanliness

A Challenge

There is a law of cause and effect in operation in all things. If we live clean we will be clean.

While returning from Conference at LaGrande, Oregon, during the hardest fighting in the Pacific, I overheard a doctor in officer's uniform on leave from the Islands, launch out on a tirade against Salt Lake City and the Mormons, which was about the most vulgar thing I have ever heard. I waited until he was through, and then I said:

"Doctor, you may be interested to know that my home is in Salt Lake City, and that I am a member of the Mormon Church, and that I know that you do not know what you are talking about."

Then I told him that I had a report in my briefcase from the superintendent of a hospital in Salt Lake City indicating that they had given the Wasserman test to over 7,000 Mormon boys, and that in only three cases had they found any trace of impure blood. Then I added, "Now, Doctor, I challenge you to duplicate that record anywhere in the world outside of a Mormon community —you can't do it, and you know you can't."

He then replied in these words: "Well, I must say that over in the Pacific everybody let their hair down." That was his way of saying what Jesus said they would say: "Come, let us eat, drink and make merry, for tomorrow we die."

Then the doctor added: "But I will have to admit that there was one girl there from Salt Lake City that no man could touch. She said, 'I left my home clean and I am going to return the way I left.' "

When the doctor told me this I thought of Joseph who was sold into Egypt. Potiphar's wife tried to seduce him repeatedly and he withstood her, saying, "How can I do this great wickedness, and sin against God?"

Joseph's integrity cost him his position as head of Potiphar's household, for Potiphar's wicked wife bore false witness against him and he was cast into prison. The integrity of the girl in the Pacific may have cost her a promotion. But both she and our ancient ancestor Joseph retained something of far greater value than life itself— their virtue. Well may their posterity honor them!

My Grandfather

An Early Convert

My grandfather, Franklin Dewey Richards, was born in Richmond, Massachusetts April 22, 1821, the son of Phineas Richards and Wealthy Dewey, and a grandson of Joseph Richards, a cousin to Brigham Young. His earliest American ancestor, Richard Richards settled in Lynn, Massachusetts in 1633 only 13 years after the landing of the Pilgrims who came over on the Mayflower.

He was baptized a member of the Church June 3, 1838, the gospel having been brought to the Richards family by their kin, Brigham Young and his brother, Joseph Young. A few months after his baptism at the age of seventeen, he left for Far West, Missouri, a distance of thirteen hundred miles to join the saints. Upon his arrival at Far West he learned that his brother George, then only fifteen years of age, had been massacred at Haun's Mill near Far West with others of the saints.

In April of 1840 he received his first call to fill a mission at the age of nineteen. Of the first fourteen years of his married life, he spent ten years in the mission field.

A Tragic Year

While laboring as a missionary in Great Britain, he received the news of the death of his wife, Elizabeth, at Winter Quarters, March 29, 1847; of his brother Joseph's death with the Mormon Battalion at Pueblo; and of the death of his daughter, Wealthy. His faith and trust in the Lord remained unshaken as he recorded in his diary: "I hope to overcome every obstacle and be not a whit behind the chiefest of my brethren in the

Celestial Kingdom of God, having kept my covenants and being sanctified thereby; and not myself only, but all those who belong to me."

Under date of June 3, 1847, he notes that it was then nine years since his baptism into the Church. Meantime, he had filled five missions in the United States, had come up through the grades of the Priesthood to that of High Priest, had received his endowments in the Nauvoo Temple, and had been made counselor in the Presidency of the British Mission then embracing sixteen thousand saints. "Most of all things this day," he wrote, "I desire the Holy Spirit which giveth life—eternal life, yea, life more abundantly to both body and spirit."

Prophetic Dream

On the thirteenth of August, 1847, he wrote in his diary: "This morning I awoke from a dream in which I seemed to have been with President Brigham Young in the Temple at Nauvoo. We sat opposite each other, with our feet in a clear lively pool of water, as we conversed together. He asked, 'Brother Franklin, would you accept it if I should appoint you one of the Quorum?' I replied, 'Brother Brigham, I have always accepted as far as I could, have obeyed every appointment that has been given me, and I always intend to.' " This dream had its fulfillment two years later when he was ordained an Apostle and called into the Quorum of the Twelve.

The Elements Rebuked

While on one of his trips across the Atlantic, returning from the British Mission in charge of a company of saints and Elders, the weather was very stormy. The waves were rolling so high that the officers of the vessel were fearful of its being dashed to pieces. When the hearts of strong men were failing them, he remembered that he held the Holy Priesthood which authorized him to rebuke the angry elements and command them to be still, as was done by the Savior and his apostles in their day. Withdrawing to a part of the ship where he would not be conspicuous and raising his hands to high heaven, he rebuked the storm and furious winds and waves in the name of the Lord Jesus Christ, commanding them to cease their violence and be calm. The tempest immediately subsided and none of the passengers were lost and no damage to the vessel.

This made a very favorable impression on the captain and the passengers on board. The captain gave him the use of his own quarters, and treated him with great kindness. He states, "When I was ready to pay for these distinguished favors, his charge was an interest in my prayers and that he and his might be gathered with us into the Kingdom of God. He gave us a parting kiss with tears and the crew bestowed three cheers. Let the prayers and blessings of the faithful be for him and his for ye have not only called us brethren, but treated us as such."

Interpretation of Tongues

While grandfather presided over the British Mission from 1850 to 1852 the mission had sixteen thousand convert baptisms.

He attended the baptism of Professor Karl G. Maeser of Dresden, Germany with other Elders. As he conversed with Brother Karl G. Maeser following Dr. Maeser's baptism, Elder William Budge interpreted. After a while he told Elder Budge that it was not necessary for him to interpret anymore as he and Brother Maeser could understand each other perfectly.

In later years Dr. Maeser testified that when he emerged from the water, he prayed that his faith might be confirmed by some manifestation from heaven. He felt confident that his prayer would be answered and it was.

At the time of his death President Franklin D. Richards was President of the Quorum of Twelve Apostles.

My Great Grandfather

A Powerful Testimony

Joseph Lee Robinson is my great grandfather on my mother's side. He knew the Prophet Joseph Smith well, and was intimately acquainted with President Brigham Young. He helped select the site on which the first state capitol was built in Utah at Fillmore. He built the first house south of Payson. He was the first bishop of Farmington and was a Patriarch at the time of his death. He gathered with the saints in Nauvoo in 1841. His brother, Ebenezer, was then editing the church paper, "Times and Seasons," in Nauvoo. He was greatly impressed with the Prophet Joseph Smith and made this statement. "We greatly appreciate the blessings and privilege of being gathered with the saints, of assisting in building the Holy Temple, of being taught in the ways of the Lord, of enjoying the blessings of the gospel, and of hearing the prophet's voice. We have long since believed and known that Joseph Smith was a true and humble prophet of God who had seen the Father, but now our eyes do see him and our ears hear his voice. There is a power and majesty that attends his words that we never beheld in any man before, for he is a mighty prophet, a Holy man of God who has seen the Father and the Son and heard their voices; has seen many holy prophets and apostles and has been ordained under their hands; has, by the gift and power of God, translated the Book of Mormon . . . has received many revelations from Almighty God, and has organized the Church of Jesus Christ of Latter-day Saints according to the apostolic order with prophets, apostles, patriarchs, high priests, seventies, elders, bishops, priests, teachers and deacons with all the gifts and graces that adorned the ancient Church of Christ. To all this we bear our solemn testimony in the fear of God and in name of the Lord Jesus Christ. I, Joseph Lee Robinson, do verily know it is true, so help me God. My love for the prophet was truly stronger than death, greater than for any man that ever lived except Jesus Christ, the first begotten of the Father."

A Kind Heart

The ancient prophet said, "Cast your bread upon the water and after many days it shall return."

Grandfather Robinson's diary tells a little story of his own experience that indicates how this promise was fulfilled in his behalf.

He heard that Jedediah M. Grant, the father of President Heber J. Grant, would like to purchase his horse to go east to fulfill a mission to which he had been called but did not feel he could afford to pay the price it was worth. So grandfather went to him and said, "Jedy, I want to sell you my horse." "What do you want for him?" "One hundred dollars." "God bless you, Brother Robinson!" Jedy said, "I will purchase him. I will pay you seventy-five dollars today, and my brother will give you twenty-five dollars next week."

He met President Brigham Young on the street and told him that he had sold his horse to Jedediah. President Young said, "What did you ask him for it?" He said, "One hundred dollars." President Young replied, "God bless you, Brother Robinson."

There was another brother in the ward who wanted to sell his horse to go on a mission and the horse was only worth seventy-five dollars. So my grandfather went to him and said, "Brother so and so, I want to purchase your horse." "What will you give me for him, Brother Robinson?" "One hundred dollars." "God bless you, Brother Robinson. You may have him." He got a seventy-five dollar horse in place of a two-hundred dollar horse, but he said, "I got three God Bless You's, and God did bless me. In a few weeks the brethren returned from the gold fields of California and brought with them their horses. I purchased two at their price. In a few weeks I could have sold them and made a thousand dollars." 'Cast your bread upon the water and after many days it shall return' when you are doing good. This my grandfather proved to his satisfaction.

Out Of Obscurity

Progress of the Church

In a revelation to the Prophet Joseph Smith in 1831, the Lord promised him that he "Might have power to lay the foundation of this church and to bring it forth out of obscurity and out of darkness." (D. & C. 1:30).

It takes truth a long time to travel, but it will succeed in the end. The Church has suffered persecutions, but thinking men today are beginning to recognize the power in the Church.

In March of 1960 a Youth Conference, called by the President of the United States, was held at the White House in Washington. President Marion D. Hanks of the First Council of Seventies was asked to give the key-note address. There were some seven thousand delegates at this convention. As President Hanks closed his remarks, the man conducting the service made this statement, "As I sat here I reflected that Mr. Hanks comes from people that were driven from our region of the country because of the things they believed, and suffered bitter persecution for their ideals, who went finally to the far reaches of this country where they thought themselves away from all this. Now we have invited a leader of that people to come here to talk to us of the same ideals and principles for which we drove them away."

It is wonderful to have a representative of the Church invited by the President of the United States to the national capitol to teach leaders of youth the ideals and principles for which they drove us beyond the boundaries of the United States.

A Tribute

In 1957, Elder Mark E. Petersen and I organized

a stake of Zion at Atlanta, Georgia, where in past years the saints had suffered bitter persecution from individuals and mobs. But progress is being made.

I quote from the *Atlanta Constitution* of May 7, 1957 following our organization of the stake. "The Church of Jesus Christ of Latter-day Saints has organized its first stake in Georgia. We join in hearty welcome and in congratulations to the new church, its officers and members.

"The Latter-day Saints, commonly known as Mormons, have had a mission in Georgia for some time. Organization of the stake testifies to the growth of the mission and its success. Members of the Latter-day Saints are a dedicated people, seriously devoted to their church and to citizenship. The new stake is a splendid addition to the Christian life of the state."

Truly the Lord is bringing His work forth out of obscurity.

Friendly Predictions

During the summer of 1959 Dr. William E. Fort, Jr., President of the Deep Springs College near Bishop, California, and a member of the Episcopal Church taught at the Brigham Young University summer school.

In an interview with a reporter of the *Deseret News* at the close of the summer school, Dr. Fort made this statement. "It may well be that the Mormon people have the key that will eventually save this country. I am impressed with the extremely high level of intellect I encounter in the students here . . . and even more important, the character of the students."

It is pleasing to see how thinking people are beginning to recognize the power there is in the church. Truly the Lord is bringing his work forth out of obscurity and out of darkness.

In Los Angeles over television KCOP on August 27, 1955 Mr. Criswell made the following statement. "The fastest growing church per capita will be the Mormon Church, the Church of the Latter-day Saints. They will carry their vital message to the world and literally fulfill the prophecy of their leader that Salt Lake City will become the cultural center of the world." We know this, but it is encouraging to have other people so express themselves and indicate the fulfillment of the promise made to the Prophet Joseph back in 1831 when he promised to bring his work forth out of obscurity and out of darkness.

Partnership

Father-Son Team

An appeal to young people's sense of loyalty and fairness often accomplishes more than laying down the law concerning their behavior. Just to illustrate . . .

When my son, Alden, was too young to get a driver's license, and yet had commenced going out with the girls occasionally I said to him, "My son, do you know what I have been thinking? I have been thinking that I need a partner in my business. The more I think of it, the more I think you should be my partner, for I am going all around the Church telling brethren how to raise their sons, and my words would fly right back in my face if, when I am out at conferences, you failed to attend your Priesthood and Sacrament Meetings."

Then I added, "And the more I think of it, the more I think you need a partner in your business, for you like to go out occasionally with your boy friends and the girls, and you do not have an auto nor a driver's license. I think I should be your partner for I have an auto and I have a driver's license, so I can be your chauffeur." Well, we agreed on this partnership. My desk calendar would show the appointments I made with him to take him and pick up his boy friend and then the girls. I would leave them at a show and inquire, "Shall I wait for you?" His reply, "No, Dad, I will call you when we are ready to come home," so I would keep close to the phone awaiting his call. When he called it would usually be that they were at the confectionery store.

Trustworthy Son

One Sunday, Mother and I were out of town attending a Stake Conference. As we neared home, I said to her, "I would give a dollar to know whether our son got up and got to his Priesthood Meeting, but I wouldn't ask him for anything. I wouldn't want him to think for one minute that I did not trust him to keep his agreement."

When we arrived home, he explained that although he had been out playing in his orchestra until midnight the night before, he had set the alarm clock and got up early and attended his Priesthood meeting. This pleased me very much. It is wonderful to have children who are trustworthy.

Point of View

In one of our general conferences in the Tabernacle, President Oscar Kirkham related this experience. He had been visiting a stake of Zion and the Stake President said to him, "President Kirkham, I wish you would talk to my son. He and I don't seem as close to each other as we used to be. I am concerned. Will you try to talk to him?" At the close of the morning session, President Kirkham saw the boy, walked up to him, took him by the arm and said, "My boy, you have a wonderful father, haven't you?" To which the boy replied, "Yes, President Kirkham, but I wish you would talk to father. He and I don't seem as close to each other as we used to. He spends all of his time with his business and his church work. He never has time to take me to a ball game or fishing or hunting, or to do any of the things we used to do together." You see, it makes a difference who it is that needs talking to.

While it is true that business and church work are very demanding on the time of the fathers of the Church, still, where there is a will there is a way, and there is no excuse for fathers to fail their sons in the years when they need them most.

Patriarchal Blessings

A Personal Guide

I wish I could urge every boy and girl and man and woman in the Church to obtain his Patriarchal Blessing. Such blessings are from the Lord and are meant to be a guide and inspiration to us. A patriarch living close to the Lord receives direct inspiration from the Lord to give each person his individual blessing.

The first Patriarch I ordained after my calling to the Council of the Twelve was in California. He said, "I don't believe I can do it." To which I replied, "I know you can't, but you and the Lord can." After he had served for a few months, he wrote me and said he had just been rereading the blessings he had given. Then he added, "Now I know I didn't give them."

Source of Blessings

While I was staying at the home of a Stake President in Canada, the President's wife told me of an experience related to her son by the Stake Patriarch, when the two went ward teaching together.

The Patriarch said two boys came to his home for blessings, and he spoke to one of the boys and told him that he had a wonderful blessing for him, and then he gave the other boy his blessing first. When he attempted to give a blessing to the boy for whom he had said that he had a wonderful blessing, he just could not give him a blessing, so he had to ask him to come another time. He explained to his Ward Teaching companion that the Lord had to let him know that *he* did not have a blessing for anyone—that it was *the Lord* who had the blessing to give *through him.*

Unexpected Sorrow

It is amazing with what degree of accuracy Patriarchal Blessings are fulfilled depending on the faithfulness of the recipients. Sometimes we do not understand them clearly until after events have taken place. Just to illustrate . . .

One of the greatest sorrows we have experienced in our married lives was the death of our oldest son, LeGrand. We had four daughters before he was born. Two months before he turned sixteen, we lost him through an accident at the Santa Monica Beach, in California.

At the time, I was serving as President of the Hollywood Stake, and I told my Counselors that I was sure we could adjust our thinking and find comfort if we only knew that the Lord wanted him and that his mission here upon the earth had not been cut short because of our having let him go to the beach that day with his friends. We had read his Patriarchal Blessing, and we could not feel that it was time for him to go.

Comforting Explanations

One Saturday evening, shortly after his death, I invited my wife to take an auto ride and we invited LeGrand's younger brother, LaMont, to accompany us, but he said he would rather remain home. While at home he got out LeGrand's and his blessings and read them. I am sure the Lord gave him the interpretation of the blessings for our comfort, for that next morning being Sunday, we did not arise as early as usual, and LaMont came into our bedroom holding these two blessings in his hands and said, "You have not understood these blessings." Then he proceeded to explain them as he had received the understanding. He read from LeGrand's blessing as follows:

"You shall be privileged to preach the gospel in strange lands and unto strange people." Then he commented that there are no strange lands or people here upon this earth. Then he read from his own blessing as follows:

"You shall be called to preach the gospel at home and abroad." Then he explained that this refers to this world, and he has since preached the gospel in Great Britain and in America.

Then he read from LeGrand's blessing: "In the own due time of the Lord your home will be the fit abode for the spirits of your loved ones." Then he explained that that meant in the next life when he would have spirit children. Then he read from his own blessing as follows: "You shall be privileged to see your children grow up around you and honor you in the same manner that you have honored your parents." This, he explained had reference to his family here upon this earth.

This explanation brought us great comfort for we felt with this explanation we could hardly reach any other conclusion than that the Lord had not intended to leave him with us for long here upon this earth. Yet, when he and his brother obtained their blessings the same day from the same Patriarch, the Lord had to give both of the boys promises, even though in words they could not fully understand at that time, or else the older son would have gone away terribly disappointed had he felt that his younger brother had received all the blessings.

Persistence

Request for Release

It is not always easy for missionaries to adapt themselves to missionary work. Some do it readily and with joy in their hearts. Others struggle to be able to do the work and to get joy and satisfaction out of it. When I was president of the Southern States Mission, I received a letter from a missionary in South Carolina, telling me that he just couldn't take it. That he wasn't cut out to be a missionary. That he would be willing to furnish the money to keep a missionary in the field for two years, if I would just release him and let him go home. I didn't write him; I got on the train and spent a few days with him. I told him that I thought the Lord was pleased with his expressed willingness to furnish the money to keep a missionary in the field for two years, but I said, "If I were to release you and let you go home, you would never forgive me. In the future when your own sons were old enough for their missions, what would you say to them?" I said, "I will help you every way that I can, but you make a success of your mission. It will get easier day by day." To make this story short, he did his best and then some and became the district president, one of our finest missionaries.

Wife Spurs Efforts

We had a young married man laboring in our mission. He left his wife and two or three children at home. After he had been there a short time, he wrote his wife and told her that he was coming home, that he just couldn't take it any longer. That good woman, true to her faith and testimony, wrote back to her husband, saying, "If you come back before your mission is finished honorably, you will have no home to come to. If we see you coming up the walk, we will lock the door and not let you in." He pitched in, did a good job and then some, and became a fine missionary, one of our district presidents.

I can relate other similar instances, but I do this only to show that it takes time and persistence for some of our young men to adapt themselves to missionary work and make a success of their missions.

Picture Puzzle Analogy

You Be the Judge

While I was attending a conference in Idaho some years ago, I had a heart attack and had to remain in the Stake President's home over four Sundays. I learned that his wife had a sister living near me in Salt Lake whose husband was not a member of the Church. They were very anxious that he should join the Church. So when I was well enough, I called on this family and expressed my gratitude to them for the kindness of their loved ones to me in Idaho. Then I said to this man (I always like to challenge a person because then it gives him something to look for), "Would you be willing to let me come into your home and tell you the story of Mormonism? You just be the judge and the jury, but wait until I get through and then tell me where it came· from." The man agreed that he would. After I had spent about five or six evenings with him, as I went to leave I said, "You would almost think the Mormons wrote the Bible, wouldn't you?" To which he replied, "It is beginning to look like it." The next night when I left, he turned to his wife and said, "You know I believe the Bishop has got something." The point I want to make is that he is now a fine Elder in the Church. I have had the privilege of uniting the family in the Temple. Their oldest son has filled a mission and was one of the traveling Elders.

The Complete Picture

This has always been my thinking. He had a brother-in-law who was a stake president. He had another brother-in-law who was a counselor in the stake presidency. He had a mother-in-law who worked in the Temple at the time. His wife was a member, but apparently did not have the ability to explain the gospel in such a manner that her husband felt like he should join the church. About all they would do was say, "Frank, why don't you join the church? What are you waiting for?" Frank knew that the Mormons were good people, but his people were good people and he did not know why he should join the church.

I always like to liken the church to these picture puzzles. You dump all of the pieces out on the table and pick them up one at a time and after you have looked at each one, you don't know what it is all about; but when the pieces are fit together, no one need tell you what it is because you have a beautiful picture. So it is with the gospel, the pieces all have to be fit together so that one can see and understand just what the church is. Then if they truly love the Lord, they cannot help but accept the gospel.

Does He Read?

I have another little illustration along that line. I attended a conference in one of our stakes about one hundred and twenty-five miles from Salt Lake. The next day one of the good sisters of the ward came into my office. She had come all that way to talk to me. She was quite broken-hearted. The Bishop had just released her from being President of the Primary and had asked her to serve in the Relief Society. She didn't know much about the Relief Society. So she couldn't love it. Then wiping the tears out of her eyes, she said, "It wouldn't be so bad but my husband is not a member of the church and I have to raise the children all alone." I said, "Why don't you convert him?" She said, "I have tried." I said, "Why don't you get the stake missionaries to help you?" She said, "I have tried that." I said, "Does he read?" She said, "Quite a little." I said, "I would like to autograph one of these missionary books that I have written. You get him to read it as a compliment to me. Then write me and tell me what he has to say about it." In a few weeks I received a letter from her that read like this: "He read your book. He didn't say much. Then he read the Book of Mormon. Then he read your book again. Then he said, 'Now I am ready to join the church.'" After he had been a member a year, she wrote me that they were going to the Temple together. Sometime later, the stake president wrote in to the First Presidency recommending this man as the stake mission president. I told President McKay that I could surely tell him a story about that man. He said, "Is it a good one, Bishop?" I said, "It certainly is," but there wasn't time for me to tell him the story.

The point is that this good sister had lived with that man possibly fifteen to twenty years and he was a good enough man all the time to be a member of the church. But no one stopped long enough to fit the pieces together so he could see what it really was. With our loved ones and friends who are not members of the Church, I think that is our responsibility to fit the pieces of Mormonism together so that they will know that it could not have come from man, that it must be from God.

Prayer

Protection from Sin

As we stood up from family prayers one night in my home after our boy of the Aaronic Priesthood had offered the prayer, calling him by name, I said, "As long as you can pray like that, I'll trust you anywhere you want to go." But what if he couldn't pray like that? It would be a warning to me that I needed to get closer to him. Isn't prayer an opportunity to feel the spirit of our children and to know whether or not it is sound?

When the Savior appeared to the Nephites, he taught them to pray—to pray with their families that their wives and their children might be blessed. We would all be blessed by following his counsel. Constant prayer is our protection from sin.

When I was President of the Netherlands Mission, one of the missionaries I had just released said to me, "I am afraid to go home." I said, "Why?" He said, "Because I had some companions at home that weren't what they ought to be. I am afraid I might not be strong enough to resist their invitations to join them." I said this to him: "If you will make me a promise that when you go home you will never be so anxious to go to work or to leave your room in the morning that you will not first get down on your knees and pray like you have prayed here in the mission field for the Lord to protect you during the day and to keep you sweet and clean. If you will promise me never to let a day end without getting down on your knees and thanking the Lord for having kept you through the day, I promise you that you will be able to keep yourself sweet and clean as you have done here in the mission field."

I did not see him for a few years. I had returned from my mission and was engaged in business. One day the front door of my office opened and I saw a young man in uniform coming in. I got up from my desk and walked over to him. It was this missionary. As he put out his hand to shake hands with me, he didn't say, "How are you." He said, "Do you remember what you made me promise you before I left the mission field?" I said, "I certainly do, and you have kept your promise; I can see it in your very countenance." He said, "I surely have; I have been in the service now for some time but I have never let a day begin or close without my prayers and I am just as clean as when I left you." Today he is a very active, faithful member of the church.

Teach Children to Pray

Of course, the time to train our children to pray is when they are very young.

Some years ago while attending a stake conference, I stayed at the home of a member of the stake presidency. His six-year-old son, when called upon to pray, offered a beautiful prayer. A short time ago the father called me by phone to ask a question. At the close of the conversation I said, "Where is that six-year-old son of yours that offered such a beautiful prayer when I stayed in your home?" "Oh," he said, "he is now a man and has been on his mission and is married and has a number of children, but he is still faithful in the church." You see, it had been many years since I heard that six-year-old boy pray, but I had not forgotten him. Children, if taught to pray from the heart, are capable of intelligent, meaningful prayers.

At the close of the dedicatory exercises for a ward chapel in Idaho, Sister Richards and I were invited to the Bishop's home. He had some of the neighbors come in and we sat up until the wee hours of the morning visiting. When I retired, I said to this good Bishop, "If you don't mind, I would like to sleep in a little in the

morning. I have been up so many nights late, I am getting exhausted." He agreed that would be all right. I got
up in the morning and walked into the back hall just in
time to hear them as they knelt in family prayer. A
young boy about eight or nine was doing the praying.
Among other things, he said, "And Heavenly Father,
bless Daddy that he might get the money to pay his
taxes." I couldn't help but be profoundly impressed to
think that that little boy shared the responsibilities of
that home to the extent that he prayed for his father to
get the money for his taxes. I went in and took the boy
in my arms and hugged him and kissed him. Now I
know that boys don't like that. You have heard the story
about the mother who was always calling her son,
Lamby; Lamby this and Lamby that. He said, "Mother,
don't call me Lamby, call me Tiger." Well, whether it
was Lamby or Tiger or what it was, I couldn't refrain
from hugging that boy.

I love to hear children and young people pray. I
know there is nothing that will bring them closer to our
Heavenly Father. There is nothing that will bring them
greater peace and happiness over the years.

Without prayer we cannot enjoy a close association
with our Heavenly Father, nor feel the joy of true worship. Prayer is essential to our spiritual well-being.
Without it we are spiritually dead. I can think of no
investment of a parent's time that will pay as rich dividends as the time he spends teaching his children to pray.

Prejudice

The Hanging Party

Much of the prejudice against the Church is because of ignorance. Just to illustrate . . .

President Taylor Nelson of the Oneida Stake returned to the Southern States on his second mission. He was a real character. The people loved him and he loved them. That was why he was back again—to labor among his friends in the South. He told us this story. He said that on his first mission they had held a meeting in South Georgia. Then they went home to have dinner with a family of saints. While they were eating, two men rode up on horseback and inquired if they were not going to hold an afternoon meeting. The missionaries said they hadn't planned on it. The men said, "Well, the people of the community thought you were going to hold an afternoon meeting. The chapel is full and they are waiting for you." So Brother Nelson told them that they would come over as soon as they were through eating. When they arrived at the chapel, they found a posse of men on horseback with their lasso ropes. They said, "We have had enough of you Mormons. We are going to string you up this tree." Brother Nelson replied, "Well, that's all right; we have to die sometime. I guess we had just as well die now as any time, but there is no hurry about it, is there? Why don't you come inside and let's talk things over first." He got the posse inside the Church. The result was that when he had explained to them what their mission was and what they were doing, the head of the posse invited them to his home to spend the night and have supper with them.

From being ready to lynch in their ignorance, they turned to friendliness when they had listened long enough to learn something, and the thing that made them willing to listen was the courage of the elders in the face of possible death.

Rampant Ignorance

While I was tracting one day in Amsterdam, a man came running for some distance, holding in his hand the tract I had left at his home as if he was afraid it would burn his fingers. As he neared me he said, "Take it! Take it! This is from Joseph Smith and Brigham Young, and they are both in hell." "Well," I replied, "I will tell you something you do not know. If Joseph Smith and Brigham Young are in hell, they will soon make a heaven out of it."

Such ignorance is rampant. Falsehoods have been spread all abroad to prejudice people against even listening to the wonderful message we bear. It is up to us to break down that prejudice, and the missionaries and the individual members of the Church are doing a wonderful job. Sometimes, as in the case of a very zealous opponent like Paul of Tarsus, the Lord himself helps to break down the wall of unfounded prejudice.

Night of Torment

In Rotterdam there was a minister — a lovely character who preached more for the love of the work than for the money. Quite a number of the members of his congregation had joined our Church. They loved him so dearly that they pled with him to attend one of our meetings. Finally he did so. At the close of the meeting he was met at the door by the missionaries. They inquired how he liked the meeting. He stood and denounced Joseph Smith as a false Prophet, a deceiver and everything vile he could think of.

He told me this story himself. He said, "I didn't know what I had done, but I knew that I had grieved God, for when I went to bed I could not sleep — peace had gone out of my soul. I laid and tossed until the wee hours of the morning. Then I got up and walked the streets until I thought the Mormon Elders would be up. Then I knocked at their door and asked them to lend me a copy of the Book of Mormon."

His honest heart could not resist the truth it held. The result was that he joined the Church.

I have had many wonderful companions in my work in the Church, but never one who thrilled me more than this grand old gentleman, standing erect, with his white beard, bearing his testimony that he knew that Joseph Smith was a Prophet of God and that the Book of Mormon was the Word of God.

Quotations

"If your self-starter works, your supervising Elder won't have to be such a crank."

"What shall we do with faith? Exercise it."

"Everything I am today is God's gift to me. What I will be tomorrow is my gift to God."

"There never has been a man upon this earth who could break a commandment of God and come out ahead."

"If you are going to leave footprints in the sands of time, you must wear work shoes."

"The largest room in the world is the room for improvement."

"The mind is like the stomach; it isn't the amount that goes in that counts, but the amount you digest."

"No matter how tall our fathers or grandfathers are, we have to do our own growing."

"Nothing has the memory of a little notebook."

"The flowers and trees look to the sun, but men look to God."

"There is no average boy; if so, what size and shape is his nose? what color is his hair and eyes? how tall is he? how much does he weigh? Each is an individual and must be treated accordingly."

"Don't prepare a speech; prepare yourself to speak."

Tennyson was once asked by a friend as they walked in the garden, "What does Jesus Christ mean to you?" He reached to a rose and replied, "What the sunshine means to this flower, Jesus means to me."

"A handful of real living is worth a bushel of learning."

"We should learn not only how to escape hell, but how to live in heaven and be happy there."

Put Everyone To Work

Work and Growth

My philosophy for successful leadership in a ward has always been — "Put everybody to work and show everybody a good time."

As President of the Southern States Mission, the first message I sent out to the members of the mission was that if my administration were going to be outstanding for one thing more than another, I wanted it to be that I stood for everybody working. Then we proceeded to initiate a program to put everybody to work. After my release, I reported to the general authorities in our meeting in the Temple. I told them we had filled in all the report blanks they had sent us, "And of course you sent us plenty," Then I said, "There is no place on the report blanks to report the achievement I feel most grateful for — the individual growth and development that has come to the members of that mission because we have harnessed them and put them to work."

Confidence Repaid

A good leader will inspire and help men to accept responsibility. When I was appointed President of the Hollywood Stake, our stake had never taken a group to the Arizona Temple, to which Temple district our stake belonged. There were only two stakes in Southern California at that time and the other stake was taking its people almost every week. I said to my counselors, "Let's ask Brother so and so to take charge of our genealogical work." One of my counselors said, "Well, you couldn't do that, President Richards. He smokes." I said, "I know that, but he will quit if we ask him to." Well, then my counselor thought it would be all right if he would agree to quit. So then we went to the high council and got

the same response. I said, "He will quit." Then they
agreed that if he would, we could so appoint him. So
we called him and his wife into the Stake Presidency's
office and told him what we had in mind for him. His
face lighted up and he said, "President Richards, I would
do anything for you and the Lord." Then I had him committed so I said, "I knew you would. That is what I told
the Brethren. There is one thing we will have to ask you
to do. Of course, we couldn't have a man at the head of
one of our stake organizations who was using tobacco."
His face colored up as if he thought we didn't know
he was using tobacco. I said, "I told the Brethren you
would quit in order to do this work." He put his head in
his hands on the desk for a moment and raised up and
said, "I'll quit."

Spiritual Growth

Shortly after that, only a couple of weeks or so we
took a whole bus load to the Arizona Temple. I went
with them and we were permitted to hold a testimony
meeting one morning before going through the Temple.
He did not bear his testimony. He could not; he was
overcome with the spirit of the Lord. The tears were
rolling down his cheeks. He was not what you would call
an emotional type man. He could keep you laughing for
hours as a master of ceremonies. Those who attended
that testimony meeting have often declared that it was
one of the finest, most spiritual meetings they had ever
attended. As we walked out of the assembly room into
the lobby of the Temple, he came and put his arms around
me and said, "President Richards, where do such feelings
come from? I have never experienced anything like that
in my life." I explained to him that I thought the Lord
was just letting him know how much he appreciated his
giving up tobacco and taking on that important work.
He later became a Bishop and a member of the high

council. The service he rendered greatly enriched his life and also contributed to the building of the Kingdom.

Sometimes we leave men with great ability and capacity on the side lines without even interviewing them to see if they would put themselves in harmony with the Church so that their talents and gifts could be used for the building up of the Kingdom of God on the earth.

Make An Inventory

A good leader is relentless and resourceful in finding men to help him with his work. Just to illustrate . . .

Some years ago a new stake president came into my office to visit with me and asked if I had any suggestions to offer because his stake was about at the bottom of the list of all the stakes of the Church in its activities. I told him that if I were being appointed President of that stake, I would first make an inventory of every man and every woman living in the stake who had leadership ability, no matter where it was evidenced, whether it was in the school room or civic organizations, or in business or on the farm. Then I said I would try and get those leaders interested in the Church. If you can get the leaders, the rest will naturally follow. Then I added, "Don't overlook the senior members of the Aaronic Priesthood. You will find many fine men in that group who may have become a little careless. They have been overlooked and they haven't been used."

Senior Aaronic Priesthood

A short time after that he came into Salt Lake with a new Bishopric to be set apart. He took them to my father, then President of the Twelve, and then brought them to my office to introduce them to me. He said rather under his breath, "Bishop, I got them out of the Senior Aaronic Priesthood." He said, "Your father turned to the first counselor and calling him by name said, 'I suppose you're a High Priest.' His reply was, 'No, President Richards, I am a Deacon.' Your father looked at him and then at the stake president and said, 'Do you vouch for this man.' The president indicated that he did." So my father looked him over again and then he said, 'All right.' He laid his hands upon his head and ordained him a High Priest and set him apart as a counselor in the Bishopric. The second counselor was only a Priest and he did the same thing with him.

I later checked with the stake president to see how this new bishopric got along. He said, "Brother Richards, they literally run rings around the other bishops." You see, they had never been in the drivers seat before; it was a new thing, and they got joy out of the challenge and the service that they were rendering.

Recently I attended a funeral here in Salt Lake Valley where I was asked to speak. At the close of the service, the Bishop who conducted the service came up to me and said, "Bishop, if I seemed a little awkward in conducting this service today, just remember that a few weeks ago I was a Senior Member of the Aaronic Priesthood." How it thrills our hearts when we see men like this brought into activity in the Church.

Could You Replace Him?

Some will remember Brother William A. Morton. He was quite witty. President Grant took him with him to Europe when he went to preside over the European Mission. He was called as the first man to set up ward and stake organizations in the genealogical and temple work of the Church. Up to that time, we only had one session a day in the Salt Lake Temple and that was not very well attended.

Brother Morton went into one of our large wards. After explaining his mission and assignment to the Bishop, he asked for a good man to take charge of the work in his ward. The Bishop explained that every man in his ward who was willing to work was already engaged. He just didn't know who he could give to Brother Morton. Brother Morton replied, "Bishop, if the superintendent of your Sunday School should die tonight, could you replace him?" "Well, of course, we would have to do that." Then Brother Morton countered, "That's the man I want. Your superintendent is not dead. Now you give me the man you would make superintendent of the Sunday School tomorrow if your superintendent should pass away."

We are so prone to overlook men, and go around calling the same ones over and over again. I always refer to the little story about the man who prayed, "Oh Lord, bless me and my wife, my son John and his wife, us four and no more."

Give Others a Chance

Some of our Bishops go around in a little larger circle in calling their members into activity, but not much larger, with the result that there is much wasted manpower in their wards.

I use this little illustration to show my thinking. I say, "If you give a very expensive toy to a boy who has been raised in a home where he has always had everything he wanted, you might find that toy laying down on the sidewalk or in the back lot at night; but give a similar toy to a boy who has never had such things and he takes it to bed with him at night and hugs it."

I try to remind the leadership of the Church that every man is a son of God, the Eternal Father, and in his bosom in embryo is every gift that his Father in Heaven possesses. If we can touch their hearts, they can develop these gifts and talents to the honor and the glory of our Father in Heaven and for their own preparation for eternal exaltation.

Resourcefulness

Increase in Converts

As Mission President, I told the missionaries that if they would learn how to tell our story, and if they could get into a home one night a week for six months, by that time the people would either join the Church or they would be no good for any other church. I believed that with all my heart because I had done enough missionary work to know that in that length of time, if they would listen, I could take from them what they already believed and build them a better house. Now the missionaries do that in possibly six visits instead of six months and in many cases less than that. They stick to the essential facts of the restoration, bearing powerful testimony of the truth, and get quick results.

To illustrate what that really means, when they first started the present program of presenting the Gospel, in one of the missions in 1950 they had some 260 converts, and they averaged 1,432 hours per missionary per convert. In two years time they had increased the converts to over eight hundred and reduced the hours per missionary per convert from 1,432 to 188 hours. Now they do it in much less time than that.

Wild Horse Ride

If a missionary can get the people to listen to him, he can capture the honest in heart among them if he is living close to the Lord. But people are not always willing to listen. That is where the missionary has to be alert and resourceful. Just to illustrate . . .

We had a District President in the State of Mississippi who was raised on a ranch. I think he would justly deserve the title of "A Cow Puncher." He didn't know too much about the Gospel when he arrived in the mission field, but after being in the field for some time, he wrote home to his mother and brothers and told them that he had found out that the Gospel was true. One of his brothers said, "It must be true or he would not say that it is."

He had a very interesting experience in attending a rodeo in Mississippi. There was one wild horse that none of the men could ride, so he offered to ride that horse if they would agree that if he were successful, they would all remain for an hour while he preached Mormonism to them. He rode the horse. He got up in a wagon box and they all gathered around while he preached Mormonism to them for an hour. By his resourcefulness he won a big audience. I am sure the Lord helped him stay on that wild horse, so he could have a chance to preach to that crowd at the rodeo. He was a great missionary and has since been a Bishop and built a wonderful building for the people of his ward.

Preaching in the Police Station

In one of the meetings in the Temple, the President of the Northern California Mission told this experience. Some of his missionaries had been cited to appear at the Police station to account for what they were doing because some ministers had reported them. The reason was that when they would go into a home and commence with the Godhead lesson, and the people did not know what kind of a God they believed in, the missionary would say, "Call up your minister and he will tell you. Then you will know that you are right." Some of those ministers had been getting five or six calls a day and they became worried. They were afraid the wolves were getting into their flock, so they reported it to the chief of police.

Two of these missionaries stood before the chief of police who demanded, "What are you men doing

anyway to upset our people like this?" One of the missionaries said, "Chief, you get over on the other side of that
table and I will show you what we are doing." So the
Chief got over on the other side of the table and the
missionary gave him the first lesson, and asked, "Do you
want the second lesson?" The Chief replied, "Go ahead."
After being given the second lesson, the Chief pulled
out his calling card from his pocket. Handing it to the
missionary he said, "Now you men go ahead with your
missionary work, but come up to the house and give
me the rest of those lessons, will you?"

Put at Ease

Once I was tracting and came to a door where I had
been several times before. The lady said, "Mr. Richards,
what are you trying to do anyway? Are you trying to
make Mormons out of all of us?" To which I replied,
"I promise never to ask you to join the Mormon Church."
That seemed to put her mind at ease. Then I added,
"But if I could show you where you could trade one
dollar for five dollars, I wouldn't have to ask you to do it,
would I?" She replied, "I get you." After I had been
home a few months, I received a letter from her calling
me Brother Richards. She said, "I decided to trade the
dollar for the five dollars — I was baptized a member of
the Church last Friday evening."

When I first saw that the lady was becoming wary
of my missionary efforts, I knew I had to set her mind at
ease. Then I had to challenge her interest in the wonderful message I had. We can either win or lose at a
certain point. That is where we have to remember that
we have the most wonderful thing in the world to offer.
I always tell the missionaries that if they cannot make
Mormonism look better than five to one as against any
other church, I think they are very poor missionaries.

Handling the Hecklers

We were holding a street meeting in New Bedford, Massachusetts and must have had over two hundred people listening. The Gospel Hall people who were holding a convention right near our corner, dismissed their meeting to come and see what we were doing. They commenced interrupting our meeting. Since the short-term visiting Elder who was speaking didn't seem to be able to control the situation and since it was my meeting, I stepped up and asked him if he would like me to relieve him. He was very happy with the suggestion.

I took the meeting over. Addressing these ministers (as I recall there were a dozen or more), I said: "Now, you men would like to be honorable gentlemen, wouldn't you? I suggest that you give us twenty minutes to finish our meeting without interruption; then we will remain a half hour and listen to you without interruption." Then I added, "And the crowd will remain also, won't you?" To which they replied, "Yes." So we finished our meeting and then turned the time over to the Gospel Hall Ministers. The man who spoke denounced Joseph Smith and the Mormon Golden Bible. Toward the close of his remarks, he said, "Why, if you would let them, the Mormons would bind the Book of Mormon in the same cover with the Bible and ask us to take it and like it."

The Last Word

I didn't like to see the meeting close at this point, so I stepped up to the man in charge and said, "You wouldn't mind if we made an announcement before the crowd leaves, would you?" He granted our request. I stepped forward and said, "If you people will come back next Tuesday evening at 7:30, we will tell you why we would bind the Book of Mormon in the same cover with the Bible and ask you to take it and like it." Then I added, "Bring your Bibles with you, for you will not need them after next Tuesday evening if you are not willing to accept the companion volume of scripture the Lord commanded his Prophet to write, which he promised to join to the Bible and make them one in his hand. You see, it was the Lord and not the Mormons who promised to join them together."

Well, the next Tuesday evening we had a larger crowd than ever and sold sixteen copies of the Book of Mormon that night.

It is the old story that when our enemies kick us, they usually kick us up the hill.

Many missionaries get discouraged when they are being heckled and interrupted, but with resourcefulness they can turn the tide. Very often a disturbance creates more interest, so they at least get more of an audience if they can just get attention. I have found that courtesy and an appeal to the other side's better nature, usually gets results. It also gets the sympathy of the audience to some degree. Another point — I try never to let the other side end up ahead. With determination, I feel we can always challenge and recapture our audience.

Sacrament Meeting

Where Are Your Children?

Many of our saints who are good about everything
else, slip up when it comes to training their children to
attend Sacrament Meeting and Stake Conference.

Shortly after I became the Presiding Bishop of the
Church, I attended a Stake Conference here in the Salt
Lake Valley. When my turn came to speak in the morning meeting, I stood up and said something like this,
"I am very happy to meet you grandfathers and you
grandmothers this morning, but where are your children
and your grandchildren?" Then I explained that their
children and their grandchildren were not there because
they had not taught them to attend Sacrament Meetings
and Stake Conferences. I explained to them how grateful I was that my father taught me to attend meetings
and conferences. I told them how he used to drive the
old gray team with the white top in from Tooele, some
forty miles, to attend the General Conferences of the
Church, and how he would bring us three boys with him
in order that we might catch the spirit, and learn to
know the General Authorities. Through this, I knew
all of the General Authorities from President Woodruff
down. As a boy I was in a conference in the Tabernacle
with my father when President Woodruff talked to the
saints. My recollection is that it was the last message
he delivered. When he told how marvelously the spirit
of the Lord had guided him all through his life, I was
thrilled. He related the incident of how he was warned
to get up in the middle of the night and move his team
and wagon from an oak tree that had stood over one
hundred years. He had no more taken care of this than
a whirlwind came and took that oak tree up by the roots
and threw it where his wagon had stood. Had he not

listened to the whisperings of the spirit, his life might not have been preserved.

Inspiring Recollections

Then he related the incident of bringing a group of saints to Zion. They were in New Orleans and about to board a boat. The spirit warned him not to go on that boat, neither he nor his company. So he excused himself to the captain with whom he had been negotiating and said they would wait for a later connection. That boat had no more than sailed up the river until it caught fire and burned. Not a soul on the boat was saved. Then President Woodruff said, "If I had not listened to the spirit of the Lord, we would not have had President so and so, naming one of the brethren, and Bishop so and so, naming another.

This experience, I never forgot.

Make the Effort

Then I related some of the experiences that had come to me in attending my own Sacrament meetings. I invited the saints to come back to the afternoon meeting and bring their children and grandchildren just to show they really had them. While we had over four hundred present in the morning meeting, we doubled it and had over eight hundred present in the afternoon! All could not get into the building. I learned that they really had children and grandchildren. They just had not trained them to attend their Sacrament Meetings and their conferences. What a blessing to our children and grandchildren—and to the Church as a whole, if we would all make the effort to bring them with us all the time to our appointed meetings! I dare say we would almost double our spirit of testimony in a few years. All it would take is a little effort and interest on our part.

Poor Attendance

At the time I became the Presiding Bishop of the Church, many wards could not get enough members of the Aaronic Priesthood out to administer the Sacrament. They had to use High Priests and Seventies and Elders. Through the Aaronic Priesthood award program we changed this pattern and got our boys of the Aaronic Priesthood to attend their meetings and officiate at the Sacrament Table.

In a Bishops' conference in the Tabernacle, I told the Bishops I would be ashamed to preside over a ward or a stake that could not get at least twenty-five percent of their members out to Sacrament Meeting. At that time, the average of the Church was between fifteen and sixteen percent. Some of the bishops took issue with me and did not seem to feel it could be done. We had stakes as low as eight, nine and ten percent.

Shortly after that, we called a bishop to speak in a conference in Ogden. He said, "He had heard Bishop Richards make that statement and had come back to his counselors and said, "I believe Bishop Richards meant what he said." "So," he related, "we went to work and decided we would get at least twenty-five percent of our members out to Sacrament meeting, and we have achieved that result."

Set Objectives

At this writing, April 1961, the average attendance at Sacrament Meeting is thirty-seven percent. It pays to set objectives and work to them. I have always told the Bishops that if they would hitch their wagon to a star, if they didn't get on the star, they would at least get on top of the mountain; but if they didn't hitch they would remain in a rut.

When I was President of the Amsterdam District on my first mission, we more than doubled the attendance of the saints at our meetings in a very short time. This is one of the methods we used to achieve that objective.

On Monday morning my companion and I would start out and visit the homes of the saints we missed in Sacrament meeting. We would say, calling the sister by name, "Sister, is someone sick here at your home?" "No, Brother Richards, what makes you think someone is sick?" "Well, we didn't see you at Sacrament meeting, and we were sure you would have been there if there hadn't been someone sick, so we felt we should call on you and make sure."

We had the saints in that branch sending us written excuses with their children at Sunday School when they were not going to be able to attend Sacrament meeting.

The Persistent Son

Sometimes a simple appeal to those present at a meeting will help increase attendance. Just as parents and grandparents may be encouraged to bring their children with them, so may young people whose parents are not active be encouraged to bring their parents to Church. Just to illustrate . . . A few years ago we had the young people at Conference all seated in the center of the chapel. I asked how many of them were there without their parents. Many of their hands went up. Then I called each of those whose hands had gone up, on a mission to bring their parents to the afternoon meeting. At the close of the afternoon meeting I saw a young boy almost dragging his mother by the hand, bringing her toward me, so I went to meet them. The boy said, "Bishop Richards, you asked us to bring our parents, and I have brought my mother." The mother was quite poorly clad, and I wondered how long it had been since she had been to church. She said, "Yes, Bishop, my son was so insistent that I come with him that I sent the other

children to the picture show so as not to disappoint him."
I couldn't even criticize her for that. Her son had a call
to bring his parents and at any cost he wanted to fulfill
his assignment. When we can encourage everyone to
bring his family and friends to Sacrament meeting and
Conference, we will reach a wonderful goal of participa-
tion and spirituality.

Sacrifice

Building the Kingdom

The Psalmist said that the Lord would gather his saints unto Him, those who had made a covenant with Him by sacrifice. It is a marvelous thing as we travel through the Church to see how the saints do sacrifice to help build the Kingdom, in sending their boys and girls on missions, in paying their tithes and their offerings, in gathering their genealogies and doing Temple work, in supporting the great Welfare program, in helping to build meeting houses and Temples, and in answering the call of duty on every hand. This spirit of sacrifice is responsible for the tremendous progress the Church is making today.

While I was attending a conference in Idaho a few years ago, the Bishop of one of the wards, a convert from Germany, invited me to go to his home with him. He had a one hundred and sixty acre irrigated farm, as fine agriculture land as I have seen anywhere, and a lovely modern brick house. He told me that one day his wife said, "Father, if the Church were to ask for it, would you give it to them?" His reply was, "Yes, Mother, and there wouldn't be a cent against it." This is typical of the spirit of sacrifice the saints have, and evidence of their love for the Church.

Family and Fortune

Many of our converts have made great sacrifices for the gospel. I once worked with a young man who one day heard the Mormon Elders preaching on the street corner in an Eastern city. As has been the experience with many a man and woman since the gospel has been restored through the Prophet Joseph Smith, the words of the missionaries pierced his heart. Jesus said,

"My sheep know my voice." After some investigation, he accepted their message. He held a very responsible position in a large company owned principally by his young wife's people. Because of his acceptance of the truth, his wife's people turned him out of the business, turned her against him, and tried to have him sent to an insane asylum. He therefore left and came to Utah as his only alternative. To maintain their good favor was to denounce the truth and this he could not do.

I was with him when he received a telegram from a friend informing him of the birth of his firstborn, a son. He shed many a tear that day. Her people did not even consider it worth while to advise him. He said his greatest desire was to some day return to his native town and stand on the same street corner where he heard the Elders, and lift his voice in defense and testimony of the truth.

One of a Family

A woman came to me in Rotterdam whose daughter, a nurse, had joined the Church. She was terribly upset. She said, "She was the finest child we had." I explained to her that that was the reason she had joined the Church, for, as Jesus said: "For blessed are they which do hunger and thirst after righteousness for they shall be filled." And, because of her righteous living the Lord had led her to the truth.

A young man had been preaching socialism on the streets of Rotterdam. But he met the missionaries and began investigating the gospel. His mother would burn any Church literature he brought into the house. It was all right with his mother for him to preach socialism but not for him to be interested in the Mormon Church. When he finally decided to join the Church his mother forbade him to ever return to his home again.

In the early days of the Church the Saints were driven from their homes time and again because of their conviction that Joseph Smith was a Prophet. I used to hear President Grant tell how his mother, coming from a well-to-do home, was offered everything by her people if she would but renounce her religion and return to her home. But the Lord had given her a testimony that Joseph Smith was a Prophet and she could not deny it.

Spirit of Sacrifice

When the Saints were driven from Nauvoo most of them could have returned to the homes from which they came had they but been willing to renounce their faith in the divine calling of the Prophet Joseph Smith, but this they could not do. Many sealed their testimonies with their blood.

Typical of the experiences of many of the early Saints was that of Daniel H. Wells. He was a great friend of the Prophet Joseph and the brethren in Nauvoo, but he had never joined the Church because of the prejudice of his wife. When he saw the Saints leaving Nauvoo, he had to decide whether to remain behind with his wife and only son or to cast his lot with the Saints. His testimony that Joseph Smith was a Prophet caused him to choose the latter course. He later became a Counselor to President Brigham Young.

We witness the spirit of sacrifice constantly in the calling of Mission Presidents. No matter what their business responsibilities are, when they are interviewed by a member of the First Presidency, they always express a willingness to even give up their businesses and make most any sacrifices necessary to answer the call of the Lord.

The sacrifices made by parents to keep their sons and daughters in the Mission field would fill a book. Through the Prophet Jeremiah, the Lord said:

Behold, I will send for many fishers, saith the Lord, and they shall fish them; and after will I send for many hunters, and they shall hunt them from every mountain, and from every hill, and out of the holes of the rocks. (Jer. 16:16.)

The Lord has been fulfilling this promise ever since the Church was organized. Up to the present time, there have been approximately one hundred thousand missionaries sent out into all lands and they have been fishing and hunting the blood of Israel among all nations. When the Lord calls a man to be "a fisher or a hunter," and sends him out in his name he does something for him that makes him different than ordinary men, as Jesus said when he sent the Seventy forth in his name, "He that heareth you heareth me; and he that despiseth you despiseth me; and he that despiseth me despiseth him that sent me."

Called to Serve

As Jesus walked by the sea of Galilee, he saw Simon and Andrew his brother casting a net into the sea: for they were fishers. And Jesus said unto them, Come ye after me, and I will make you to become fishers of men. And straightway they forsook their nets, and followed him. (Mark 1:16-18.)

In the same spirit, the leaders of his Church in this dispensation have left their businesses at his call. President Brigham Young spent nearly ten years of his life in the mission field after joining the church. When President Grant was a member of the Quorum of Twelve, he was offered a salary of $40,000 per year if he would go East and become a chief executive in an insurance company. His allowance from the church at that time would have been a small percent of this amount. Many of the leaders of today have made similar sacrifices at the call of the Church.

I have always said that as long as the Lord continues to put such faith in the hearts of the members of his church no one can stop its growth.

Science And Religion

A Young Student

While I was presiding over the Netherlands Mission, I met a young man who had gone to The Hague to attend college. The first thing his professor told him was that he would have to forget his idea about God and the story of the creation told in the Bible, etc. So he went home to his parents. They took him to the minister. All the minister did was to warn him that if he heeded such counsel, he would be on his road to the bad place. The result was that he decided to go forward with his college work. Then if he could find a place for religion after doing so—he would take it up again.

He completed his college work and came to America to do post graduate work. Upon his return he made the acquaintance of one of our Mormon girls. She brought him to me. We had quite a number of interesting discussions together at my office. I explained to him the teachings of the Church—that the Lord didn't create the earth in six of our days, but in six periods; the end of each period, He called a day. That appealed to him. I told him he had been studying the workings of a great machine, which he called nature, but he had never stopped to ask himself the question, "Who put that machine in operation?" I said, "Wherever there is evidence of intelligent organization, there is a purpose back of it."

Need of Intelligent Organization

Then I used this argument. I told him that while I was not a scientist, I understood that the scientist accepted the fact that there were two things that were eternal and could not be destroyed—force and matter. You could change the form of matter, but you could not

SCIENCE AND RELIGION

destroy it. Then I added, "Now, admitting that is true, why not add one more eternal 'intelligence'? Then you would have something that could organize matter and put it into operation." I pointed to the stove standing in our office. There was a scuttle containing coal and kindling wood, paper, and a box of matches. I said, "There is enough matter and force there to warm this building, but it never will be warmed until intelligence is applied to put those elements together and strike the match." Then I pointed to the river Maas and said, "There is enough element there, and force, to warm the whole nation of Holland, but it never will do it until intelligence is applied to organize it." I used other similar illustrations.

Then I handed him the book written by Dr. Widtsoe on "Joseph Smith as a Scientist." After he had read it, he said he would surely like to take it to his professor in The Hague and get him to read it. I permitted him to do so, requesting that he let me know when he brought the book back what his professor had to say about it. When he returned the book, I asked him what his professor thought. He reported, "If that book had not been written by a religious man, he would believe every word that was in it. What he would like to know is how Joseph Smith got hold of those facts." Joseph Smith taught scientific truths far in advance of science. The Prophet Joseph taught that one glimpse into the eternal worlds would do more to teach man his relationship to God than reading all the books that had ever been written. Joseph Smith had that glimpse; hence he was able to teach scientific truths in advance of scientists.

In my office, that young man put his head down on his hands on the desk. After solemn thought, he raised up and said, "Mr. Richards, there is a God."

Service

The Wise High Councilman

I am a great believer in passing the honors around in the Church and giving each member an opportunity to use his gifts and talents for the building of the kingdom, for the blessing of our Father's children, for the honor and the glory of His Holy Name, and for his own preparation for eternal exaltation. Some of our leaders go around in little circles as it were, using the same people over and over again for positions of responsibility and for speaking assignments while many never get an opportunity to participate.

Just to illustrate . . . A member of the High Council in one of the stakes said that his wife had three important jobs in the ward. She was a member of the Relief Society Presidency and of the YWMIA Presidency, and she taught a class in Sunday School. This member of the High Council went to his Bishop and said, "Now my wife can keep any one of the three jobs you desire, but she must be released from the other two because she cannot carry these three positions and take care of her family." The Bishop replied, "Well, we haven't anyone else in the ward who can take her place." Then this good member of the High Council said, "Bishop, what about Sister so and so living over here?" pointing in the direction of her home. The Bishop replied, "We couldn't ask her to take one of the jobs; she doesn't even attend church." To which the High Councilman replied, "Bishop, do you know why she doesn't attend church? It is because you have never asked her to do anything. You give her one of these positions and she will attend church." So the Bishop did and she became just as faithful in her service as the High Councilman's wife had been. Then he pointed in the direction of another woman

and had the same response from the Bishop. He said,
"If you will give her one of these jobs, she will attend
Church," and she did.

Service Is a Privilege

Sometime ago Elder Clifford E. Young and I were
to meet a stake president at the Bishop's home. We
arrived there before the stake president. The Bishop's
wife, wishing to be kind to us, served us a wonderful
meal. While we were eating, she named ten jobs on the
fingers of her hands that she held in her ward as the
wife of the Bishop. She had been so gracious and kind
to us that we could not criticize her. But as we left that
home, I turned to Elder·Young and said, "Her husband
may be a wonderful man, but he is a very poor bishop."

Service in our Church is a privilege and a blessing.
No person should hold more than one job unless every
attempt has been made to get someone else to accept
it. The only way for anyone to enjoy this Church is to
be active in it. I once heard an elder comment on this
in a missionary meeting. He was quite a philosopher
and a little slow of speech. He said, something like this,
"Well, I am enjoying my work." Then he waited a few
minutes and added, "You know that is all I can enjoy.
I can't enjoy what I don't do." This statement made a
profound impression upon me. I have realized that none
of us will ever be able to enjoy that which we have not
done. If we want much joy, we must perform much
constructive work, for that is what will bring us joy.
Whether it is preaching the gospel to those who know
not the truth, or whether it is helping to train and edu-
cate the members of the Church to prepare them for more
efficient service, or whether it is to look after the poor
and the unfortunate, whatever our work may be, we can
only enjoy what we do.

Importance of Being Valiant

It is up to the ward leaders to see that everyone is given an opportunity to serve. We have many men who have never been asked to serve. When asked, they often do outstanding work. This I have found to be true in my own ministry in the Church, until I have made this statement to the bishops I have visited. "If the stake presidency were to divide an average size ward and let the bishop take his first choice of half the members— those to whom he gives all the jobs and assignments, and let me have the inactive half, I believe that within a year or two we could bring them up to par. I have worked with so many inactive people, that I know it is mainly a matter of gaining their love and confidence and you can get them to do almost anything for the Church.

Sometimes our people forget that they are the ones who gain through service. Just to illustrate . . . One branch president in Miami, Florida said to me, "All of the officers here want to be released." Then he began naming them. Miami is a pleasure resort city and they seemed to have caught the spirit of pleasure seeking. I said to the branch president, "don't let them get to me until after the morning meeting." So in the morning meeting, when my turn came to speak, I said, something like this, "How would you like to be a devil?" Then I said, "Do you know why you are not a devil? Because you were once faithful in the spirit world. If you had not been, you would have been cast out with Satan and a third of the hosts of heaven." Then I said, "How would you like to be a negro? Do you know why you are not a negro? Because you were once more valiant than they, and earned the right to this white body instead of a colored body." Then I added, "now after having been faithful in your pre-existent life which entitled you to obtain a body, and through your faithfulness, to obtain a beautiful white body; are you going to fail now by not being faithful here to gain exaltation in the eternal worlds? What you will receive in the next life will be as much conditioned on what you do here as what you have received here is the result of what you did before you came here." Obviously, no one resigned while I was there.

Spirit Of Research

The World at Work

The last two verses of the Old Testament record the promise that Elijah would come and turn the hearts of the children to their fathers. Today we are witnessing the result of Elijah's visit to Joseph Smith and the keys he restored. Throughout the entire world there is a spirit of research. Countless people not of our Church are busily engaged in searching out their lineage, and spending untold time and money to do a thorough, accurate job.

While I was living in Portland, Oregon, I met a man who had traveled all over the United States gathering the genealogy of his father's people. He explained that he didn't know why he was doing it, but that he just had a mania for it and could not let it alone. That is what the spirit of Elijah does.

We converted a couple in Florida. After his conversion the husband became interested in searching the genealogy of his people. He found a book in the library in Jacksonville which had been prepared by a Judge in Texas and his wife, who were his relatives. In the preface of the book was a statement like this: "This book has been prepared at great effort on the part of my wife and myself, and at great expense. Why we have done it, we do not know, but we trust that in the providences of the Lord it will serve a useful purpose."

Again the spirit of Elijah was at work.

While presiding over the Hollywood Stake in Los Angeles, we met with the Stake Genealogical Committee at the home of Bishop David P. Howell, and there was present the director of the Los Angeles Library. During the evening we discussed Genealogical work. The Director of the Library explained that he had spent thousands of dollars in genealogical research—that he had a vault full of records and manuscripts, but that he did not know why he had done it except that he had a driving desire to do so.

I explained to him that some day he would realize that he had been in partnership with Elijah the Prophet without realizing it.

Spirit of Inspiration

Members of the Church have testified repeatedly that they have had inspiration to guide and help them in their research. Our General Authorities and other leaders have been inspired in assigning missionaries to locations where they have been blessed to find rich family genealogies. Just to illustrate . . .

When I went on my first mission there were two other young men who accompanied me, one from Idaho and one from Southern Utah. Upon our arrival in Rotterdam, Holland, the one from Southern Utah was assigned to labor in the Rotterdam District, and the one from Idaho in the Groningen District. I was assigned to the Mission office.

When the young man from Idaho was called to the Netherlands Mission, his parents were somewhat disappointed. Being of German descent, they felt that it would be better had he been called to Germany, so that he might have done some genealogical research work while there.

When he arrived in the Groningen District, he was assigned to labor in the city of Veen Dam. He and his companion commenced looking for furnished rooms. After passing a number of houses with signs on of furnished rooms for rent, this young man said, "This looks like a good place." They arranged to rent rooms there.

After he had been some weeks in this home, he found a record containing many names of his father's family, which had been brought across the line out of Germany. His people didn't know that any of their people had ever been in Holland.

See how marvelously the spirit of the Lord can direct in matters of importance pertaining to the salvation of our Heavenly Father's children! The inspiration of the Lord directed the First Presidency to send this young man to Holland. The same inspiration inspired the mission president to assign him to the Groningen District. The same spirit directed the District President to assign him to the city of Veen Dam. And again, the same inspiration guided him and his companion to this home, which in itself could hardly be regarded as a coincidence in a city of over fifty thousand people.

A Promise Fulfilled

In 1926 I filled a short term mission in the Eastern States. On my way to the mission field, I met an Elder Wadsworth. We were assigned by President B. H. Roberts to the Boston District, and by the District President to labor in the city of New Bedford, Massachusetts.

When Brother Wadsworth was set apart for his mission by Elder George F. Richards of the Council of the Twelve (my father), he was promised that he would not only be able to do a good work in preaching the gospel to the living, but that he would be able to do a great work in gathering the genealogy of his father's family.

The first real stormy day that came (and it knows how to storm in that country), I suggested to Elder Wadsworth that we go to the Library and see what we could find in the way of information regarding his father's family. They had a very fine genealogical department in the Library at New Bedford. We found letters from Brigham Young, from my grandfather, Franklin D. Richards, and others. We also succeeded in locating a book containing several thousand names of Brother Wadsworth's family. This book covered, as I recall, the genealogy of the poet Longfellow, whose mother was a Wadsworth; and it also contained the record of Elder Wadsworth's grandfather, indicating that he went west with the Mormon Pioneers and gave the names of his two wives.

We wrote to the publishing company and found that the book was out of print, and that the author had passed away. The next time we went to Boston I suggested to Elder Wadsworth that we try the second-hand bookstores. We went into one large bookstore, and when we told the proprietor what we wanted, he scratched his head and replied, "I believe I have one of those books." Reaching up on one of the high shelves, he pulled a copy down all covered with dust. Elder Wadsworth arranged to purchase the book by making a deposit on it.

Truly the words of Elder Richards were fulfilled when he set him apart for his mission. Not only did he fill a good mission, he also did a great work in gathering the genealogy of his father's family.

Stake Missionary Work

Perseverance Pays

Some persons are inclined to minimize the importance of stake missionary work. They seem to think that because it is just a part-time service and done fairly close within one's own neighborhood it is not of great importance. But I have never known the Lord to make any distinction between fields of labor as long as the one called to serve was giving as much of his time as he could and was magnifying his call. All around us are people who will accept the gospel if we can just get them to listen. Just to illustrate . . .

My secretary at the Presiding Bishop's office and her companions spent eighteen months doing stake missionary work here in Salt Lake. They were successful in bringing seventeen people into the Church during that period of time. She told me this one experience. She said they went into one home where the woman was a member of the Church, but hardly knew why. Her husband was a non-member having been raised an Episcopalian. They tried to get him to let them give him some of the lessons but he was not at all interested. He said he was raised an Episcopalian and expected to die an Episcopalian. I always add that he was like the story they tell of the Englishman who said he was born an Englishman, raised an Englishman, and he hoped to die an Englishman. A Scotchman said, "Have you no ambition?" Finally these two lady missionaries prevailed upon this man to let them give him two or three of the lessons with the explanation that his wife would be teaching Mormonism to his children when they were old enough and that it wouldn't hurt him to know a little bit about what the teachings of the Church were. He consented and after about the fourth lesson, he applied for baptism. A few weeks later I met him at a conference in the Assembly Hall where he served as an usher. Since then I have met him and learned that he brought his neighbor into the Church and baptized him.

Break Through Indifference

I always add that there isn't an honest man or an honest woman in this world who really loves the Lord who wouldn't join this Church if he really knew what it was. Our responsibility is to break through indifference and prejudice, and teach what the Lord really has done in restoring his truth to the earth.

I visited in the home of a stake president and his wife while attending their stake conference. I learned that he and his wife, being missionary minded, had brought thirty converts into the Church during the two years that they had served as stake missionaries. This is truly a wonderful achievement.

One of our young men in California who was studying pre-medics was asked by his Bishop to spend his summer vacation doing stake missionary work. He agreed to do this. He lived in a very aristocratic part of the town and he called on the boys and girls with whom he had attended high school. Making a statement like this, "My Church has asked me to do some missionary work for it, and I am not very well prepared. How would you like to give me a few nights of your time and let me practice on you, so I can prepare myself to do my missionary work for my Church?" During those summer months he brought four of those young people into the Church by practicing on them.

If these good brothers and sisters had not been willing to accept a call as stake missionaries there is no telling how long it would have been before those whom they converted would have had the opportunity to hear the gospel. Oh! that we would recognize that every call to serve is a blessing, whether it is great or small. We will be rewarded not according to the size of the position we fill, but according to our diligence in striving to magnify our calling.

Telling Of Unclean Stories

An Evil Pastime

In the little country town where I was raised as a boy, the men from the farms would gather frequently at the old Co-op corner waiting for the snow to melt. Since that was a sunny spot with sandy ground, it was the place where we boys played our first games of marbles in the spring. As we played we could not help but hear the smutty stories exchanged by the men gathered there. As I walked away from that corner one day, I resolved that no friend of mine would ever be able to accuse me of having befouled his mind with an unclean story, and I think I have kept that resolution. It took me years of my life to try and forget some of the unclean stories I heard as a boy at that corner. If I had been smart, I would have left the corner rather than listen, but I guess I was too young.

The telling of unclean stories is a pastime indulged in by many people who are apparently clean otherwise. Perhaps they do it because others of the group do it. Just to illustrate . . .

A Roommate's Censure

During the war we called a young lieutenant in uniform to speak at Stake Conference in San Diego, California. He told of attending Officers' Training School in the East. One day the young officers were sitting in the lounge telling dirty stories, and he said, "When my turn came I told one, too. That evening when I went to bed, my roommate, to whom I had been preaching the gospel, turned to me and said: 'I didn't think you would do it.' "

Telling of this experience, the young lieutenant declared: "That was one of the best sermons I have ever listened to. Those words have kept ringing in my ears— 'I didn't think you would do it'—'I didn't think you would do it', and I haven't done such a thing since."

I wish we could all resist the temptation to listen to or tell unclean stories. It is completely out of harmony with the Lord's admonition—"Let virtue garnish thy thoughts unceasingly."

Testimony

Of Great and Small

A true testimony is the strength of the gospel. President Clark has often said, "It is like the mortar that holds the bricks together." One of the outstanding meetings I ever attended was a Missionary Stake Conference in Washington around 1957.

As I recall we had about 2,500 people in that conference. The Stake President, Willard Marriott, who has been most successful financially stated that his membership in the Church was the most priceless thing that he possessed. .Then we heard from Elder Ezra Taft Benson who bore a powerful testimony. Next we called on President Ernest L. Wilkinson of the Brigham Young University who was visiting there and we heard a wonderful testimony from him. After this we heard a report from a young man who had just recently returned from the Argentine Mission. I had visited with him a week or ten days prior to this conference in my office in Salt Lake. I asked him if he thought his mission had been a waste of time. They held him over an extra six months to help train the other missionaries. He said, "Brother Richards, if the brethren want to make me happy, just let them load me on the plane in the morning and send me back to Argentina." He bore a wonderful testimony. Then we heard a new convert, a little mother of two children, bear her testimony. She told how the Elders promised her, reading the promise from the Book of Mormon, that if she would read that book and ask God, the Eternal Father, in the name of the Lord, Jesus Christ, in faith, that the Lord would manifest the truth of it unto her by the power of the Holy Ghost. "So," she said, "I went into my bedroom, got down on my knees and asked the Lord to let me know whether that book was true or not." She said, "I read it and my whole soul was illumined. I knew it was from the Lord."

I asked that great audience, "How many of you could come up to this pulpit without reservation, if you were asked to do so, and bear testimony that you know that the Church of Jesus Christ of Latter-day Saints is the Lord's only true Church?" Practically every hand went up. I assumed that we had a few non-members in the audience.

A Group of Ministers

I contrasted that experience to one a short time prior when a group of ministers stopped in Salt Lake City on their way to California to a convention. They wanted to meet some of the leaders of the Church so they could ask questions. Accordingly, a meeting was arranged for them in the missionary room of the Church Office Building. Elder Lee was assigned to meet them and answer their questions. After he had done so, he bore his testimony to that group of ministers. Then he said, "Could any of you stand and say that you know that you represent the only true church of our Father in Heaven?" After a brief silence, the man in charge of the group said, "Well, of course, we hope we are right." What a difference!

The story is also told of the English government having sent a man to Utah to study the Mormon question. They could not understand why the Mormons would keep sending their missionaries when they were being so persecuted. After the man had studied the situation here in Utah, he returned with this explanation. "The black secret of Mormonism is the individual testimony of its members. Each member knows that Mormonism is the truth."

The Basic Testimony

The whole strength of the Church hinges on testimony. When a member has a testimony that this is the true Church, the rest of the commandments are easy to keep. Just to illustrate this thought . . .

I quote from a letter dated February 8, 1961 from my grandson in the Swiss Mission. "Last Sunday we baptized here the most beautiful couple I have met in the last two years. A young man and his wife with two small daughters accepted the message after a good deal of fasting and praying. We challenged him three times to be baptized, as we were in their home for the last time. The first time he said he wouldn't. The second time he said, "Perhaps." The third time he eagerly accepted the challenge and was baptized the next morning. After his baptism he remained in the font and with tears streaming down his face said a silent prayer. After the confirmation he came over to me, gave me a big hug, sobbed on my shoulder, and said throughout eternity he wouldn't be able to thank me enough for what I had brought into his home. Both he and his wife said they were ready to give their lives for the gospel. When we first started to tell him of the commandments, he said, "You don't need to tell me about those things; *all I want is a testimony of Joseph Smith.* Once I receive that, I can keep any commandment you can give me." He got his testimony.

It is a testimony that inspires the saints to make the great sacrifices of time, talents, and means to help build the Kingdom, to share the gospel with others, and to change their own lives to conform with the commandments of the Lord.

Humble Testimony Converts

I try to impress the young missionaries with this truth: It is the humble, solemn testimony that will convert people more than logic and the ability to argue. We are told in the scriptures that the letter killeth, but the spirit giveth life. I once ran onto a missionary who depended on his own logic and brilliance rather than on the sweet spirit of the Lord. He was just being released and came through Rotterdam, the mission headquarters. He knew the language when he arrived in the mission field, and delivered a wonderful oration which impressed me. Although I was laboring as the secretary of the Netherlands Mission, I had many good investigators all of my own working without a companion, so I asked him if he would be willing to visit some of them with me the following day. After we had made one visit, I found an excuse to take him back to the office, for all he did was to try to show that he knew more than my investigators did and to embarrass them. I didn't want him to visit any more of them, for I felt his approach would do far more harm than good. All his intelligence was wasted because he didn't have the humble spirit of testimony bearing.

Bear Witness

And in their testimony bearing, missionaries must not neglect to bear witness of Joseph Smith and his divine calling. Just to illustrate . . .

When I was a bishop, I asked one of our returned missionaries how he had enjoyed his mission. He said, "The first half of my mission was a failure. The second half I enjoyed immensely." I asked him to explain. He said, "The first part of my mission I thought the wonderful truths of the gospel could be taught without giving the Lord credit for having restored His Church through the Prophet Joseph Smith. So I never mentioned the Prophet's name. I never got any real joy out of my preaching. Finally my companion said to me one day, 'Elder so and so, don't you think you would enjoy your work more if you would bear testimony that Joseph Smith was a Prophet of God, and that the Lord has established His Church and Kingdom in the earth through him to prepare the way for the coming of His son?' " He said, "I took that companion's advice. From then on, I bore witness of the truth in all my sermons and I was thrilled during the last half of my mission."

Yes, it is the humble, solemn testimony that will convert, but there will always be those people who will not receive our testimony. You remember the story of Nicodemus, a ruler of the Jews, who came to Jesus by night. After the Savior explained to him how a man should be born again and Nicodemus couldn't understand him, Jesus said, "We speak that we do know, and testify that we have seen; and ye received not our witness." In other words, it is the testimony that brings conviction to the souls of men, and if they will not receive it, they cannot obtain the blessings it brings.

A person who has not gained a testimony does not know the joy he is missing.

After the close of a Fast Meeting in our Ward, our son LaMont who was a teacher in the Aaronic Priesthood said: "Father, if the Bishop hadn't closed that meeting just when he did I couldn't have kept my seat another minute." And I felt grateful that he had experienced such feelings in Testimony Meeting, for I recalled as a boy how I had felt something pulling up on me and something pulling down, as I would try and decide to arise and bear my testimony. The Spirit of the Lord is wonderful.

Doubting Thomases

Sometimes our missionaries arrive in the mission field without any real testimony, but there's nothing to prevent them from getting busy and obtaining one. Just to illustrate . . .

While I was serving as President of the Southern States Mission, a new group of missionaries arrived from Salt Lake. We held a meeting with them before assigning them their fields of labor. When one of the missionaries was called to express his feelings, he said something like this:

"I guess I am here to please my parents. My College Professors have told me that my mission would be a waste of my time. You know, I am a very practical sort of a fellow—I like to go out in the orchard and pick the pears off a pear tree; then I know that it is a pear tree." "Well," I replied, "Don't let that bother you—pears grow on our trees also. Now, you are a college man— you take the Book of Mormon and study it and analyze it as you would any scientific matter. Then tell me where it came from if Joseph Smith's story as to its origin is not correct. How could he have known about the destroyed cities, the cement highways, etc., that we know about today, that were unknown at the time the Book was printed and given to the world. Then," I said, "When you get through with the Book of Mormon, I will give you something else to account for."

I assigned him to labor in Alabama. Shortly thereafter we held a conference where he was laboring. I asked the District President to call this Elder to speak. He bore a wonderful testimony, so I went up to him at the close of the meeting and said: "Elder so and so, you must have found some pears on our pear trees." His answer was: "Oh, forget it, President Richards." When he finished his mission, he asked permission from his Bishop to run a tourist service to the temple in his home town, not for money or gain, but because he wanted to share his knowledge of the truths of the gospel with the people. He was a fine missionary.

Ask the Lord

In the Eastern States, a young missionary came up to me at the close of a meeting on the Boston Commons, and said: "Brother Richards, I don't know the gospel is true." My reply was, "You don't! Well, it is about time you are finding out. I advise you to take your Book of Mormon and read it. Ask the Lord to manifest the truth of it unto you by the power of the Holy Ghost as he has promised."

Only a few nights after that we were about to hold another meeting on the Boston Commons. The same young missionary came up and asked for the privilege of speaking. Of course, I was happy to give him the privilege. He walked out before the crowd and pulled some post-cards out of his pocket showing the ruins of the uncovered cities in Central and South America, and said something like this: "If Joseph Smith was not a Prophet of God, and the Book of Mormon is not true, you tell me how Joseph Smith knew about the cities that had been destroyed and covered in the depths of the earth at the time of the crucifixion of the Savior!" All doubts as to the origin of this work and the Book of Mormon seemed to have left his mind. He had gained a testimony just as easy as that. There is not a person in the Church who cannot gain a testimony in the same way if he wants one.

The Honest in Heart

I met a recent convert to the Church in Bessemer, Alabama. She was a woman of dignity and regal bearing —one who had been very active in her church and had taught a Sunday School class for years. After hearing the message of the Missionaries, she left her former church, much to the dismay of her family and many friends. She called upon her minister requesting him to remove her name from his church records. Then she asked permission to go to the classroom where she had taught for years, telling the minister that she wanted to thank the Lord for the privilege she had enjoyed through the years of teaching there. They had a large, attractive church building while ours was but a humble place, but she was humble enough to leave the old and accept the new.

Several months after our first visit I had a letter from her from which I quote the following: "Elder Richards, I have been a member of this wonderful Church one year. I can truthfully say it has been the happiest year of my life. Hardly a day passes that something doesn't happen that strengthens my testimony. I only regret that I did not have an opportunity to receive this Gospel about thirty years ago. I will just have to be content with doing what I can the rest of my life. I have been given some assignments in the Church and appreciate the opportunity to progress and learn more about the Gospel."

Tithing

A Remarkable Fulfillment

As a missionary in the Eastern States, I observed that one of our branch presidents paid a large tithing regularly every month. I said to him, "Brother so and so, you must have a wonderful testimony of the principle of tithing." He said, "I have." Then I asked him to tell me what it was. He said that his wife and children joined the Church in England some years before, but that he did not join. He said, "The reason I didn't was because I didn't have the faith to pay my tithing, and I didn't want to be a hypocrite." When he told me who the missionaries were that brought the gospel to his family, it was an M.I.A. teacher I had when I was a boy, and his wife who were laboring together in the mission field. Then this man said, "A young missionary who was being released came to me and said, 'Brother so and so, I want to baptize you before I go home.' I replied, 'You can't.' He said, 'Why can't I?' 'Because I haven't the faith to pay my tithing and I don't want to be a hypocrite.' Then this young missionary spoke up and said, 'Brother so and so, if you will let me baptize you before I go home, I promise you that within a year from now you will be in America earning three times as much as you are earning now.' I said, 'Okay, that is good enough for me. Where shall we go?' "

So he was baptized. He said, "At that time I couldn't believe that that promise could be fulfilled because I was under contract to work for my company for three years and I knew that I would not break a contract." It was during the first world war when the American manufacturers had such a difficult time to make dyes that would hold their color. So they sent representatives to England to get some of the dye workers to come over and teach them how to make dyes. They came to this man's father. He said he was not interested, but that he had a son who might be. They came to the son. He said, "I can't go; I am under contract to work for my company for three years." Then the agent said, "If we will buy you off so that your company will release you from your contract, will you go?" Now he said, "The Lord just threw in a little for good measure. Within a year from the time of my baptism, I was in America with my family earning four times as much as I was at the time that young Elder made me that promise.

I told that story in a general conference of the Church in the Tabernacle one day. At the close of the meeting one of the mission presidents sitting down in front, came up and said, "Bishop Richards, I am the Elder who made him the promise." I said, "Did I tell the story correctly?" He said, "Just exactly."

Tithe Payers Blessed

I have always said that I would rather have 90¢ with the blessing of the Lord than $1.00 paddling my own canoe. I think a man can keep out of debt longer and get out of debt easier by paying his tithing than he can without. Just to illustrate . . .

We had a couple in Rotterdam without children. One of our good sisters died and left a little baby. At that time it seemed as if we would be able to place that baby in the home of this couple who had no children, but the sister of the mother of the baby came and claimed the baby. So we had to let her have it. The result was that the couple who wanted the baby so badly became inactive in the Church and the man ceased paying his tithing. I was transferred to Amsterdam and I returned to Rotterdam some months later and went to visit this couple. He showed me by his bank book that he had been able to save money every month for years to accumulate sufficient to pay their way to America until he quit paying his tithing. Then he had to draw money out of the bank each month to live on. He worked as a riveter building large boats. "I have had my work," he said, "but we had sickness and other things so that our money just didn't reach." Then he showed me that when he started paying his tithing again, every month he started putting away money again in the savings bank.

The Lord's Law

I had a young lady come to me in Rotterdam when I was president of that branch. She said, "Brother Richards, I have only earned a quarter this week." That is 10¢ American money. "Should I pay my tithing?" I looked at her and said, "Sister, if this were my church, I wouldn't take your tithing; but it isn't my Church. It is the Lord's Church and tithing is the Lord's law for blessing his people. If you have only earned a quarter this week, I surely do think you need a blessing from the Lord. So I advise you to pay your tithing and be blessed." I wrote her out a receipt for 2½¢; we had a coin for that amount in Dutch money. I lived to see that young lady immigrate to America, marry, and send her children to college and on missions. I have seen that repeated so many many times that I have great faith in the principle of tithing.

Most of our members in Holland just lived from hand to mouth. When we taught them the gospel, they didn't think they could pay their tithing. But the Lord blessed them. When they kept the word of wisdom and lived the kind of lives that Latter-day Saints should, they not only paid their tithing, but they saved money to immigrate to America.

While Sister Richards and I were touring the Scandinavian Missions in 1959, a number of the brethren who

were called to speak testified that one thing that held
them back from joining the Church was their fear that
they could not pay their tithing. Then they would add,
"But now we have more money than we ever had. In
addition to meeting our obligations and paying our tithing, we can now make trips to the Temple. We would
not have been able to do that before."

The Tithing Preacher

Our Church has been blessed by the principle of
tithing. We are free from debt because of it. In the
Southern States Mission we were invited by one of our
Presbyterian friends to attend her Church and listen
to an itinerant preacher who was going through the country telling the churches how they could get out of debt.
This was his program: If they would pay their tithing
for ten months, they could get their churches out of
debt. The arguments he used sounded like he had been
reading one of Brother Talmage's talks on tithing. He
quoted the words of Malachi and said that tithing was
the Lord's law of blessing his people. At the close of
the meeting, I was introduced to this man and said:
"Reverend so and so, I would like to bear you my testimony that you are getting near the truth. I am a Mormon
Elder. We have been paying tithing all our lives. There
is just one thing I cannot understand. You say that
tithing is the Lord's law of blessing his people. Now if
that is true, why don't you give them both barrels at
once and ask them to pay their tithing all their lives?
If it would be well to be blessed for ten months, wouldn't
it be much better to be blessed for their entire lives?"
His reply was, "Mr. Richards, we can't go that far yet.
If we can get them to pay their tithing for ten months,
we will do pretty well."

Time and again I have heard our people testify
that they were blessed because they paid their tithing.

I was visiting with one of our good brethren in Florida following a very cold spell that destroyed many of the citrus crops there. As we went through one of the groves owned by this good brother, I said, "Brother so and so, it is remarkable how well your crops thrive." His reply was, "My crops are tithed." I had a letter from a good sister reading as follows: "Brother Richards, when the season commenced, we hardly knew how to get the seed to plant our crops. Now our bins are full of grain and our smoke houses are full of hams. I don't know why except that we pay our tithing."

Tolerance

'Protecting' An Enemy

As a Church and people we have suffered greatly from the intolerance of others, but our leaders have always taught us to be tolerant of others, and I think we do a good job of it. Here is a very good example. Some years ago Lula Shepherd was traveling all over the United States holding public meetings and talking against the Mormons. She wrote a letter to the Chief of Police at Jacksonville, Florida, telling him that she planned to spend a few days there and asking for a personal bodyguard, because she said, "The Mormons will try to kill me while I am there."

The Chief of Police wrote her and assured her that it would be his great pleasure to be her personal escort while she was in Jacksonville. After having escorted her for several days, and when she went to leave Jacksonville, the Chief said, "Now, Mrs. Shepherd, it may interest you to know that I am an Elder in the Mormon Church." This was our good Brother Roberts, treating an enemy with courtesy and without malice, according to the Savior's injunction: "Love your enemies; do good to them that hate you."

A Good Deed

During the war a Catholic Priest met with all of the service men on the Catalina Islands— service men of all faiths. He asked for three volunteers to help him set up his altars on Saturday so he could be prepared to administer Mass to members of the Catholic Church. Three boys volunteered. After the altars were set up, the Priest said to the boys, "Well, I will see you at Mass in the morning." To which one of the boys replied, "I guess not, Father," He said, "Why not?" "Well," he said, "we happen to be three Mormon boys." Then the Father wanted to know why they had volunteered to help him set up the altars. The boy's reply was, "Well, we have been associating with some of your boys around here and we thought a little religion wouldn't hurt them any, so we thought we ought to help you get ready to give it to them."

These servicemen could have spoken ugly truths against the boys whom they felt could use a little religion, or they could have refused to help the Priest in his efforts, but I am sure they accomplished the most good by their spirit of tolerance, good will, and willingness to help.

Trust

Personal Integrity

"To be trusted is better than to be loved." A person's loyalty to his family and his church is a fairly accurate measure of his integrity in all things. Just to illustrate . . .

My cousin residing in Los Angeles was asked by one of his business associates if he knew a good Mormon boy he could get to work for him. My cousin told him that he would send one and so he did. The first thing this man did was to offer this boy a cigarette. He took it, feeling that he ought to be a good sport along with the employer. This man of business did not employ the boy. A short time after my cousin said, "Did that young man come to see you?" "Oh yes." "Did you hire him?" "No." "Why not?" "Because he smokes." "Well," my cousin said, "You smoke too." "Oh yes, but I have never been taught not to smoke." "If his church can't trust him, I can't trust him in my business."

We had a non-Mormon banker here in Salt Lake some years ago who used to hire quite a few Mormon boys to work for him, but he would never hire one who smoked or used liquor. He said, "If their church can't trust them, neither can I." He would hire boys of other churches who smoked but none from the Mormon Church.

Million Dollar Loan

Clyde Edmunds, who served as a member of the General Church Welfare Committee, and I attended a number of conferences together. I was always greatly impressed with one story he told about going East to arrange a loan of a quarter of a million dollars for the poultry business he managed. After the board of directors looked with favor upon his loan in the bank, they called the President since there was a rule in the bank that no loan of that amount should be made without the President's approval. When the President came into the presence of the board and Brother Clyde, the first thing he did was to offer Clyde a cigarette which Clyde refused to accept. So the President lighted up his cigarette. In a few minutes he said, "Let's see, where did you say you come from?" The answer was, "Utah." "Oh, then you are a Mormon, aren't you?" The answer was, "Yes." "That's why you don't smoke. Then I don't smoke in your presence." Clyde always explained that if he had taken that cigarette, he was sure it would have cost him the loan because the President would have immediately said to himself, "Well, if his church can't trust him to live up to its standards, we can't trust him with our money." Clyde got the loan for a quarter of a million dollars.

A Name to Live Up To

After a conference in Miami, Florida, one of the members of the branch who was engaged in business and had many business and social fields (for he served in several civic organizations) asked me if I would remain over another day and come to his home that evening and let him invite his friends and have me tell them why he was a member of the Mormon Church. He explained that they all knew that he was a Mormon, but they did not know why.

About thirty-five of his friends were present in his beautiful home. To them, he made a statement like this, "You all know that I am a Mormon, but you don't know why I am a Mormon. I just want to tell you that my membership in the Mormon Church is my most treasured possession. I have invited President Richards to come here and tell you why I am a Mormon.

I spoke to them for nearly an hour. At the close of my remarks, a man by the name of Mr. Knowlton explained that his first acquaintance with the Mormons was when he went out to work for an implement firm in Arizona. He explained that the company did only a cash business, but one day a man came in and wanted a few hundred dollars credit until his crops were harvested. He said he explained that they did not do any credit business, but that since he was a new employee he would take the matter up with the owner of the business. When he did so, the owner said, "Who is the man?" When he gave him the man's name, his answer was, "Oh, he is a Bishop in the Mormon Church. Let him have anything he wants." He said, "After that whenever a Mormon came in and wanted credit, I just gave it to him." And of course, I was grateful that he didn't report any unfavorable experience for so doing.

The matter of trusting a person is especially important where moral conduct is concerned. Our church from the beginning has consistently held to a single standard of moral conduct for both man and woman.

A Serious Situation

As President of the Southern States Mission, I received a telegram from a man in New York who was there attending an educational convention. I had had the privilege of calling him to serve as a Bishop in the Hollywood Stake. The telegram invited me to meet him and his wife in Birmingham, Alabama where she was raised. He wanted me to meet her relatives, so Sister Richards and I went. Her relatives were prominent church and business people in the town, owned much valuable business property and served on the church board of their own church. One man was a doctor, another was the county treasurer. I had the privilege of explaining Mormonism to them. Then one of them, a director of his own church, asked this question, "What about your young people? I don't know a young man in all Birmingham that I would trust with my daughter." I pointed to the young missionary about 21 who was the district president and I said, "There is a young man you could trust with your daughter. He is as clean as your daughter is." He looked at him for a few minutes and said, "I believe you." When one of the directors of another church can make a statement like that, it certainly makes you grateful for the gospel and its influence upon the lives of our young people.

Young Girl's Ideal

It was our policy in the Presiding Bishopric to have young people give talks at the stake conferences we attended. One girl gave a wonderful talk on "The Kind of Woman I Want to Be." That talk was published in the Era. A minister wrote back from the East asking permission to publish it in pamphlet form. He said he wanted every woman and every girl in his parish to receive a copy of it. I have always said, "Wouldn't it be wonderful if every girl in Israel would give a talk on that subject and then try to live up to the ideals she had expressed! And wouldn't it be wonderful if every boy in Israel would give a talk on the subject, "The Kind of Man I Want to Be," and then try to live up to it. Such expressions of goals would strengthen our youth to be trustworthy and live up to their ideals.

Then people everywhere would say of all our young people what the lady in the United States Passport Office said of our boys. On November 25, 1953 I was in San Francisco arranging for my trip to the South Sea Islands. The lady at the desk said she fell in love with our Mormon boys who came in for passports because they were all such fine, clean-looking young fellows.

Truth

Lasting Impression

While laboring as President of the Southern States Mission, we buried Brother Yarn in Atlanta, Georgia, the father of the Branch President, Homer Yarn. About three weeks after the funeral I was in the Muse Store where Brother Homer Yarn was in charge of the hat department. Many of the employees had attended the funeral. Homer said, "President Richards, the man upstairs in charge of our lingerie department attended my father's funeral and heard you speak. He said if you ever came into the store he would like to meet you. Would you like to meet him?" I assured him that I would be delighted, so we went up to his department. This is what he said:

"Mr. Richards, I am a religious man, and all of my friends are. We attend church regularly, and I think it would be fair to say that thirty minutes after the sermon is given, eighty percent of us couldn't tell what the minister had said. All we know is that he had delivered a good sermon. It is three weeks since I heard you speak at Mr. Yarn's funeral. I went home and told my wife I had heard something I wished all Atlanta could have heard, and notwithstanding the fact it was three weeks ago, I can still tell you what you said."

The truth is simple when properly taught, and is easily understood.

A Son's Assurance

As a missionary in New Bedford, Massachusetts, I had made a number of visits to the home of a man who was confined to his bed. After each visit he would say, "I believe I have been a Mormon all my life and didn't know it." He did not belong to any church, but his

wife and son and daughter did. His wife would never
come into the room with her husband and listen to me;
she would go in an adjoining room and iron. This being
a quiet job, I made it my business to see that she heard
what I was telling her husband.

When I made my last visit to his home before returning home, I invited her to come in, explaining that she
might never see me again in this life, and that I would
feel honored if she would come in and listen to me. She
finally decided to do so. I suggested to her husband
that he let his wife have the Bible so she could follow
in the scriptures.

We had no more than commenced our discussion
when in walked her son from Harvard University. The
mother said, "You are just in time. You have a trained
mind; now, sit down and listen to this man and tell us
how he is trying to lead us astray." Then I suggested
that she give the Bible to her son.

On that occasion, I was discussing the promises of
the Lord unto the twelve sons of Jacob, stressing the
promise unto Joseph of a new land in the utmost bounds
of the everlasting hills. They knew nothing about the
land of Joseph. Then I discussed the command of the
Lord unto his prophet Ezekiel that two records should
be kept, one of Judah and his followers and one of
Joseph and his followers. They knew nothing of this
record of Joseph. I took an hour and a half to discuss
all the phases of this wonderful subject, and how this
record was brought forth in the latter-days, as the Lord
had promised Ezekiel he would do. When I had completed my discussion, and I don't recall that one question
was asked, I turned to this young man from Harvard,

and said, "Will you please tell your mother how I am trying to lead you astray." His reply was, "Mother, this man isn't trying to lead you astray—he is teaching you the truth." Then the mother said, "Well, Mr. Richards, even if I don't believe all you say, there is something about you I can't help but like anyway—will you pray with us before you leave?"

Unknown Is Unloved

Change of Heart

When we were in Holland, we tried to rent a building to be used as a mission home and office. We had everything agreed to between the owner and ourselves except for the fact that he did not know we were Mormons. We did not think it would be right to rent his building without telling him, so we said, "Would it make any difference to you if you knew we were going to use your building as a headquarters for the Mormon Church in Holland?" His reply was, "I should say it would—I wouldn't have the Mormons in any building of mine," so our negotiations ended right there.

He did not rent his building for about ten months. I don't know whether the Lord had anything to do with that, but I have always thought that he did. He then hunted us up to see if we would still like to rent his building. We did, and he said we would not need to mail the rent checks—that he would pick them up. I think he was afraid they might be a few days late. He would ring the bell and step back as if he were afraid he might become contaminated. One day it was raining hard so we got him inside. Thereafter, he always came in and waited while the rent check was being written. It finally got so he would stay an hour or so visiting, so I said to him one day, "Mr. so and so, do you remember what you said when we first tried to rent your building?" His reply was, "Och, onbekend is onbemind," meaning "Unknown is unloved," and I have never forgotten that. That is why the Mormons are not loved by the world. When the honest in heart get to know us, they love us.

Values

Ability to Appreciate

I have often said that I thought one of the most important things in life was to learn to properly evaluate and appreciate things. I have always been intrigued by the little statement written by Elizabeth Barrett Browning:

"Earth is crammed with heaven,
And every common bush afire with God.
But only he who sees takes off his shoes;
The rest sit around and pluck blackberries."

At a conference in Los Angeles some years ago, one of the young ladies was asked to give a talk. Among other things, she said, "There are two kinds of things in this world. There are the things that matter, and then there are the other things." It is wonderful when one has the ability and the desire to choose the things that matter.

When I was a missionary in Holland, I led one of the other missionaries up to an oil painting in the Rijks Museum in Amsterdam. It was a very insignificant painting compared with some of the larger and finer pieces of art such as Rembrandt's Night Watch. I asked him what he would give for it. He replied, that if he had to take it home and hang it up, he didn't think he would give over $10.00 for it. I imagine that if that same piece of art were passed around out here in the West, where we know so little about art (since we have been so busy subduing the wilderness to make it blossom as a rose) that it might pass many homes without getting a bid of more than $10.00, but the National Art Museum paid three hundred and fifty thousand gilders what at that time meant $120,000 for that one piece of art. The value something has for us depends on our understanding of its worth, and our desire for it. Another example along the same line. . .

Musician vs. Ragtime

When I was a boy, we had a young man and young lady teaching school, board at our home in the country. This young man was a real artist with the piano. During the summer months he went up and down the State of Utah selling pianos. One night in the lounge of a hotel in St. George, he was asked to play for the guests, which he did. I don't remember just what it was, but I think it was one of Bach's. (I am admitting that my knowledge of music is such that I can hardly appreciate Bach's music. It seems to me that just as they get warmed up ready to give you a little melody, they are all through.)

Well, when he got through playing, they wanted to know if he made it up as he went along. They didn't encore him, but there was a boy there who could play ragtime, I suppose we call it swing now, and they kept him playing for an hour or two. You see, it wasn't because the school teacher didn't have greater ability, but because they lacked the ability to appreciate. Often the choicest things in life are trampled underfoot because of lack of appreciation and ability to understand.

Contrast

I attended a Tabernacle organ recital some years ago. The lady sitting next to me said, "Mister where is the choir?" I said, "Oh, there isn't any choir here today." "Oh, yes," she said, "Listen, I can hear them singing." I said, "No, that's all coming out of the organ." I looked around and there were people sitting on the edge of their seats they were so thrilled with the music of that great organ. Then there were others sitting half asleep, waiting until the recital was over so they could go to something more interesting.

I give these illustrations only to show that we must understand a thing to be able to appreciate it. This is especially true of the gospel. Until we can help people recognize its beauty and worth, many do not want it, and are not willing to pay the price for it.

Ward Teaching

A Pattern

A good brother in one of the wards asked his Bishop which was more important, to go ward teaching or attend to his other Church duties. The Bishop answered him in the words of Andrew Carnegie, "Who can say which is the most important leg of a three-legged stool?"

My first experience ward teaching was when I was attending Business College here in Salt Lake City. I was a priest at the time. By companion who was a mail carrier had not been on a mission, so he had not had much experience. We were given a large ward teaching district which took us two or three nights each week to cover. We went to the counselor in the Bishopric in charge of ward teaching and asked him for advice. He said, "Before you go out, kneel down together and ask the Lord to bless you and the people." This we did religiously. Then he said, "After you enter a home and have greeted the people, one of you stand up and talk to them, because then you will not be interrupted and you will talk about things pertaining to the Church and the Kingdom." This we did. Then he suggested that we should always offer to pray before leaving.

We went into one home of a little widow and her children who had joined the Church in the East. She had saved her money by nickles and dimes to come to Zion, so she could be where the Temple was and where the Prophets of the Lord were. When we asked if she would like to have us pray with her, and her little children, she said, "Brethren, this is the first time since I came to Zion that a servant of the Lord has offered to pray with me and my children in my home." She said in the mission field the missionaries did that often. We felt compensated as we left that home.

Conversation or Inspiration

Ward teachers who perform their duty can inspire
the members to improve in the things they lack. We
went to the home of a prominent merchant who was
a member of the stake high council. His family has
become nationally prominent. After we had visited with
this good brother, we asked him if he had held his family
prayers. He said, "No, our children go to the University
(this was before the day of automobiles)—one goes on
one car, another on another; it is difficult for us to get
together." We asked if he would like us to pray with
him before we left. He invited his children in. I was
asked to lead in the family prayer. The next month
when we called at his home, he met us at the door. The
first thing he said was, "Brethren, we haven't missed
our prayers one night since you were here last month."

Ward teachers who merely visit are not fulfilling
their calling. I moved into another ward and went out
teaching with a returned missionary. We never talked
about the gospel in any home we went to. I remember
leaving many times with the thought that I would be
happy when I could be a senior ward teacher so we
could talk about the gospel and the Lord and his work.

I heard a statement on ward teaching once that has
remained with me and I have used it all over the Church.
It went like this, "One of the good brethren in Brigham
City went up to the Washakie Indian reservation where
practically all of the Indians are members of the Church.
He came up to one of those huts just as the ward teachers
were leaving. He said to this good Indian brother, 'How
do you like ward teaching?' The Indian shook his head
and said, 'Me no like it anymore. All time too much
hundred percent; not enough ward teach.'" I tell the
ward teachers that we do not go out for one hundred
percent only, but to teach.

Companion Learns

Ward teaching is really an opportunity to do missionary work. I went ward teaching in the Yale Ward where we lived for many years. On one visit the father was not home, we met the son who had not been attending church regularly. I asked him if he would like to go ward teaching with me. He agreed he would. So I took him ward teaching. In my talks in the homes, I talked primarily to this young man. Following one of our ward teaching visits, I invited him to our home. I talked to him about the Church and about our responsibilities in life. I learned that he had been attending other churches. As a result of our conversation that night, he went to his Bishop and told him he would like to go on a mission.

Witnesses

World Will Be Judged

There are two kinds of witnesses in the world—true witnesses and false witnesses. The Lord foretold that he would establish His word in the mouth of three witnesses, and their testimony plus this latter-day work and scripture would be a testimony against the world at the last day.

Once in a conference, when I was a young boy, we recited the testimony of the three witnesses to the Book of Mormon. We memorized that testimony and it made a profound impression on me from that day until the present. When those three witnesses testified that they had seen the plates and the engravings thereon, that they were shown to them by an angel of God, and that the voice of God declared unto them that they were translated by the gift and power of God, I wondered how anybody could doubt such a testimony, particularly after reading the book.

But there are many who do reject the testimony of the three witnesses and accept instead the malicious lies of false witnesses. The world will be judged according to the witnesses it chooses to believe, for there are those who choose to believe the false witnesses not because they really believe them but because they love a lie—they love darkness better than light. The Lord has given ample witness to the world that Mormonism is true and good, for he said, "By their fruits ye shall know them." No honest person could believe the slander against the Church after meeting a few members or missionaries. But the dishonest in heart will continue to cleave to the heap of lies because they do not love the truth. Just to illustrate . . .

Unfounded Prejudice

Some years ago I filled a short term mission back in New England. The people were so prejudiced toward the Church in those days that we could not even get permission to hold a baptismal service in the YMCA pool. When I asked the reason, the minister in charge said, "Well, you are Mormons, aren't you?" Of course I admitted we were. He said, "That's the reason."

After I had written my book, "A Marvelous Work and A Wonder," I sent a copy to a distant relative of ours in New England, who had been located by my cousin, Merlin Steed. After reading the book he wrote to Merlin and made a statement like this, "I have just read your cousin's book. It is an eye-opener to me. It is the first book I have ever read in favor of the Mormons. I doubt if you have any idea the erroneous stories and tales that are told about the Mormons here in New England. I question in my own mind if the people who tell them really believe the stories they tell."

While serving as a missionary in New England, I left a tract with a woman one day. (At that time we did not work in pairs.) When I came back, I asked her what she thought of the tract. "Well," she said, "there is only one objection I have to it." I said, "Shall I tell you what that is." She said, "What?" I said, "The source from which it came. Had you heard those same truths from anyone but the Mormons, you would have been glad to accept them." She said, "How did you know?"

We often had such experiences, which gave us fully to understand what Jesus meant when he said, "If ye were of the world, the world would love you, but because ye are not of the world, the world hates you."

The world builds a formidable wall of prejudice

against the truth that only the truly honest in heart can surmount.

Shortly after my return from my first mission to Holland, I accepted a position as Assistant Secretary of the Portland Cement Company. The company made arrangements with a bonding company from San Francisco to sell its bonds. I gave up my position as Assistant Secretary and went out selling bonds on strictly a commission basis. I had letters of introduction from the most prominent bankers and business men of Portland.

Hearsay and Ignorance

I called on a doctor in Oregon City who had formerly been mayor of the city. He was leaving to visit some patients in the country and invited me to accompany him. It was before the days of automobiles so we rode in a lovely rubber-tired buggy with a team of beautiful horses. The doctor gave me an opportunity to tell him of the plan of our company for the erection of a cement plant. I told him of a directors meeting that had just been held, and the decisions reached. I informed him that Bishop Nibley had been there from Salt Lake as one of the principal promoters of the project. He inquired: "Who is this man Nibley? Is he a Mormon?" My reply was that he was the Presiding Bishop of the Mormon Church. He then started in with a tirade against the Mormons that almost made my blood run cold. I had not realized that in the minds of intelligent people we were so undesirable. He then commented on what a H— — of a time the Mormon missionaries had. I listened until he came to what I considered a good stopping point, and then I said, "Doctor have you met a Mormon?" His reply was, "No." Then I asked, "Have you ever read a Mormon book?" and his answer was "No." Then I said, "Now Doctor, I don't want you to feel at all embarrassed, but you are sitting right at the side of a Mormon Missionary, and while I am not laboring as a missionary at the present time, I just recently returned from serving nearly three years as a missionary for the Mormon Church in the little land of Holland." The doctor went red in the face and I added, "Now Doctor, you do not need to feel in any way embarrassed, for I have qualified you—you have never met a Mormon or read a Mormon book, so you could only be expected to know what the general reputation of the Mormons is." When I had asked the doctor what he knew about the Mormons, his reply was, "Everybody knows what they are—you read about them in the newspaper and in the magazines and hear about them on the streets."

While returning to Oregon City, the doctor gave me an opportunity to tell him about the Mormons, our standards and way of life, and so on. When we reached Oregon City he tossed me the lines and asked me to drive his team to the livery stable, explaining that he had to catch a train to Portland. His parting words were, "Mr. Richards, if that is Mormonism, I could be a good Mormon. Don't ever come to Oregon City again without calling on me."

A Friendly Witness

While I was laboring in the south a very unfavorable article appeared in one of the national magazines. One of our Presbyterian friends had the courage to write a letter answering this article, from which I quote two paragraphs.

"I am a Presbyterian in good and regular standing, strong in the faith, but it has been my privilege to know well over a period of twelve years many young missionaries of the Mormon faith who have passed through the Southern States Mission Home in Atlanta.

"If there are any young people today who know where they are going, it is the Mormon young people, brought up to seek education, to love music and the fine arts, to do without stimulants of any kind, and to lead clean lives. They have the foundation for useful and happy homes and are certainly not proceeding under the momentum supplied by Brigham Young."

I feel sure this woman was sincere in her statements because she told Sister Richards she wanted her girls to marry Mormon boys. Sister Richards said, "Well, the Mormon boy's mothers may want them to marry Mormon girls." Her reply was, "Of course, I would expect my girls to become Mormons."

Word Of Wisdom

Outcast

Whenever one of my investigators complained about the restrictions of the Word of Wisdom, I would answer them that it was the Lord's blessing to us to help us keep free from the things that would really restrict and enslave us. Just to illustrate . . .

I was walking along the street in Salt Lake one day and met a man who was a former member of one of the wards I had lived in. At that time he had served as superintendent of the Sunday School, had been active in his Elders Quorum, and because of his wonderful singing voice sang at most of the funerals. At the time I met him, he had become an alcoholic. Calling him by name I said, "Things go badly with you, do they not?" His reply was, "I made my first mistake when I took my first glass of beer." The result was that he lived any place he could find a place to lay his head. His family apparently had cast him off. He had a wonderful wife and wonderful children, and wonderful talents. He gave it all up because he became a slave to the terrible habit of liquor. My heart has gone out to him. I helped him by sending him to Provo for treatments, but because I could not live with him afterwards, he soon fell back into his old habit.

Before he started drinking he was free, happy, and healthy. After he disregarded the Lord's law of health, he was in pitiful bondage. And it was the first seemingly innocent drink that caught him. If he hadn't taken the first drink he could never have become addicted to it, could he? They say, "Where a principle is involved, compromise is fatal." While this may not always be one hundred percent true, it usually is, so it is certainly wiser to play safe and avoid the least thing that could bring us trouble.

Quick Decision

Just to illustrate . . . When I was a young man on the Saltair Dance Floor when it was considered to be the finest dance hall in America, a young lady friend invited me to have dinner with them. I accepted her invitation. So we took hold of hands and went hop-scotching down to where a long table was set. As we neared the table, I noted that there was a beer bottle by each plate. I stopped suddenly. I looked at the table and then looked at her. She said, "What is the matter, are you too good to drink a little beer?" I had to make a decision in a hurry. So I replied, calling her by name, "Well, I guess I am; I thought you were too. Goodbye, I will see you again." I went up the steps faster than I had come down. I don't recall that I have seen that girl from that day until the present.

I have often thought of that little experience and wondered if I would have become the Presiding Bishop of the Church to preside over the Aaronic Priesthood of the Church if I had taken that first bottle of beer. If one never takes the first drink of beer or liquor, he will never have to worry about the second. The same with the matter of smoking cigarettes.

A Steady Hand

Elder Reed Smoot attended one of our conferences in the Hollywood Stake accompanied by his wife. She told this story that greatly impressed me.

"One of our Mormon boys was studying medicine in a college in the East. One day they were in the operating room waiting for the professor to come in and perform an operation. The students were holding out their hands to see if they shook. The Mormon boy held out his hand and it was perfectly firm. When the professor came in and picked up his knife to perform the operation, the students noticed how his hand shook.

They began to twitter. The professor wanted to know what was the matter. They told him that they were just watching his hand shake. He said, "If there is any man here whose hand doesn't shake, I will step aside and let him perform the operation." The students pushed this Mormon boy forward. The professor directed him while he performed the operation. That is the dividend for keeping the Word of Wisdom. All the others were restricted in their skill by shaky nerves, but the Mormon boy was free from this affliction, and steady and capable.

Cold Water

When I was a boy in one of our country towns, we held a Sunday School Convention attended by Karl G. Maeser and George Goddard. The way Brother Goddard led the Sunday School in the singing and the songs that he selected made a tremendous impression on my mind. One was "Take Away the Whiskey, the Coffee and the Tea, Cold Water Is the Drink for Me." Since that time it has been difficult for me to drink anything but cold water. I was riding on the train between Salt Lake and Los Angeles and went into the diner for breakfast. The waiter said, "Will you have coffee?" "No thank you." "Tea?" "No, thank you." "Postum?" "No, thank you." "Chocolate?" "No, thank you." "What *do* you want to drink?" I said, "Cold water, please." His reply was "You are the funniest man I ever saw."

Another song Brother Goddard had us sing was, "Who's on the Lord's side, who? Now is the time to show, We ask it fearlessly, Who's on the Lord's side, who?" I recall that that made such an impression on me as a boy I resolved that I would always be on the Lord's side.

I was talking along that line at Conference up in Wyoming one day. At the close of the morning meeting a young boy about eight or nine years old came up and said, "Bishop Richards, could I shake your hand?" I assured him that I didn't know anything I would rather do than to shake his hand. Looking up into my face he said, "Bishop Richards, my Bishop will never have to worry about losing me." I thought, "Wouldn't it be wonderful if every boy in the Church could say that to his Bishop!"

Idle Hours

I was raised out in the country where we had no high school. After graduating from the grade school, I came to Salt Lake to attend business college. I boarded with a young man who was a member of my Deacons Quorum of which I was the President. On Saturday night he would beg me to go up town with him and see the sights. It was almost as if he were looking for trouble. I always excused myself on the grounds that I had too much studying to do. The result of his going up town to see the sights was that he fell into bad habits. He became a drunkard. After his marriage I have had him call at my office on various occasions asking for a dollar to buy bread to feed his family. If this boy had determined to keep the Lord's law of health, he would have avoided places that encouraged drinking and carousing. He would have been free from the awful grip of poverty and drunkenness.

A person's desire to live the Word of Wisdom is in proportion to his testimony. If he has strong faith in the wisdom and purposes of God, it will not be hard for him to follow the Lord's advice concerning the care of our bodies.

The Easy Way

Some years ago a Stake President said to me, "Bishop Richards, my neighbor is a Senior Member of the Aaronic Priesthood. I have visited him a number of times to try and get him to give up his tobacco so we could give him a recommend to take his family to the Temple. I have been unsuccessful." I replied, "Has it ever occurred to you, President, that you might be starting at the wrong end of the horn. You go in that home and teach the man what the gospel really is and what it can do for him and his family. Then you will not have to ask him to give up his tobacco; he will just do that automatically." I have seen this fact demonstrated many, many times in my missionary labors in the Church. When a person gets a testimony of the gospel the rest is comparatively easy. The wonderful part about the Word of Wisdom is that if a person truly desires to keep it, it becomes easy. It is "Given for a principle with promise, adapted to the capacity of the weak and the weakest of all saints, who are or can be called saints."

Ye Are Not Sent Forth To Be Taught

Missionaries, Remember!

In a revelation to the Prophet Joseph Smith, February, 1831, instructing the Elders who were being sent forth to preach the gospel, the Lord said:

Again I say, hearken ye Elders of my Church, whom I have appointed: Ye are not sent forth to be taught, but to teach the children of men the things which I have put into your hands by the power of my Spirit." (D. & C. Sec. 43:15).

If the Missionaries would always remember that they are sent forth to teach and not to be taught, they would be much more successful in their work. Consider these illustrations:

My Debate with Seventh Day Adventist Minister

As a Missionary in Amsterdam, I called one evening at the home of a family of saints, only to find that they had a Seventh Day Adventist Minister there. We had a discussion about Priesthood. I made the statement that the Melchizedek Priesthood was not upon the earth from Moses to Christ— that the people lived under the lesser law or the Aaronic Priesthood. He countered: "What about the minor Prophets?" My answer was, "I don't know—I will have to look that matter up." So right there he challenged me to a debate in his Church a week from the following Saturday evening. At that time we were not counselled against debating, so I accepted his challenge. When we arrived at his church, it was filled to capacity with his members and our members. How our members learned of the debate, I never knew.

In introducing me and the purpose of the evening the minister said, "Inasmuch as Mr. Richards is a guest in our Church, we will accord him the privilege of opening the debate. We will each speak for twenty minutes at a time and continue as long as it is mutually satisfactory. Is this agreeable with you?" I assured him that it was, and I felt grateful to the Lord that he had permitted me to open the debate.

Sound Foundation

I commenced by telling the people that the last time I talked with the minister, we had a difference of opinion regarding Priesthood—that I had come prepared to discuss that matter further, but that I did not propose to open the debate with that subject. I indicated that if one were going to build a house, it wouldn't matter much what he used for the roof and the decorations if one side of the foundation were left out, for the house would surely fall anyway. "So," I said, "I propose to commence this debate by laying the foundation of the gospel of Christ. I choose for my text the sixth chapter of Hebrews, verses one and two, which read:

"Therefore leaving the principles of the doctrine of Christ, let us go on unto perfection; not laying again the foundation of repentance from dead works, and of faith toward God,

Of the doctrine of baptisms, and of laying on of hands, and of resurrection of the dead, and of eternal judgment."

I discussed hurriedly the principle of repentance from dead works, faith toward God, the doctrine of baptisms, and then I dwelt at length on the principle of "laying on of hands," showing how all the Apostles of Jesus Christ taught this principle. I referred especially to the eighth chapter of The Acts of the Apostles, where "Philip went down to the city of Samaria and preached Christ unto them. . . . But when they believed

Philip preaching the things concerning the Kingdom of God, and the name of Jesus Christ, they were baptized, both men and women. . . . Now when the Apostles which were at Jerusalem heard that Samaria had received the word of God, they sent unto them Peter and John: Who, when they were come down, prayed for them, that they might receive the Holy Ghost: (For as yet he was fallen upon none of them: only they were baptized in the name of the Lord Jesus.) *Then laid they their hands on them, and they received the Holy Ghost.* And when Simon saw that through laying on of the Apostles' hands the Holy Ghost was given, he offered them money, Saying, Give me also this power, that on whomsoever I lay hands, he may receive the Holy Ghost. But Peter said unto him, Thy money perish with thee, because thou hast thought that the gift of God may be purchased with money."

Faulty Foundation

Then I asked, "Who has changed the Gospel of Christ? Why would the Apostles send Peter and John to Samaria to bestow the Holy Ghost upon those who had been baptized by Philip if this were not the proper manner of conveying the Holy Ghost in the Church of Christ? Why would Simon have offered money to the Apostles to purchase this power if the Holy Ghost could be obtained in any other manner?" Then I concluded my twenty minutes by inviting my friend, the minister to explain why his church did not practice the principle of "Laying on of hands" to bestow the Holy Ghost, calling attention to the fact that they had left out one side of the foundation, so his house was sure to fall.

I never felt more power in speaking to an audience, and the people were nodding approval all during my remarks. I then turned the meeting back to my friend, the minister.

Turning the Tide

He stood up and took twenty minutes discussing the claims of Joseph Smith; the Mormon Golden Bible; the Mountain Meadows massacre, and so on. Then turning to the audience he said: "Now if Mr. Richards will enlighten us on these matters, I am sure this audience will be most grateful."

I was on my feet in a hurry and called attention to the fact that in the days of the Savior his enemies tried to ensnare him through trickery, but that I was sure there was no one present in that audience who would like to see either of us resort to any such tactics. I explained that it was my understanding that a debate consisted of the presentation and answering of an argument. Then I asked: "Has my friend answered any of my arguments?" The audience all shook their heads in the negative. I explained that the very courtesy my friend had extended to me as a guest in his church to open the debate, he was now trying to take from me — that he now wanted to open the debate and that I didn't propose to let him do so. I therefore offered him his twenty minutes over again to answer my presentation. He refused. His wife stood up in the audience and said, "What Mr. Richards is asking is right — you should answer him," but still he refused. I knew he could not answer.

I then stood up, picking up my hat and overcoat, and asked the Elders to also stand, then I said, "I offer you one more chance. I am prepared to remain until ten o'clock tomorrow morning when I have to be in my own church. I am willing to discuss any subject you want to discuss, provided this debate can continue as you first proposed. If you are not willing to do this, we will leave and ask our members to leave with us. He refused, and we all left.

I met that man many times on the streets of Amsterdam after that but when he would see me coming, he would drop his head so he would not recognize me.

I can't remember ever having discussed the gospel with a man better versed in the scriptures than this man. In our first discussion, if I were to use the wrong tense of the verb in quoting a passage of scripture, he would call me on it immediately.

My point is, that the Lord had not sent me forth to be taught, but to teach the children of men. Had I let this man have his way and try to teach me instead of teaching him, the debate might have ended in a much less favorable manner.

Essential Facts

When I went on my first mission to Holland, a friend of mine was in the same company only he went to Norway. He was sent to labor in the northern part of Norway where, for months, it is dark nearly all day. The Missionaries go tracting with flashlights.

One day I received a letter from this friend reading something like this, "The other day I met a man who knows more about religion than I ever dreamed of. I told him that if he had something better than I had that I would join his church." He seemed to have forgotten that he was sent forth to teach not to be taught.

My reply was, "You told him just the right thing— if he has something better than you have you should join his church. But, does he have something better than a personal visit to this earth of God the Father and His Son Jesus Christ, to usher in the Dispensation of the Fulness of Times and to pass judgment upon all the churches, telling the Prophet Joseph Smith that he should join none of them? Does he have something better than a personal visit of the angel Moroni, telling

of the plates containing a record of the early inhabi-
tants of this land of America, being the stick of Joseph
which, the Lord promised he would bring forth and
join to the record of Judah? Does he have something
better than a visit to this earth of John the Baptist, a
resurrected being, to restore the Aaronic Priesthood
to the earth? Does he have something better than a
personal visit of the Apostles Peter, James and John,
restoring the Holy Melchizedek Priesthood and Holy
Apostleship, with authority to organize the Church of
Jesus Christ? Does he have something better than the
coming of Elijah, the Prophet, according to the promise
of Malachi, to turn the hearts of the fathers to the
children and the hearts of the children to their fathers,
lest the Lord come and smite the earth with a curse?
Does he have anything better than a visit from Moses
the Prophet restoring to the earth the keys of the gathering of latter-day Israel? Does he have something better
than a visit from Elias, the Prophet, restoring the keys
of the Gospel of the Dispensation of Abraham saying
that in him and his seed should all the nations of the
earth be blessed? Now," I said, "if he has something
better than this, you should join his church."

We may not all have the ability to meet the arguments
presented to us, but if we have a testimony of the above
facts, nothing can shake our faith. These are the facts
we should teach. If we will bear testimony of these
wonderful truths we will be too busy to be awed by the
learning of those who would teach us.

Youth

A Sore Festers

There is not much sense in spending our money and energy in gaining new converts while we let our own precious youth slip from us practically unnoticed. Love and diligence is needed if we are to keep our young boys and girls active.

In order to try and help Bishops realize how they should gain the love of the boys of the Aaronic Priesthood over whom they preside, I relate this incident.

A boy speaking in one of our Stake Conferences on "The Kind of Bishop We Boys Like" made this statement. "We boys like a Bishop who doesn't feel that a boy is just a pain in the neck." I have never forgotten that. I have thought that every Bishop should take stock of himself and see what the boys really think of him in order that his teaching and influence might touch their hearts for good. It is so easy to lose a boy if we do not always manifest a spirit of love. Just to illustrate . . .

At a leadership meeting in Washington some years ago, one of the brethren reported standing in line to get into a theatre. He got into conversation with a man standing next to him and learned that he was from Utah. Then he said, "Then you are a Mormon, aren't you?" To which the man replied, "No, I am not a Mormon." The man making the inquiry wasn't so sure so he tried to make it easy for this man to admit that he was a Mormon, so he said, "Well, I am from Utah and I am a Mormon. I thought most of us from Utah were Mormons." To which the other man replied, "Well, I was once, but I am not anymore." Then he was asked to give the reason. He said that when he was a boy he attended the Aaronic Priesthood meeting and a member of the Bishopric threw him out by the nape of the neck. He said, "As I left that building, I said to that man, 'If you put me out of here, I will never darken the door of your Church again.' He did, and I never have." Of course under our present Aaronic Priesthood program, he could not be away 30 days without someone there to check on him before the sore calloused over.

Healing Balm

Another illustration—a contrast to the one just mentioned. I attended an award night in a certain ward here in Salt Lake some years ago. This was when we had charge of the girls' program. So it was an award night for boys and girls. After a program in the chapel, we went into the recreation hall to a lovely banquet with fine linen and silverware. It was just beautiful. The Stake President sat at the right of me. The Bishop was supposed to sit on my left but there was no Bishop. Finally he came in, nibbled a little at his food, then pushed his plate away. I turned to him and said, "What is the matter, Bishop?" He replied, "I just had a very unpleasant experience. When we were having the closing prayer in the chapel, one of the boys talked all through the prayer. I spoke to him about it. It offended him and he grabbed his hat and ran home. I followed him and remained with him until he had apologized to me, and I had apologized to him and we are both back together." You see, nothing was lost except the Bishop's appetite, and he could soon regain that. The injury that had been done was corrected before the sore had calloused over, and we had lost that boy.

Some wonderful work is being done in many wards of the Church in helping our young people remain active in the Church. Brother Ballard used to say, "If we can just help them over fool's hill." That is the work of our leaders.

Youth Program

New Ideas

Since the restoration of the gospel our leaders have stressed the importance of recreation. Our Church has set a pattern for the entire world in its comprehensive youth program. Young people must keep busy in wholesome activities, or boredom may lead to a seeking for the wrong kind of fun. It used to shock people when they heard we held dances in the same buildings as we held church services. Even our own members resisted the idea in certain localities. Just to illustrate . . .

When I became President of the Southern States Mission, we introduced the youth program of the Church in that mission. It was something new and the people did not respond too enthusiastically. When I told some of the local leaders that we were going to dance in our buildings, they said, "We don't want our children dancing." In South Carolina they said, "If you let them dance in our buildings the people will burn them down." My reply was, "If they burn them down, we will build them up again, only we will make them larger so more can dance." In West Florida, the Superintendent of one of our Sunday Schools said, "President Richards, if you let the people dance in our chapel, I will have my father's body removed that is buried in the little cemetery adjoining the chapel." My reply was that he didn't need to get excited—that we would not force the program upon them. But I said, "Before I leave the South, you will be asking us to dance in your building." Before I left the South, he was dancing in it himself and enjoying it very much. In Atlanta, I told them that before I left the South, we would hold a dance in Atlanta with three or four hundred couples of our young people and we would invite all the ministers of Atlanta to attend.

Well, we had the dance with over a thousand people present, but we had no room for the ministers. We couldn't even find a building large enough to take care of our own people. We had the queens of the five different States of our mission present, and there were no signs of drinking or smoking anywhere around the building.

In Los Angeles, I heard a minister speaking over the radio who said, "What we need today is a church for the youth of the land. We have been preaching to the old people and letting the young people go to the devil. That is why our churches are empty today."

I couldn't help but feel grateful that we do have a church for the youth of the land.

Deseret Club Dance

Some years ago in California, the Deseret Club was organized on the U.C.L.A. Campus. They held a dance in the Wilshire Ward Recreation Hall with three to four hundred couples present. Mr. Evans, who had charge of all the groups of various churches on the campus was present. I spent considerable time visiting with him during the dance. It was a beautiful party. I used to say that I wished it could have been televised so that everyone could have seen our young people in action.

Mr. Evans was so thrilled, he said, "I wish all the ministers of Los Angeles could see what I am seeing tonight. I wish they were doing for their young people what you are doing."

During the party, I kept going outside, as it was my custom to do to see that there was no smoking or drinking on the grounds. I found one young man smoking a cigarette on the front steps. I stepped up to him and said, "Pardon me, my boy, but this may be the first time you have ever attended one of our dances. You probably do not know that we teach our young people not to smoke. Would it be asking too much of you to ask you not to smoke while attending one of our dances?" His reply was, "I did know it; I apologize—it will not happen again."

I never found it difficult to get boys to cooperate when approached in the proper spirit.

Field Days

Besides dances, we held field days in the various districts of the Southern States Mission lasting for several days at a time. Our young people engaged in all kinds of sports: swimming, dancing, races, ball games, and so forth. It was a new day for the young people of our mission.

When we announced at a District Conference in South Carolina what we were going to do, the principal of the school, a lady, and not a member of the Church, came up to me and said, "I would like to volunteer my services to help put over that program. We have tried to do it through the school, but without success." My comment was, "Do you know why you have been unsuccessful?" She said, "No, why?" I replied, "You cannot lift water above its source. The parents of your children do not think they have had a good time when they go out for an evening unless they indulge in the drinking of liquor, and you know what follows." Her reply was, "That is right."

Well, she did help us with our program, and trained our young people, and took them all around the state, attending our various MIA functions, showing what could be done. When I left the mission, she said, "I feel myself slipping."

Spirit of Cooperation

At Sarah, Mississippi we told the people the kind of parties we wanted to hold and asked for the people to indicate by a show of hands how many were willing to cooperate with us to the extent of seeing that there was no smoking or drinking within a hundred yards of our building. One non-member who was present, in reporting his experience to a friend the next day, said, "I have always said I would smoke any place I d——ed please, but when that Mormon Elder asked for a show of hands of those who were willing to help see that no one smoked within a hundred yards of their buildings, my hand went up. If you had been there, your hand would have gone up too."

Scouting

Our church has a reputation for being outstanding in the Scout Program. I personally feel that one of the most important positions in the church is Scout leader. The boys are at an age when they need what Scouting has to offer. If we can give it to them through a really superior man who is an example of the best in manhood, it will be a blessing to our boys throughout their lives, and will help to keep them close to the church during a very difficult period.

Dr. Shuck, Chief Scout Executive of the United States and his assistant, who was reported to have supervision over ninety thousand scouts and scouters, attended our MIA June Conference in 1954 or 1955. It was a wonderful conference. Following the dance festival with fifteen thousand young people participating, there was a Scout Pageant in the stadium of the University of Utah.

Monday morning following the conference, the MIA officers gave a farewell breakfast for these gentlemen at the Hotel Utah. I was invited to attend. Following the breakfast, Dr. Shuck's assistant stated that the past four days, witnessing the activities of our young people, had been the most interesting four days of his entire life.

I suggested that he try to stimulate other churches to provide similar activities for their young people, indicating that we could not offer to join them because of our standards, having in mind particularly the Word of Wisdom.

The Answer

For the past seventeen years, Dr. James W. Fifield, Jr., Minister of First Congregational Church of Los Angeles has conducted a question box every Saturday evening from 7:00 to 7:30 called "Even Song."

One evening in July 1953, the first question was: "What church does the most for its young people?" The answer was: "The Mormon Church." He then explained that the Mormon Church provides recreation in connection with its church buildings; that the church teaches against the use of tobacco and alcoholic liquors; and that if a merchant should hire a Mormon boy he would find him honest. He concluded by saying, "The answer is "The Mormon Church."